W9-AFJ-110

Also by Ron Powers

Far From Home (Anchor Books)

The Beast, the Eunuch, and the Glass-Eyed Child: Television in the '80s and Beyond (Anchor Books)

The Newscasters: The News Business as Show Business

Face Value

Toot-Toot-Tootsie, Good-bye

Super Tube: The Rise of Television Sports

White Town Drowsing

RON POWERS

ANCHOR BOOKS
DOUBLEDAY
NEW YORK LONDON TORONTO SYDNEY AUCKLAND

This book is for
Dean Paul and Kevin

AN ANCHOR BOOK
PUBLISHED BY DOUBLEDAY
a division of Bantam Doubleday Dell Publishing Group, Inc.
666 Fifth Avenue, New York, New York 10103

ANCHOR BOOKS, DOUBLEDAY, and the portrayal of an anchor are trademarks of Doubleday, a division of Bantam Doubleday Dell Publishing Group, Inc.

White Town Drowsing was originally published in hardcover by The Atlantic Monthly Press in 1986. The Anchor Books edition is published by arrangement with the author.

First published in the United States of America by The Atlantic Monthly Press 1986. Published in Penguin Books 1987.

Library of Congress Cataloging-in-Publication Data
Powers, Ron.
White town drowsing / by Ron Powers. —
1st Anchor Books ed.
p. cm.
Originally published: Boston : Atlantic Monthly Press, © 1986.
1. Hannibal (Mo.)—Politics and government. 2. Powers, Ron.
I. Title.
[F474.H24P69 1992]
977.8'353—dc20 92-10191
CIP

ISBN 0-385-42423-X

PRINTED IN THE UNITED STATES OF AMERICA
FIRST ANCHOR BOOKS EDITION: SEPTEMBER 1992

1 3 5 7 9 10 8 6 4 2

Acknowledgments

THE people of Hannibal were unfailingly open and generous in their response to my presence and to my endless questions — even when, in certain instances, the questions were necessarily adversarial. In the face of this generosity I am humbly grateful.

In addition to those who are quoted in the text — and whose contributions are self-evident — I am especially indebted to several people who supplied an extra measure of guidance. These include Cathie Whelan, Henry Sweets, Hurley and Roberta Hagood, Ginger Jones, Jim Cary, Estelle Winkler, Hiawatha Crow, Mike Sohn, John Briscoe, Gale Newman, and Chris Straub.

My historical research was greatly enhanced by Ann Sundermeyer of the Hannibal Public Library; Mary Lou Montgomery and Beverly Darr of the *Courier-Post;* the Hagoods and their historical study, *The Story of Hannibal* (1976); and, for architectural history, Esley Hamilton of the Missouri Office of Historic Preservation.

Research conçerning the California dealings of Capital Planning and Development / Cypress Investments was assisted by the Center for Investigative Reporting. Certain documents covering the history of the Joanna / Clarence Cannon Dam were provided by the St. Louis District, United States Army Corps of Engineers; I also acknowledge the doctoral thesis by Michael D. Shulse, "The History and Development of the Clarence Cannon Dam and Reservoir, 1957–1968."

For certain insights into Mark Twain's social views, and for the text of a correspondence with his wife, Livy, I cite *Mark Twain, Social Critic,* by Philip S. Foner (International Publishers, New York, 1958).

This book was conceived in a happy moment — in a speculative conversation with a dear comrade several autumns ago, as we sped northward in a van toward Vermont and a reunion of the Bread Loaf Writers Conference. I owe a great deal to my friend, the historian David Haward Bain, for his bolstering attention and criticism of the manuscript. I'm grateful to Joyce Johnson (also aboard that van) for her rigorous and empathetic editing; and to my mentor Robert (Shad) Northshield, the senior executive producer of "CBS News Sunday Morning," for his affecting moral vision of American continuity and loss.

And to Honoree, whose imprint is on every page.

White Town Drowsing

"After all these years I can picture that old time to myself now, just as it was then: the white town drowsing in the sunshine of a summer's morning; the streets empty or pretty nearly so . . ."

— Mark Twain

Life on the Mississippi

CHAPTER I

For the past quarter-century I have clandestinely carried a town inside my memory — a town, and a fragment of river, and a bridge. These images glow and fade in my consciousness like distant signals in a radio tube, and in fact the remembered town takes on the ensemble bedlam sometimes of an old radio show, the sort of show my father would dial into and then abandon, dial and abandon, as he searched the airwaves for evidence of larger universes, better times.

But the town was no cathode fantasy. It was real. I was born in this town and lived there virtually until the last moment of my boyhood, which occurred on a morning in June of 1959, when I was seventeen and my father, who was the town's Fuller Brush man, packed the family into two Studebakers and headed us west across Missouri toward the state capital and better times.

We reached the state capital. There, my father continued to sell his Fuller Brushes at an imperceptibly diminishing rate until he died twenty-five years later, in September, in a hospital room with the radio on, in the heat of the National League pennant race, having reported taxable income for the previous year of just under one thousand Fuller Brush dollars. That was the destiny of my father, who had always dreamed of leaving the river town.

I, who had always dreamed of staying, found the better times. I enrolled in a university that I would never have dared to consider had we remained in the river town with its beguiling, illusory systems of growth and education and commerce — and its Baptist junior college. I thought I would become a journalist. I wanted to meet all the famous people whose voices had floated into the river town on the radio airwaves, and I wanted to live in the larger universe they inhabited. All this on behalf of my father, who cared terribly about these voices, and memorized their jokes and their hidy-hidy-ho signature lives and made bets on their salaries with men in saloons.

So I did. I learned journalism and blindly practiced it in a broken path of cities tending north and east, the cities growing brighter and stranger as the town receded. And I met them, the famous images, and the newer, colder images of television. And I became an image on television. But the town rushed at me in dreams. And one day when I was reporting back to my transplanted father on how it was to live and work among the famous voices, he interrupted, shyly, cupping the deaf ear, to ask me to refresh him on the name of the newspaper I worked for.

He remembered details of the people with the famous voices better than he remembered the details of my life. It had been the jokes and the signature lives that were real to my father all along, back in the river town; things in themselves; not symbols of personal possibility.

And then my father died, and the blind weight of a quarter-century descended, and now I was both fatherless and estranged from the river town. And a son arrived, and then another son, and I saw that it was imperative on their behalf as well as my own that I begin going back.

I had always believed that I could go back. Going back to the river town and reentering my life there had remained as plausible an option, at least in my clandestine communings, as advancing my career with a better job in a larger city. I had visited the town a few times in the first years after the family left — I brought squinting, eye-shading girlfriends; we inspected scenic sites and points of historic interest — but the visits decreased as my urban path tacked north and eastward, and at some point the visits ceased. But the idea of going back, like the intact presence of the 1959 town inside my memory, never diminished. The idea was as necessary to my subsistence as drawing breath.

Long before I knew that the town enjoyed any fame beyond the fame I conferred on it as a young child from my grandfather's front porch on the top of Union Street Hill; before I understood that the river was something greater than an interesting shard that supported barge traffic between its two framing bluffs in the daylight and lay invisible as evil beneath the winking bridgelights at night; before the bridge came to represent in my dreams the skeletal conduit to flight and the even more horrifying orifice of return — before I knew all this, I knew that the town and the river and the bridge were indivisible from one another and from me. As I grew older I sensed that they established my moral coordinates, and in some vague way defined my expectations of the world. Their permanence seemed a precondition of my own. The town and the river and the bridge formed a triptych that forestalled the intrusion of change, decay, death.

Not that I seriously resisted. Not that I could rid my memory of this glowing and fading image even if I wanted to. The town's hagiography of street names (I was born in a family house on Lamb Avenue, passed my early childhood on a street called St. Mary's; my parents moved next to Sunnyside and finally to Pleasant Street, where we lived next to a family named Paradise), the bridge's phantasmic geometry, the river's seditious and constant subtraction of time — these are the fixed evidences of my own being, necessary as shadows.

The Mississippi flows due south to Hannibal until it bumps against the limestone bluffs beneath Riverview Park. Deflected, it slants southeasterly along the town's old railroad yards until it disappears beyond a brutal, transfixing high tooth of limestone called Lover's Leap.

The Mississippi River flows through nearly every remembered picture I have of Hannibal. It is visible from all the hilltops that ring the old central business district, including the top of Union Street Hill, where my maternal grandparents lived. More than a visual memory, though, the Mississippi asserts itself in my thoughts as an almost sentient presence of weight and movement — a savvy channel out there on the innocent prairie, profound with some secret intelligence, or at least the sort of volition associated with lifeblood.

The river lent animation to the town; the river blessed and cursed Hannibal with animation in much the same way that Mark Twain blessed and cursed Hannibal with his legacy. The blessing lay in the river's usefulness as a marketing conduit, and in its beauty, and in its irresistible metaphor as memory; Hannibal has forever been dreamily in love with its unrequiting past. The curse lay in flooding. Six or seven times a century, the Mississippi River would swell up out of its channel and drown the very epicenter of commerce (railroads, hotels, restaurants, shops and stores) that its animating force had coaxed to the riverbanks. Hannibal's most peculiar trait has been its susceptibility to ruination from its assets.

The Mississippi worked on the deeper instincts. Its soundless summer-day shimmerings, its deadpan placidity and friendly lappings in nonflooding times, only sharpened its intimation of sentient weight and movement, and lent the river a patina of terror — the kind of terror felt not so much when one was gazing at the river and astonished by its daylight majesty, but later, at night, and forever, in one's dreams.

I remember — I have dreamed — sitting in my grandfather's black Packard on Third Street, facing south toward Bear Creek, which bisected our route to Union Street Hill on its flow to the Mississippi, and watching oilskinned men in flat-bottom boats heap sandbags around the Admiral Coontz Armory. In 1947, my sixth year, the spring floodwaters submerged the railroad tracks and the sidewalks and pavement of Third Street virtually up to the wheels of the stopped Packard. I remember pleading with my grandfather to back the Packard up, turn it around, and get us away from the alien plane that had obliterated this part of Hannibal's surface by a power I did not yet understand. The dark floodwaters gave the familiar buildings an amputated look; disconnected them from any unifying context. They unfixed my universe and caused it to float apart; it was as if my identity, so dependent on the town's permanence, were dissolving.

This was the terrible duality of the Mississippi: its capacity both to define my location in the world and to suddenly deny it, by some capricious swelling of its weight and movement.

And yet, like the town, I was a fool for the river. The river satisfied what limited need we felt for connection to the nation. The river carried traffic down to us — past us — from Minneapolis and up from Memphis and New Orleans. Even when no grain-bearing barge, its connected scows lying low and tricky in the channel; or excursion steamer; or fishing skiff; or parading amphibious tank from the late Pacific theater happened to be passing our levee, we Hannibal people (we *Hannibalians*) received the Mississippi as my father received the airwaves: as connoisseurs of information. We knew that the waves and currents and driftwood themselves, the catfish and turtles, the winter's ice floes, all nature's bulletins, were reaching us from Clinton and Muscatine and Rock Island. St. Louis, that snob of a city to the south, would have to wait for this particular news. Hannibal had it first.

This Ptolemaic sense of the river — that the small curving shard visible from the town was somehow the Mississippi's center, if not the universe's — allowed us to forgive the river its terrors. Besides, it was gorgeous. Not many people born and reared in Hannibal ever had much experience with great landscape that they might compare with the Mississippi; and still the river struck us as a judgment against all other displays of natural beauty.

From the vantage point of my grandfather's front porch the river, now a mile in the blue distance and safely below me, formed the unifying line in a great dioramic composition.

My grandparents' house was at the foot of Booker Street, on the crest of Union Street Hill on the South Side of town. Jasper Toalson's was the bottommost house on a short, down-sloping block that ended at the precipice of a reinforced embankment. A Jonathan apple orchard began at the foot of the embankment and slanted down Union Street Hill toward the town until it gave way to bungalow backyards. I could sit, in summer, on my grandfather's green porch swing facing south, turn my face to the breeze rising from the east, and let my gaze widen upward from hollyhocks to Illinois. The hollyhocks grew wild at the top of the embankment, across a small graveled lane bordering the yard, where my grandfather parked his black Packard. Below the hollyhocks the apple-tree branches floated in the wind; below the trees lay the rooftops and church steeples of Hannibal, and the railroad roundhouse, from where the distant thunder of boxcars coupling at night commingled deliciously with voices on the radio. At the town's eastern border flowed the Mississippi, framed in my vision by two opposing bluffs — Cardiff Hill with its centennial lighthouse on the left, or upstream side, and Lover's Leap with its inspirational myths of Indian suicide awaiting downstream. The Mark Twain Bridge arched over the half-mile river channel from the foot of Cardiff Hill to the blue-green Illinois flatland on the far side. My perspective from Jasper Toalson's front porch revealed the entire bridge's southernmost flank. At night the winking bridgelights and the headlights of crossing automobiles cut the blackness like purposeful comets. Bing Crosby sang "Did You Ever Sail Across the Sea to Ireland" on my grandfather's console Zenith radio in the darkened living room, and in my child's mind, Ireland became the mound of pinpoint streetlights on the hill beyond the orchard valley, the hill to Lover's Leap. I looked out my grandparents' living-room window toward the invisible bridge, waiting sleepily for the tiny headlights I somehow could always identify as belonging to my parents' Nash, coming back to Hannibal after a mild jukebox evening in Illinois, coming to reclaim me from the best house on the best hill I ever knew, until later in my childhood I would walk into a house on another hill, the house of my great friend Dulany Winkler.

My father met my mother on the doorstep of Jasper Toalson's house at 1503 Booker Street, not three paces from where I later would pass time in the green porch swing, gazing out at the Mississippi. The year was 1937. He had driven his brakeless Ford up Union Street Hill to sell his Fuller Brushes. I imagine pompadoured Paul Powers rapping on the doorjamb of the Toalsons' small white frame house, then backing up two steps as prescribed in the Fuller Brush sales manual (to dispel the housewife's fears), then extending his arm to offer the bait, the "free gift" — a wire brush or plastic comb that the salesmen were required to purchase with their own money. And falling, by the manual, in love.

There is a verse in the 1939 edition of *Fuller Songs,* the official company songbook, intended to be sung to the tune of "The Man on the Flying Trapeze." My mother used to croon it to me when I was very small:

Oh, he comes to my door with the finest of aids,
That charming young man of the Fuller brigades.
His manner so pleasing, his brushes so fine,
My cares he is taking away.

That, in its outline at least, almost eerily sums up Paul Powers's courtship of Elvadine Toalson. But to think of my father *precisely* as "charming," in the manner of, say, Trevor Howard pursuing Celia Johnson in *Brief Encounter,* would be to seriously overstate the case. My father was a shy man. That fact alone would not have set him apart from his fellow Fuller recruits of the 1930s. The company legend virtually depended on the romantic image of manly but laconic young self-starters in two-tone shoes, reinventing themselves and breaking the Depression's stranglehold by summoning up their pluck at the nation's screen doors.

But even within this abashed pantheon, Paul Powers merited some special niche. He took his shyness seriously; he burnished it until it approached the status of charm. His early brakeless second-hand Ford is good evidence of this. Broke, brakeless, and a stranger when he first tooled into Hannibal, and too withdrawn to impose on some service-station grease monkey for repairs on credit, my father solved the considerable problem of navigating Hannibal's omnipresent hills by easing down them in zigzag patterns (I imagine his fedora at just the right rakish tilt, his babyface deadpan), relying on low gear, telephone poles, and the kindness of strangers to see him and his dust mops safely to the bottom.

Not long ago my uncle Aubrey, Dad's brother-in-law, happened across a townsman in his eighties, an ancient customer of my father's, while strolling on the riverfront. "I'll never forget the first thing he ever said to me," the old friend told my uncle. " 'I'll give you *aaaanything* to get me down off this hill.' " If my father was in anything like his usual form that day, he accepted whatever help the man offered him. And sold him a brush. My father and the town shared some central characteristics: a certain opacity of temperament that was often hard to distinguish from passivity; that talent for converting curses to blessings — and vice versa; a dreamy indifference to time and change, as if the worthwhile life lay somewhere within, inexpressible and darkly sublime. Although my father was not born in Hannibal, the people of the town understood him at once as he shrank back on their doorsteps. They found his deference charming, and bought his brushes. He never should have left.

But perhaps Hannibal never really struck him as home. My father was a southern Illinois farm boy set adrift by the Depression. He was hired into the Fuller company by his lifelong friend Bill Helm, an unvarnished specimen as primordial and single-faceted as his name. Bill Helm had escaped a life working the dry bean fields himself by taking an iron grip on the fabled Fuller Brush sample case, a grip he would not loosen for the next half-century. By 1934 Bill Helm was already a sophisticated two-tone shoe man, a sporter of white shirts on weekdays, and the latest in hand-painted ties, a driver of coupes. All these bounties flowed from Bill Helm's absolute and almost terrifying surrender to the Sales Gospel According to Alfred C. Fuller.

Bill Helm passed these verities along to my father. He was still passing them along when I was a child listening to them at our kitchen table at night, the ball game on the radio; he even tried to pass them along to me at my father's funeral, but I had long since memorized the cadences; I knew the strategy of getting the lady to reach for the big twelve-ounce size.

"When the lady of the house comes to the door, you say, 'Hello there,' or 'Hi,' if she's a young lady, your age," Bill Helm would instruct, leaning to press my father's arm. They would be drinking beer out of beaded bottles. I would be sitting silently, looking at their arms, looking at the lines where the suntans ended and the flesh turned white as a boy's.

" 'I'm your *Fuller Brush boy,*' " Bill Helm would recite, his eyes closing as the litany took his spirit, " 'and I have a *free gift* for you.' " (Here Helm would shoot an arm into the air.) " 'Which one would you like?' And you hold up three: Vegetable brush. Pastry brush. Spatula."

"And she'll have to make a choice," my father would put in, shutting his own eyes and pursing his lips to sip.

"And *she'll have to make a choice,*" Bill Helm would inform my father. "And then you say, '*May I step in and get it out of the case?*' After you get in the house, then you try to rub some of that witch hazel on her. Women love that witch hazel. Then, why, you've got her where you want her."

Bill Helm was in fact an absurdly successful sweet-talker of housewives, especially considering a couple of built-in handicaps — a certain low-grade reflexive raciness coupled with his lifelong inability to make the *th* sound due to severe overbite. (As the years went by and Bill Helm rose in the ranks, destined for his fifty-year desk lamp, his salesmen never tired of imagining their erstwhile field manager setting up an assignation: "I'll meet you at free-furty on Fursday.")

But the only Fuller Brush romance that Bill Helm ever instigated was consummated by my father, and it led to my arrival in the world. Helm's role was to assign my father to Hannibal, where he came, with the finest of aids, to the Toalson door opened by red-haired Elvadine, just four years graduated from Hannibal High School and ready for destiny's next whim. Elvadine was an aspiring pianist, an aspiring practical nurse — and just at that particular moment working as a heel-trimmer at the International Shoe Company. She was one of eight children — six survived into adulthood — of Jasper and Tracy Toalson, the Baptist baker and his dreamy, superstitious, hallucinating Catholic wife.

Paul and Elvadine were married in 1938. Bill Helm personally drove them to St. Louis for their honeymoon — out of concern, possibly, for my father's brakes. I was the first of their three children; I arrived three weeks before Pearl Harbor in 1941. My brother, Jim, was born at World War II's end (my father did not serve; his arches were fallen), and my sister, Joyce, arrived at the threshold of the 1950s.

I grew up in a town that seemed less a town to me than a kingdom. Its hills turned neighborhoods into discrete principalities and lent its modest area a bogus sense of vastness — the South Side, with its peeling bungalows and steeply angled vegetable gardens and tire swings depending from front-yard sycamores, was as culturally separate from stolid, plumb-level St. Mary's Avenue as Portugal from Spain. Hannibal regathered itself, transformed itself as the light of day shifted its intensity on familiar surfaces; as the universe of one fenceless backyard merged almost imperceptibly into the similar and utterly distinct adjoining backyard; as the myriad possibilities and aromas contained within a dark carless garage, opening onto a sunlit back alley, yielded to an equally rich profusion suggested by a lightly traveled neighborhood street, two fielder's gloves, a hardball, and the good right arm of Bobby Schweitzer; as the presence of night, and silence, conferred a different sort of feeling — unaccountably tragic — on the railroad yards than had the mundane day.

(But if Hannibal was a kingdom, who was king? The question never presented itself in my childhood. The town did not seem to require authority. It ran on invisible allegiances, or allegiances whose objects were less visible than the forty-eight-starred flag whose allegiance we pledged every morning at Mark Twain School, and to the republic for which it stood. The allegiances seemed founded on order, on cycle, on some unresisted sense of duty — my father, driving a sturdy beetle-shaped Nash now, threading and rethreading the finite itinerary of Hannibal streets on his Fuller rounds, the Nash perfumed by the disinfectant scent of new dust mops; my humpnecked grandfather, rising at half past four each weekday morning for years and generations to eat his Shredded Wheat with banana slices and then drive his black Packard down Union Street Hill to Zimmerman's bakery, returning to the house on Booker Street at midafternoon with flour to his elbows, the hump at the back of his neck a condition of his lifting sacks of flour for years and generations. These men understood obligation, understood allegiance, and I thought I understood as well. Perhaps if I had been asked who was king, I might have suggested the shadowy late author with the white mustache whose inescapable image the town seemed to worship, and whose image I tended to confuse with God's. Perhaps I would have been correct. And a terrible authority this king would yet prove to be; in some respects a despot.)

Hannibal's architecture reinforced its aura of fantastic exemption from mere municipality. Our police station at Fourth and Church streets was a child's confection of minarets. It had parapet gables and a three-story octagonal tower whose ogee dome was taken off one day by a tornado. (Before 1903, it had served as the City Hall.) The police station's most glamorous denizen — and, save for ministers, the town's single living icon of authority — was Officer Floyd Capp. Officer Capp was a motorcycle patrolman. That was the bureaucratic way of putting it; that was the job description. Officer Capp elevated that role to the genus of cavalry; there was a Prussian fatalism about the way he spearheaded a funeral caravan or directed church traffic on Sundays.

Officer Capp never revealed himself beyond the police station's meringue girdlings in anything less heroic than a wardrobe whose principal details remain as vivid and unwavering to me as my Sunday-school tenets of virtue: a pair of obsidian sunglasses, a polished Sam Browne belt lashed to his fat middle by a diagonal strap the width of a pot roast, and riding jodhpurs festooned with yellow stripes, tucked into knee-high leather boots that were laced as tightly about his calves as puttees. Appareled thus, Officer Capp loved to burst unannounced through the doors of our grade-school classrooms, where he would stand in front of the blackboard, rocking sidewise from booted heel to booted heel, and recite the

Five W's of Traffic Safety. When he had finished, he would spin about and take French leave, the teacher hastily bidding us rise in a collective *so long,* and there would be a bright hole in the air where Officer Capp had been.

The storefronts and hotels along the main commercial streets sustained Hannibal's abiding air of kingdom, of sovereign idiom impervious to fashion's whim. These buildings stood, and stand today, along the T formed by lower Broadway, which points directly at the riverfront, and Main Street, which parallels it. Mark Twain was at work on *Huckleberry Finn* in Elmira, New York, when the bulk of these buildings went up in the 1870s: two- and three-story brick structures with flat roofs, mainly Italianate vernacular in design but punctuated by a few Victorian specimens, with their low-relief friezes and cornices; an occasional stab at neoclassical (the Orpheum, later the Tom Sawyer Theater) or Egyptian revival (the BPOE Hall at Fourth Street and Central Park).

These were the first implantations of serious wealth in Hannibal — they and the pretentious pilastered mansions that arose during the same building boom on the high bluffs above the town's center. They sprang from Hannibal's golden age, the lumber age, the age in which men with names like Pettibone and Cruikshank and Dulany began to amass great entrepreneurial fortunes by lumberjacking the white-pine forests of Wisconsin and Minnesota. These men arranged to float the masses of felled timber down the Mississippi to Hannibal, where their company roustabouts hauled the logs out of the river and fed them into the sawmills that lined the banks of Bear Creek. The finished lumber was loaded onto freight trains for shipment to the pullulating neighborhoods of Oklahoma, Nebraska, Kansas, Texas, and the Dakotas.

It was the town's only age of grand gesture, of imperial presumption. For a couple of decades in the late nineteenth century, Hannibal actually mattered to the nation, and for reasons that had nothing to do with the accident of Samuel Clemens's legacy. The town was the fourth-largest lumber center in America; twelve lumber mills processed two hundred million feet of wood in the

1870s. The new aristocracy showed promise of an interesting talent for profligacy. In 1877 a lumberman named Sumner McKnight decorated the crest of a prominent Hannibal hill with an imperial two-story residence. It featured five giant bay windows on its front and three on each side. Its mansard roof, elaborate cornices, and graceful staircases were the standard of town fashion for years. McKnight eventually moved away, but his creation remained — to endure a brutally crushing snub. In 1898 Hannibal's greatest lumber baron, John J. Cruikshank, decided to build an even more imperial mansion — neoclassical, in beige brick with wood trim and a grand central cupola. Since the McKnight mansion disturbed Cruikshank's prospective view to the Mississippi, Cruikshank had it moved two hundred feet to the west.

By 1904, two years after Mark Twain's final visit to Hannibal (he addressed three hundred prominent citizens at the Cruikshank mansion), the town seemed impossibly graced with hope and good fortune, a town of destiny. Its population stood at 18,000, an increase of nearly 50 percent over the 12,790 recorded in 1900. The assessed valuation stood at $4 million. There were four banks, three shoe factories, a newly opened public library, the largest Portland cement plant in the world, twelve cigar factories, two breweries, one hundred twelve factories, a street-car system. Four thousand Hannibalians worked for factories and railroads; the town handled fifty-six passenger trains and thirty-four freight trains a day. The Mississippi flowed down like milk — twenty million gallons a day, someone estimated. "Two thousand miles of river transportation," the Chamber of Commerce boasted, "to all parts of the world." The horseless carriage had appeared in town; a man drove his through a store window and entered local history. One hundred businessmen purchased stock in a prospective new hotel, a centerpiece for conventions and civic luncheons and fashionable dining. They chose a site on South Main Street, a few falsely prudent blocks from the river. They called the hotel the Mark Twain. In 1904 Hannibal could still salute its most famous son and make the gesture seem gallant, inclusive; the town sweeping the famous son along in its triumphant ascension to the zenith.

In 1904 Hannibal, booming, dreaming, was already a husk. The white-pine forests of Wisconsin and Minnesota were nearly depleted. The sawmills along Bear Creek were producing far below capacity. In 1901 the lumber-pulling season had closed early because the Mississippi had dropped to a low ebb — a symbolic beginning of Hannibal's demise, and an eerie counterpoint to the river's virulent ravages later in the century.

The full piper-paying consequence of this inevitable cessation in Hannibal's lifeline, this prefigured termination of boom, was concealed, cushioned for several decades. The railroads and the shoe factories sustained the town's transition into its smokestack years, while the great lumber families played out their charades of aristocracy in their gilded dreamhouses on the green hilltops. If the lumberless Mississippi was beginning to isolate Hannibal from the nation's growth patterns, the Great Depression arrived to camouflage that trend; it absorbed Hannibal's inertia into the country's.

And even in the Depression Hannibal seemed especially favored, protected by destiny. The very avatar of American regeneration himself, President Franklin Delano Roosevelt, intervened personally in Hannibal's fortunes on two occasions. On the night of January 15, 1935, President Roosevelt touched a gold key in the White House and ignited the beacon atop a twenty-foot memorial lighthouse on Cardiff Hill — the ceremonial beginning of the Mark Twain Centennial, the one hundredth anniversary of the author's birth and the symbolic beginning of Hannibal's planned regenesis from hard times. On September 3 of the following year, Roosevelt appeared in Hannibal in person to sever the silk ribbon formally opening the new, million-dollar Mark Twain Bridge across the Mississippi, consummating an integral link in a continental route known in more lyric times as the Pikes Peak Ocean-to-Ocean Highway and more lately designated Route 36.

(One of my father's most sustaining personal memories was that he had appeared in the *Hannibal Courier-Post's* front-page photograph of Roosevelt at the bridge; a face in a crowd of seventy-five thousand. I grew up believing this. But as the occasion for verifying my father's claim began to take on a kind of inevitability —

as I began to pore through the newspaper's back issues for the daily record of the town's past — I began to dread the discovery; a certain pattern of doomed imaginings had long since, by then, revealed itself in my father's life. My fears proved legitimate enough. My father's face is nowhere visible in any of the newspaper's photographs of the Roosevelt motorcade. But then, in an odd manner of thinking about it, neither is Hannibal's.)

The Mark Twain Bridge supplemented an earlier, smaller upstream bridge built mainly for train traffic; it only incidentally accommodated wagons, pedestrians, and a few cars. Hannibal's city fathers quite naturally hoped that the new bridge would prove a conduit for motoring tourists from the East — people with money to spend in the boyhood town of America's greatest humorist (for that is how Mark Twain is inevitably regarded in Hannibal — as a humorist). And for a few years, that was indeed true. Typical of Hannibal's fortunes in the matter of harnessing Mark Twain's commercial legacy, however, the bridge was completed a year after the Mark Twain Centennial had closed down.

Mark Twain recalled Hannibal as a white town drowsing in the sunshine of a summer's morning, the streets empty or pretty nearly so. My own boyish memories are pretty nearly the opposite, and yet I sense that the town's elemental claim on reverie must be essentially the same for anyone who lived there as a child. I remember a town teeming with life and voices — my wild-eyed grandmother's voice in her darkened living room as she spun Germanic fairy tales at night; the voice of toothless Old Lady Collins, behind hollyhocks across the back alley from my grandparents, shrieking the melody to "Jesus Loves Me" in precise wordless syllables; the voices of my father's fellow Fuller men singing, half in parody, their company songs over beer in the kitchen of the house on St. Mary's; the voices of all the straw-hatted shoppers on North and South Main and inside the rows of stores — the Woolworth's, the Penney's, the Famous, and the Eagle — and the grown men's voices inside the scale-scented fishmarket on the river's edge or the blood-scented poultry house where my father took me on Sundays after church; all these voices of public movement and commerce, the grown-ups fulfilling Hannibal's apparently limitless logic of exchange and growth (although it must have been hollowing out even then, in those early postwar years, the logs no longer floating down the river); and I remember the voices on the radio, always the radio — Jack Benny and Amos 'n' Andy and *The Shadow* of course, not to mention Harry Caray doing the play-by-play of the St. Louis Cardinals through all my boyhood summers, but also our own radio voices: Genial Gene Hoenes, KHMO's Man on the Street, there at Main and Broadway at noon with his baton of a hand mike and his Question of the Day; the Reverend Johnny Golden, "The Old Ridge-Runner," beckoning me sonorously from sleep each morning from my mother's kitchen . . .

And so we come through the rest of the night
To look once again through the Window of Light
With ears to hear and eyes to see
What today has in store for you and for me.

. . . The Window of Light serving, in my dream-shedding first wakefulness, as the conduit for the aroma of skillet-fried eggs and percolating coffee. Johnny Golden's sermon would be followed by a local commercial, certifying our town's mercantile preeminence: *Yates-and-Hagens-as-you-all-know-is-just-the-place-for-you-to-go-for-shirts-and-shoes-and-ties-and-slacks-we-have-'em-ON-OUR-RACKS!*

And yet my abiding image of Hannibal is nocturnal. Twain recalled empty streets in the sun; I remember a town bursting with humanity but nearly always in the night. Perhaps I am coming back to town in my father's old Nash after a nighttime baseball game in St. Louis in one of those soft-consonant summers of my boyhood — Nash, Hannibal, night, never. Never grow up. I grew up and left Hannibal. Not out of choice, but I left nonetheless, and the town and the river and the bridge kept the account. The boy in me would dream his way back home forever afterward, but he would never make it. Perhaps he would make it as far as the top of the Mark Twain Bridge, crawling across the superstructure. Always, waking, he fell.

A quarter-century after I left Hannibal, I began to enact that dream. I began to reenter the town.

The year was overwrought with anniversaries. Nineteen-eighty-five marked the one hundred fiftieth year of Samuel Clemens's birth, and the hundredth anniversary of the American publication of his greatest work, *The Adventures of Huckleberry Finn.* Somewhere out beyond Jupiter, Halley's Comet was speeding on its seventy-five-year orbit toward the interior of the solar system and its eight-month loop around the sun. The last approach of Halley's Comet had occurred as Mark Twain lay dying in 1910; its visit previous to that had attended the author's birth.

And here I was in middle age, launching a fugitive summer of quick trips back halfway across the continent to a place I hadn't really known for more than half my life. I had planned it carefully: weekends stolen from my small boys, vacation time at my wife's expense.

And for what? For hanging out in a small town that most of my friends and relatives had departed, through death or the quest for better times; to ask questions I had not yet formulated of strangers who had no reason to trust my motives and even less reason to comprehend my essential, half-coherent reason for being there:

To try to reenter the last system of life that had ever made sense to me; to regain an old quotidian passion for the ordinary, and to see whether the town, the river, and the bridge still held their power as guardians of the old moral coordinates — the values and assumptions that cast Hannibal as an extension of my own identity.

Reasons enough, I decided, and I started going back.

CHAPTER II

I HAD never thought much about Hannibal's history while I lived there. Why should a child afflict his mind with intimations of a time before time? Why try to parse infinity? It would have been like trying to think about myself contained in my ancestors' blood; it would have been like trying to remember memory. Hannibal was a solid state of being. It had always been there — here — and it always would be: just as the pastel houselights at the Rialto had always been about to dim for the matinee double feature; just as my grandfather had always been shifting his Packard into second gear up Union Street Hill; just as the arc-lighted blur of the batted ball down on Clemens Field had always darted over the second baseman's head long before the cracksound of the bat reached the ears of any two boys watching in the night from the precipice at the end of South Fifth, a block from the lighted pilasters of the public library.

I accepted the town as it was, and asked no questions. I did not wonder why it existed on several planes — neighborhoods stacked above neighborhoods, streets ending at cliff-edges, lawns tilting downward at sixty- and seventy-degree angles — while the countryside around us was gently rolling prairie. I did not wonder why a lighthouse decorated the crest of Cardiff Hill, three hundred feet above the Mississippi, nor why no light from the lighthouse ever shone. The Mark Twain Bridge in its half-mile span across the river seemed to me to be an awesome, primal thing, like a dinosaur skeleton, but without beginnings — it was the only bridge I could bear to cross as a small boy without burying my face in the backseat upholstery, because it seemed to have stood there in the current forever, a god-bridge. I wonder whether I would have trusted its spans so implicitly had I known that it preceded me in history by only six years.

But these were necessary mysteries, the more wonderful to me for their lack of explication. They blended with the other odd wisps of information that drifted on the airwaves into my senses and lodged there without ever revealing their complete meaning. (I still pause sometimes to shudder over the tantalizing wrapup of a crime report that I overheard on my grandfather's console Zenith radio when I was about eight: ". . . Some of the men used garbage-can lids as shields.")

When I began to reenter Hannibal, however, I knew that I would have to engage its history. The intact town of my clandestine memory was itself history now; and if I were ever going to truly plumb its context, I would have to extend my lines of inquiry in two directions: forward, toward time present, and backward, into the deeper past.

And so on each visit to Hannibal, I would mount a short flight of granite steps at South Fifth and Church streets. I would pass between two sets of twin Ionic pilasters and push through the curved oaken doors of a sublime building that had unaccountably shrunk to about half its former size in the intervening quarter-century: the library. I would stand in the tiled circle of the foyer, in the center of the inlaid bronze star, for a couple of minutes. I would let my nostrils fill with the pervading scent of ancient bookbinding glue that had once intoxicated me as I prowled the Dewey Decimal System en route to the "602" shelf. There I used to pounce on the only books I was interested in checking out of the library (the stamped dates indicated, to my enormous satisfaction, that I was the only kid in town interested in checking them out). These were the Joseph A. Altscheller series of Civil War novels for boys —

The Guns of Bull Run, The Guns of Shiloh, The Scouts of Stonewall, and the rest — books that nearly came apart in my hands as I pulled them from the stacks, having been published near the turn of the century; each brittle book with a tissued page still protecting the illustration labeled "Frontispiece"; but books, nevertheless, that I treasured and nearly memorized, perhaps as much for their musty fragrance as for their romanticizing of a war that I gathered had been fought with plumes and brocade. It was the Altscheller series that brought me my first flawed, sweet whiff of history.

And then, having scented this trace of my own former existence, and feeling like some hulking Gulliver in this contracted shrine, I would spend the next couple of hours happily copying out the notes to the town as it unfolded in all its becomings before my time.

My guides into the past were mostly fellow townsmen: Twain himself; Thomas H. Bacon, who in 1905 published a pointing-with-pride history called *A Mirror of Hannibal* (and who served as first president of the library in which I sat); John Winkler, the late father of my best friend Dulany and president of the Mark Twain Home Board — but mostly the magnificent Hagoods, Hurley and Roberta, who in 1976 published a great compendium of town chronology called *The Story of Hannibal.*

I was especially at home with the Hagood book, because it was good and because I knew the family. Hurley Hagood had been a professional Boy Scout leader for forty years of his decent and useful life. His brother, Don, had been my scoutmaster (Troop 100, flashy in khaki and neckerchiefs; I knew what Twain meant when he wrote, grudgingly, about admiring the stunning red scarves of the Cadets of Temperance). I used to play wild November games of two-man football with Don's rattle-boned son Steve, who, upon throwing or catching a completed pass against phantom opponents, would shriek to the leafy neighborhood, "Yard gainage! Yard gainage!"

My townsmen guides to Hannibal's past led me gloriously into a time before time.

Hannibal was born of an earthquake that set the Mississippi churning backward and sent a newly homeless population flocking north toward Missouri in search of quiescent land.

Before dawn on December 2, 1811, the most violent tremors in recorded North American history began to split trees and vaporize streams around the village of New Madrid in the southern Missouri Territory. In the ensuing days, the earth rippled and burst over a million square miles beyond the epicenter. The Pemisco River was blown out of its bed; it vanished. The Mississippi and Ohio rivers foamed to a halt and reversed their flow; the Mississippi's resulting flood tide created Reelfoot Lake in northwestern Tennessee.

The convulsions shattered windows in St. Louis, Louisville, Cincinnati. Shocks were recorded in Washington, D.C., and Detroit and New Orleans. Hannibal, Missouri, was in chrysalis.

After the upheavals ceased, The United States Congress moved to authorize land certificates for New Madrid residents whose property had been destroyed in the earthquake. The certificates entitled their holders to claim up to 640 acres anyplace in the territory that had not already been settled.

Many of the claimants staked out homesteads in the quiet blackberry uplands of Missouri. A larger number repaired northward to St. Louis as soon as it was convenient, to float their certificates among speculators. It was in St. Louis a few years after the quake that a man named Thompson Bird struck up a friendship with a goateed, hair-slicked young handsome named Moses D. Bates. Bates persuaded Bird, who held his father's New Madrid Certificate, to file a claim for land near the confluence of Bear Creek and the Mississippi River.

This was the same lowland that disappeared under the alien plane of floodwaters in my childhood; the same land on which I sat in my grandfather's Packard in nonflooding times, waiting for a hundred-car freight train to complete its crossing of Third Street on the Burlington tracks that ran parallel to the creek — the two of us growing happily dizzy with the engine off, counting the black flatbed and the chipped yellow freight cars (Soo Line!) that streamed past us until the cars themselves seemed to suspend their motion and it was the Packard that drifted sideways along their flanks, dreamily and forever, click-*click,* click-*click,* click-*click.*

Moses Bates is officially recognized as the founder of Hannibal. More accurately, perhaps, Bates was its first impresario, the frontier fixer who first spotted the area's dollar potential and put together a viable package: a mode of operating that would be renewed periodically, and with varying results, throughout Hannibal's history. Bates had arrived in St. Louis in 1816, dripping enterprise. He opened a lumberyard, he built important homes for important people, he was sheriff of St. Louis County. When he learned in 1818 that the government was planning to survey the northern sector of the territory for demarcation into townships, Bates, no slave to false pride, landed himself a job as a chain carrier. And when, trudging the territory, he laid eyes on a small northern trading post on the western Mississippi shore, a mile or so above some superlative limestone bluffs and a small inland waterway lined with sycamores, Moses Bates grasped the inherent rightness of the site, its possibilities for combining river commerce with overland trade.

Bates threw up a log cabin on the site and hustled back to St. Louis, looking for a middleman, a man holding the right kind of paper. He found one in Thompson Bird with his father's New Madrid Certificate. Bates talked Bird into claiming the acreage surrounding Bear Creek. The two men immediately began carving out lots within the tract. They sold the lots. Their buyers were speculators. Most of the town's first landowners never bothered to come within a hundred miles of the site.

No one knows for sure who named the site Hannibal, or why. The official histories of the region — that is, the white histories — are content to point out that settlers of the early nineteenth century had a taste for classical allusions; and it is true that many of the smaller towns near Hannibal suggest this taste: there are Palmyra and New London and Cyrene and Canton. (There are also Monkey Run, Clarence, Cherry Box, Elmer, and Sue City, suggesting that the settling pioneers were not always above a little whimsy.)

At any rate, the official histories seldom go further than identifying Hannibal as the famous Carthaginian general. One needs to check a few independent sources to confirm that Hannibal was a *black* Carthaginian general — a fact that has tended to legitimize a cherished but carefully guarded oral legend passed through the generations of the town's small community of black citizens.

According to this tradition, a campsite had existed below the Lover's Leap outcropping before Moses Bates arrived — a campsite struck sometime after 1804 by members of the Lewis and Clark expedition of the Louisiana Territory. Among the members of this expedition was an African slave, a former explorer and ocean pilot who had been taken into slavery by Thomas Jefferson himself, then sent west with Captain William Clark.

William Clark was disposed to call this man by the name of York, but the man resisted the designation. "I am Hannibal!" he insisted. In the dark wilderness beside the Mississippi River, York — or Hannibal — was assigned to guard the expedition's campsite. Members of the party who had ventured inland — so the legend goes — could always find their way back to the base by fixing upon the sight, or sound, of the fierce African who waved a flag from side to side and announced into the western continent, "This is Hannibal! This is Hannibal!"

I find the legend appealing — the town, at its earliest nascence, bawling out its being in a human voice.

By 1819, Bates's speculator friends had persuaded a few seriously settlement-minded families to risk the upriver journey by keelboat and begin a pioneer life on the bartered land. Bates himself built a large trading post near the present site of Hannibal High School — not far from the football field where, one apple-cider night in 1958, I watched my classmate, the heroic Pirate quarterback Ted Hardy, still aching from a first-half kick to his groin, furiously run back two consecutive Fulton Hornet punts for touchdowns. My friend Dulany, a golden son of the town aristocracy, blocked for Hardy all the way, shattering his right arm on the second charge ahead of the workingclass ballcarrier. The dimglowing football field was its own history that night. I wondered how anyone could willingly walk back out of the glow and into the abiding dark quotidian after soaring like that — how they could endure the flow of ordinary time, the ordinary scent of decaying goldenrod in the night meadow up beyond the football field.

Moses Bates went into the keelboat business and later started a steamboat line. The steamboats prefigured Hannibal's golden era. In 1856, an Irish immigrant, a former grocery clerk named John J. Cruikshank, stepped off a steamboat and opened Hannibal to the lumber industry. Cruikshank had landed up in Pittsburgh (then spelled Pittsburg) from Dublin in 1826 with his two brothers, an immigrant boy of fourteen. He drifted from there to a flatboating life on the Mississippi near New Orleans.

No history book has recorded the process that led John Cruikshank from New Orleans to the white-pine forests of Wisconsin; but by 1851, Cruikshank owned lumberyards in two Mississippi River towns on the Illinois shore, Galena and Alton. Five years later he arrived in Hannibal with five hundred feet of house-building lumber, which he thought he could sell over a five-year period. The lumber lasted less than twelve months. Cruikshank contracted for more white-pine trees to be cut and floated down the river. By 1870 there were twelve lumber companies operating in Hannibal, including one founded by a prospector who had struck it rich in the California Gold Rush, William H. Dulany. William and his brother, Daniel, created the Empire Lumber Company. Daniel's daughter, Ida, would later marry an attorney named George A. Mahan, consolidating two great fortunes and forming the most influential family (save the Clemenses) in Hannibal history.

The lumber industry quickly reached a combined capital investment of $3 million. Ancillary industries grew up around it: sawmills, railroads. Pork packing and shoe manufacturing soon followed. For a few thunderous decades, Hannibal boomed and boomed.

Now the town still lies there, as far from tremors and shock waves as any of its founders could have wished. Now the town lies, still, in its cluster of limestone bluffs by the curving river, in the great urban absence at the middle of the loud nation. It is as if a vast and delicate bell jar had been placed over Hannibal and the miles of oceanic prairie around it, sealing out the noise and the deadliness and all the million-square-mile convulsions of the late twentieth century. Of a cold late night on a Hannibal hill one can hear a dog barking a mile across town, the sound traveling as if on water.

Hannibal's aura of soundless isolation is partly a trick of the mind — a wish — but mostly it is genuine. No divided interstate highway approaches within two hours' drive of the town. The Iowa border is eighty miles north. The nearest metropolis, St. Louis, lies one hundred twenty miles downriver, and the best driving route (61, inland, the least scenic) is single-lane for almost forty big-rig-clustered cornfield miles. One does not find oneself in Hannibal without seriously *intending* to find oneself there.

A phantasmic intruder upon Hannibal's isolation is a redbrick industrial city two and a half times Hannibal's size, and sprawling within twenty miles of the town's northeastern border. This is Quincy, the Gem City — settled two years after Hannibal, in 1821, site of a Lincoln-Douglas debate in 1858, and a relative colossus of worldliness for all the decades of its proximity to the town. And yet Quincy scarcely bears on Hannibal's consciousness.

Quincy gestated in a sort of parallel universe — its universe being Illinois, separated from Missouri by the Mississippi River and linked by politics and railroads back to the progressive, corporate East. Quincy matured as the last outpost of the plumbed continent; Hannibal, as the first clearing on the Paleozoic prairie to the west. Transportation across the Mississippi was limited to ferryboat traffic until the Wabash Railroad built a train bridge in 1871 — the Mark Twain automobile bridge did not arrive for another sixty-four years — and so the neighboring towns gazed Janus-like toward their respective destinies, the towns sealed off from mutuality by the thin wall of the river, eerily like contiguous, stubborn spinsters in an otherwise spacious but vacant rooming house.

The automobile had forged a link, of sorts, between Quincy and Hannibal by the time of my boyhood. Quincy was our El Dorado. It was low-slung roadhouses and blue-neon bowling alleys for the ducktailed rodders off the Marion County farms. *It ain't the best, but you c'n git it for less, in Quincy.* Quincy women rolled their shirt sleeves all the way up and stared at you out of their car windows at drive-ins. Once I tried meeting a Quincy woman's stare with a pouty, saturnine gaze of my own. The crack of her chewing gum shattered the sexual tension I was trying to establish. "Why don't you go home and get in bed and get happy?" she called to me from the far shore of the Hannibal A&W parking lot, and I shrank beneath the window of Bobby Schweitzer's Studebaker, red-eared with horrified pleasure at her ambiguous suggestion — my first encounter with a truly *low-down* woman.

But this sort of cultural interchange arrived late in the two towns' relationship. No such proximity to a metropolis abetted Hannibal's early growth. Nor was it, strictly speaking, the Mississippi River. Northern Missouri's original attraction lay largely in its network of inland waterways: beautiful, coiled little streams, many of them mineral springs fed from underground systems, that provided rich alluvial soil for the great southern migration of the 1820s: alluvial soil and, even more compellingly, salt.

Europeans had been prowling about the upper Mississippi valley at least since the late seventeenth century, when the French explorer-priest Father Jacques Marquette floated downriver, taking note of the jagged tooth of limestone that would become known as Lover's Leap. A few years later the area accommodated its first tourist. During the great expedition of discovery by La Salle, which established the Louisiana Territory as a French possession, a small coterie led by the monk Louis Hennepin pulled its canoes out of the icy river at a bay two miles above Bear Creek. Hennepin declared this to be the Bay de Charles, in honor of the French prince — a name it retains today. Hennepin's leader was less successful in naming the river itself. La Salle fancied the title *Colbert,* but the Indian name prevailed in history: *Missi Sepe,* the Great River.

Still, the region waited another century and a half for settlement by a white population — and when that population began to arrive, it arrived largely by wagon, not by riverboat. In 1793 a Frenchman named Mathurin Bouvet came searching for a naturally saline spring that he had heard mentioned by Indians trading at St. Louis. If the spring existed, it would be one of the extremely rare sources of salt on the continent, and thus a great treasure; the salt could be sold at St. Louis to settlers heading west.

Bouvet found his spring less than thirty miles southwest of Bay de Charles — a thin, exquisite mineral stream that arced and curled for perhaps a hundred miles between banks of black willow and sycamore; through forests of oak and hickory and dogwood; through fields of goldenrod and bloodroot and columbine — through a land dense with deer and wild turkeys and brown bears and opossums and mink and muskrat. The stream emptied into the Mississippi. The indigenous Sac and Fox Indian tribes called it the *Au-Ha-Ha* — the Laughing River. Bouvet, an early exponent of development, applied a more functional name: he called it the *Rivière au Sel.*

I came to know the Salt River and its encompassing terrain. My father and I hunted the land a century after the forests had been hacked down into cornfields and still we came home with game — bloodied rabbits and quail. We stalked the denuded swells of land in winter, trudging over corn stubble, my silent father at rare peace in his hunter's cap, the earflaps tied alertly up above the bill, cradling his shotgun, a timeless figure; me, anxious and quite temporal in my cap with the flaps down, holding on to an air gun, conscious of being on somebody's property, conscious of the blood, the filmed-over eyes.

Mathurin Bouvet set up his salt-boiling kettles on the banks of the *Rivière au Sel* and hastened to St. Louis for more supplies. The Indians confiscated the kettles and Bouvet's horses. Bouvet brought more men, more equipment. He built a furnace and a warehouse and began to boil salt on a grand scale for transportation to St. Louis. In the winter he repaired south to the great trading post himself. The Indians destroyed his plant again. Bouvet stayed away two years. When he returned in 1795 he built a warehouse at Bay de Charles — thus establishing the first white settlement on the Hannibal site — and returned to his salt-making operations on the *Rivière au Sel.* This time Bouvet lasted five years before the Indians tracked him to the bay and killed him, along with his assistants.

But Bouvet had established a frontier. Now other white men came, in clusters and with their families, to boil the *Au-Ha-Ha* into salt and to work the splendid cheap land. By the time Lewis and Clark explored the territory, by the time Moses Bates arrived carrying his chain, there were settlements all along the Salt River. Over the ensuing quarter-century a great migration struggled up into the Missouri Territory from the South, principally from impoverished Kentucky. The people came by overland wagon on a laborious route that required three river crossings: the Ohio River at Shawneetown, the Mississippi at St. Louis, and the Missouri a few miles farther west, at St. Charles. Then they struck a rough and mostly untended trail known as the Salt River Road, which they followed some eighty miles northward — bringing with them their southern mountainfolk usages and religions and zodiacal charts and their mountain fiddles and their fondness for green tobacco smoked in clay pipes; bringing with them even in this hated diaspora their deep, hooded, mountainfolk blood allegiance to family and to place, and their concomitant defiance of the new, the alien, the usurping. These allegiances define much of Hannibal's character, and that of its surrounding villages, to this day — a surviving thrust of Appalachian fierceness in a relatively northern enclave.

Thus it was the Salt River, and not the forbidding Mississippi, that established northeastern Missouri's population, if not its pervading culture. Hannibal remained a clearing of five or six families until the late 1820s — until Moses Bates and others established a steamboat line between St. Louis to the south and Galena, Illinois, to the north, bringing immigrants and river trade to the village for the first time. A Salt River settler typical of the migratory patterns was John Marshall Clemens of Virginia, Mark Twain's father. In 1823 Clemens set up a law practice in Columbia, Kentucky, with his Kentucky bride, Jane Lampton. A few years later Clemens moved on to Fentress County, Tennessee, where he invested a significant bulk of his worldly assets — about $400 — in seventy thousand acres of virgin land. Clemens expected that this estate, rich as it was in coal, iron ore, copper, and timber, would enrich his family for generations to come. It was not to be. A financial panic in 1834 wiped out most of Clemens's savings. He gathered his family and joined the great migration to the northwest and into Missouri, where he settled in a Salt River village of one hundred inhabitants called Florida. It was there, in a log cabin, that his second son and sixth of seven children, Samuel, was born in 1835. The Clemens family did not move on to Hannibal until four years later. It was to be their final journey in search of better times.

The small boy Sam spent his summers at the farm of an uncle, John Quarles, four miles from Florida. In his *Autobiography,* Mark Twain composed a loving elegy to the remembered land and to childhood days.

"I can see the farm yet, with perfect clearness . . . ," Twain wrote. "Beyond the road where the snakes sunned themselves was a dense young thicket and through it a dim-lighted path led a quarter of a mile; then out of the dimness one emerged abruptly upon a great level prairie which was covered with wild strawberry plants, vividly starred with prairie pinks and walled in on all sides by forests. The strawberries were fragrant and fine, and in the season we were generally there in the crisp freshness of the early morning, while the dew beads still sparkled upon the grass and the woods were ringing with the first songs of the birds. . . ."

I decided to begin my pilgrimages back to Hannibal with a visit to this land, this countryside along the Salt River valley half an hour's drive to the southwest of the town. Here, in many ways, lay the cradle of Hannibal. Besides, to approach Hannibal from this valley would be to retrace the Clemens family's migratory route that led them to the house on Hill Street.

Such a retracing seemed appropriate, given this one hundred fiftieth anniversary year of the author's birth and the town's plans for a great civic celebration, the Mark Twain Sesquicentennial — a seven-month-long pageant that would culminate on November 30, Mark Twain's birthday.

I had in fact visited Hannibal twice within the previous year: once in July and again in November. These visits had been quick and perfunctory, defined by specific obligations. The visits had served one purpose: they had erased any inclinations I might have had to postpone further, more intense pilgrimages. But they had not allowed much chance for exploration in themselves.

Now it was the first day of March 1985, and I sat in a parked car by myself in Missouri, gazing once again, after all the years since my boyhood, at an alien plane. Floodwaters covered the familiar surface of land that I thought would be visible forever, part of my identity.

But this time the floodwaters were not natural; they had been created by men. This time they would not recede; they were permanent. Here was the Salt River — but the Salt River transmogrified into something called Mark Twain Lake.

A few feet beyond the artificial shoreline, half submerged by the dammed waters, I could see a sort of outdoor bulletin board, coated with use regulations. It looked dumbly out of place, like the lake whose uses it was intended to regulate. At any rate, it was too far offshore for any of the regulations to be legible.

Mark Twain Lake lay upon twenty-three hundred square miles of prairie land, the handiwork of the United States Army Corps of Engineers. Created several years after I left Hannibal, the lake had been a visionary hope among many northeastern Missouri businessmen since my childhood — indeed, since before my birth.

Mark Twain Lake was not connected to Hannibal in any municipal sense. The town most likely to feel its effects was Monroe City, a sturdy, square-cornered little hamlet of bean fields and grain elevators that lay a few miles to the north. A prairie village for all the years of its existence, Monroe City now found itself, in 1985, a prospective lakeside resort.

As depicted on a promotional map of the region, the lake resembled a digitally rendered Chinese dragon, one whose front legs had been splayed outward from the body, owing perhaps to a smart blow to the base of the neck. I left my rented car and walked in the cold wind down a graveled incline so that I could stand at the sheet-metal water's edge. I was near the hinge of the open lower jaw, at the southwestern extremity of the dragon. Fully ten miles separated me from the tip of the tail, which lay to the northeast, at the Bluff View Recreation Area and just yards from the Re-Regulation Dam. (The principal dam, known as the Clarence Cannon Dam, defined the beast's hindquarters.)

Somewhere in between — amidst the shoulder blades — at the tip of an engineered peninsula, near the ruins of the old hamlet Florida, and presently enshrouded by a swoop of architecture known as the Shrine, rested the tiny log cabin in which Clemens was born. The tip of the dragon's tail lay twenty-eight miles southwest of the authentic waters that called forth such torrents of his literature. Now the contrived water had all but surrounded his birthplace — a venue for water-skiers.

I climbed the gravel incline to my car and eased it back onto the service route numbered 154, dawdling my way onward toward the dragon's watery midsection. There was no other traffic on the road. The sky and the lake were nearly identical shades of gray. There was no color either in the amputated sycamores branching above the water line nor in the cornfields or woods that had survived the lake, owing to high ground. When the lake opened up on my left from a narrow talon to a vast slatelike belly, I slowed the car. I tried to conjure a color-drenched summer universe: blue skies filled with cottony clouds above a sunfish-sailboat regatta, above outboard motorboats towing water-skiers, while on the shores, copper-toned young girls in iridescent bikinis reaching to accept iced-down brews from their Polaroided boyfriends — and, in the background, happy family units enjoying the picnic facilities, the group picnic shelters, the electrical hookups, the trailer dump stations; the elder members clinging to their valid Golden Age Passports. . . .

But it was not working for me. The amputated sycamores kept getting in my way; the sycamores and Mark Twain's memories of the great level prairie covered with wild strawberry plants, the dew beads that sparkled upon the grass and the woods that rang with the first songs of the birds.

Well, the dew beads would no longer sparkle upon those grasses. The wild strawberry plants, if any vestiges remained, lay buried beneath an average twenty-nine feet of normal pool elevation.

Thus the first vista of my first pilgrimage revealed how thoroughly the old system of life had been buried. The old moral coordinates had been replaced, it seemed, by illegible instructions. Reentry might prove an elusive undertaking.

CHAPTER

III

I HAD traveled down this road before.

I remembered skimming along it toward town from the west, as now, but in Duly's white Chevy convertible, riding shotgun, stunned at my temples from the force of summer air after some insane sundown sprint flat out the old straight slab of 36, the gold-tinted soybean fields flattening toward either horizon and the railroad tracks running parallel to the road — no particular reason for us to still be alive, Duly having gunned it down the flat stretch, the low sun goldening his face, to give us some boost when the Chevy's tires hit the roller-coaster hump in the pavement where 36 curled up and over the tracks just east of Monroe City.

And if there was no traffic ahead we'd hit the base of the hump full speed and the Chevy would seem to launch itself off the rim of the earth for a moment and we couldn't draw breath. And then Duly would fight to control the wheel one-handed, his big left elbow casual on the window jamb. And he would settle the yawing Chevy back on the road at seventy-five; and if a freight train happened to be curving under the hump as we flew over it, and if Elvis Presley was singing "All Shook Up" on the radio, the universe would be briefly perfect.

Then slowdown; standstill. We would sit hushed and motionless for a few minutes, the countryside pressing in on us, the silence enormous beyond the idling engine. And then Duly would dial the Chevy in a half-circle on the old tar-caulked two-lane. He'd lay down just a little judicious patch of rubber to boost us back up off the shoulder. Maybe the rubber would blacken the same slab where John Winkler, Duly's highway patrolman father, once spot-weighed an eight-wheel rig back in the 1930s, before he married into the town's ranking family and took up his inherited calling as Mark Twain's hometown curator and defender and advocate.

And then Duly would slow the white Chevy down enough so that when we breathed, we could taste the pollen and the dewfall in the vast Missouri air. And we'd let Hannibal's gravitational belt reclaim us from the rim of wildness, from our brief thrust toward a distant but onrushing galaxy whose polestars were named Kerouac, named Kennedy, named King. We succumbed to Hannibal stunned with the sunset on our necks and our temples numb from the wind, silent and in cahoots, yet already imagining our separate family suppers — Duly's roasted, mine fried — taking for granted the fact of our lives and the permanence of the town that now presented itself as we topped the rise above the Junction of Highways 36 and 61 and Fern's White Rose Diner. Fern's and the Junction told us we were most of the way home.

They had moved the Junction.

Highways 36 and 61 now intersected nearly a mile north of where I was presently dropping into Hannibal. The two-lane road I was driving on — the old 36 — was now something called MM, cracked and weedy on the shoulders. Several miles back to the west, they had forked off a new section of 36 and thrust it clean through Hannibal, a limited-access dagger. This new route caught the action from Macon and Chillicothe and St. Joseph over on the Kansas border, and moved it along divided lanes straight through town to the base of the Mark Twain Bridge, where the historic district beckoned.

"New," it occurred to me as I slowed the car, was an unreliable value, as so many of my perceptions of Hannibal might prove to be. They had begun grading for the new section of 36 before my family left town.

There was still a *junction,* of sorts, on the original site, where MM crossed the north-south stretch of 61. In fact, it was a bigger deal, in certain ways, than the Junction I remembered. A complicated electronic stop signal, complete with all sorts of left-turn arrows and delayed greens, had replaced the four-way stop signs of the old 36/61 days. As I sat idling under the red light, I looked to my right and saw that Fern's was still there.

Fern's White Rose Diner: that holy all-night cheeseburger chapel to truck drivers and my more Brando-embracing ducktailed classmates, its men's restroom presenting the widest assortment of machine-vended prophylactics to be found in northeast Missouri, still stood. In fact, it had expanded. Grafted onto the low-slung dining room now was a clean well-lighted convenience place (beer, soda pop, Riunite) and a brace of self-service gasoline pumps shielded by a high canopy roof of corrugated aluminum. At the edge of Highway 61, Fern's had placed a signboard marquee of black plastic letters fitted into grooves. It announced:

BEER LIQUOR GROCERIES
ANTIFREEZE
BUDWEISER
BUSCH

I was deeply gratified to find that Fern's had survived. It occurred to me that I had never met Fern. I think that Duly might have pointed her out to me once; I have a fleeting impression of plumpness, bobby pins, and *authority* near the homemade pie case—but mainly Fern was an abstraction, a celebrity proprietress tangible only to Hannibal's hangover breakfast crowd. The regulars. I was never a Fern's regular. Never wore a ducktail. I had a flattop and only went there in the daytime.

The light turned green and I considered wheeling into the diner plaza, and breezing past the glass door and introducing myself—provided she was still there, of course. But how would I presume?

And how would I begin? *"Fern, you probably wouldn't remember me, but I used to be a fan of yours. . . ."*

Instead, I eased the car across the intersection. I pulled off into the lot of a Scooters Sub Shop, and spent a few minutes looking through my rearview mirror.

The rest of the Junction was unrecognizable. All the other family-owned eateries and gas stations had vanished: the wonderful Osborne's Service Station and Cafe with its green awnings and its big Sinclair sign on the roof and its gastronomically ambiguous slogan —

HOME OF SINCLAIR PRODUCTS
STEAKS-CHICKENS-FISH-SALADS

— and gone also were Lloyd & Gene's Mobil Service, and DeLaPorte & Sons Shell Service (*"Better Care — Longer Wear!"* I went to school with one of the sons), and the Dairy Queen, already a portent of standardized changes to come when it appeared in the 1950s, but welcome with its one-cent sales and the indigenous flutter of moth wings against its yellow fluorescence on summer nights. Long-shoed Jon Eddington and I would stroll away from its window spooning weeknight raspberry sundaes and discussing, with total absence of irony, our ideas for the perfect Norman Rockwell *Saturday Evening Post* cover, or shy Jon's procedural theories for time travel ("Have friends all over the world . . .").

All this had been replaced by the embassies of franchise. Around the electric signal were a Cassano's Pizza & Seafood, a Kentucky Fried Chicken, a Hardees (one of three in the town), a Wendy's, and a second convenience shop, attached to a Shell station. The marquee signboard at the Wendy's said:

WAKE UP TO WENDYS
GET DETAILS
ON KGRC

No local legends to be found behind these counters! The legends were all in the logos, and the logos came from someplace else. I was looking through my mirror at a conquering colony of franchise, imported piecemeal but no less systematically from distant marketing empires and affixed here upon this disjuncted Junction, this crossroads that had itself been rendered vestigial by time and engineering. I assumed that I was looking at a reflection, as it were, of Hannibal's flight from isolation, and at its price.

The assumption was false. Or it was no more true than any single conclusion to be drawn about the town. I had forgotten the lesson of my own childhood: Hannibal imploded. It subdivided itself into a microcosmos of facets that were as subtly distinct from one another as vegetable gardens, as the smell of frying chicken on a weekday night from the same smell on a Sunday noon, as Baptists from First Christians. As the running board of a black Packard from the running board of any other car.

It was the neighborhoods that blew away my first impression that Hannibal had succumbed to the modular orthodoxy of the revised American town.

Route MM — old 36 — rises to its stop-sign terminus at St. Mary's Avenue, the true western rim of residential Hannibal and my old neighborhood from grade-school days. I glanced right and left along St. Mary's and immediately felt as though I could breathe again; I had broken the surface of consciousness after submersion in a twenty-five-year dream.

Here was the intact town of my clandestine memory. Here, at least the surfaces had not changed, the structures.

I turned right on St. Mary's and pulled to the curb. Across the street was the St. Mary's Pharmacy — or the odd little wedge of a building that had once housed the pharmacy (it seemed to be a beauty parlor now): an inexplicable taste of Old Mexico with its dusty-pink stucco facade (now repainted a bright blue) in this block otherwise represented by righteous white bungalows.

I knew, without having to look behind the streetside facade, that the pharmacy was not a four-cornered building at all. It was shaped rather like a wedge of pie — strawberry chiffon, judging by the old color. Its southernmost flank narrowed almost to a point so that the building could fit into the property angle formed by Hawkins Avenue as that street slanted across St. Mary's, rising toward Mark Twain School and rising again — the beginning of a long grade that climbed through tilted neighborhoods until it crested beneath the glorious great house called Skylands, where Dulany had lived.

The pharmacy! I remembered how we used to invade that cavern of clovesmell and comic books in bunches of six and seven on sweltering Missouri August afternoons, our ball gloves buttoned by their straps to our belts. I remembered what it was like to push through the main door from the blaze of pavement and be blinded by the dimness while Melvin Bird's air-conditioning shocked our skins under our T-shirts, turning our sweat cold. To our left, the fat part of the wedge, was a soda fountain with a marble-topped counter and wire-backed stools. Melvin Bird himself was behind the counter drawing the Cherry Cokes, Melvin Bird small and quick and watchful in his outsized short-sleeved business shirts, his black hair slicked and parted in the middle. From this command post, Bird had a direct line of sight, through his round glasses, to the narrow end of the pharmacy, the point of the wedge — back beyond the cosmetic cases and the first-aid shelves and the bubble-gum cards, back to where he kept his magazine racks.

We would guzzle our Cherry Cokes and then congregate down in the narrow end, a clot of damp baseball kids, pretending to flip through the comic books (Little Lulu and Superman and Scrooge McDuck) but secretly in pursuit of the lurid. Secretly we were turning the enameled pages of *Argosy* and *Real Detective* and *Police Gazette* and *True Confessions,* on the lookout for illustrated lurid bare female thigh — the thigh bared, in most cases, in consequence of that most routine of grown-up social encounters, that between a cringing woman in a slit skirt and the looming chieftain of a Nazi slave cult. (The willingly bared bare enamel-pulp breast was still in the future.)

The second entrance to the pharmacy was a door built into the wedge, opening onto a narrow aisle between the two full bins of magazines and newspapers and comic books — a breach of security unimaginable in present-day mercantile America. A True

Confession here: through that door and onto Hawkins Avenue passed the occasional pilfered copy of *Argosy* and *Real Detective* and *Police Gazette* and *True Confessions,* the copy palmed by a prepubescent in a trancelike study of deadpan. That is not the morally decisive element of the story, however. The morally decisive element is that Melvin Bird never stopped us. Never confronted us, never called our parents. Years later I talked to a fellow perpetrator, and he agreed: there was no way Melvin Bird could not have seen, could not have known. Nor was he in any way a meek or timorous man. Perhaps, like most merchants who sold magazines in Hannibal, he was a bit ill at ease with the raciness of some of those titles the distributors brought to his shelves and did not wish to draw any further attention to them. But that is a cynical, late-twentieth-century way of looking at it.

The only plausible conclusion is that Melvin Bird simply did not want to see us in trouble. We were good kids. We would outgrow it, we'd pan out all right. If you would know Hannibal, Missouri, at midcentury, if you would understand the majesty and essence of lost community everywhere, you must know about the pink stucco St. Mary's Pharmacy and the man behind the soda fountain who allowed his lurid magazines to be stolen, and the thieving children who eventually understood.

But the pharmacy was long gone on this March afternoon. Behind the doorway at its narrow-wedge entrance was something called the Cut Up Ltd.

I glanced into the rearview mirror — into the reflected way home, home to the white bungalow on St. Mary's where I passed my T-shirt, grade-school, pharmacy days — and eased the car back into traffic. I was heading for downtown, the river, the bridge. The old moral coordinates. I would come back to this neighborhood, but now I wanted to see some other facets of this town of mine, this sesquicentennial town. I wanted to see what else had changed, and what else had remained the same.

Moses Bates bought himself a small sidewheel steamboat in 1825 and started running it up and down the Mississippi River between

St. Louis and Galena, Illinois, with a stop at Hannibal. This venture marked Hannibal's transition from settlement to town. By 1830 there were thirty people living in Hannibal. They built a log schoolhouse on the town square, where Central Park is now. The following year a ferryboat began operating across the river to Illinois.

Hannibal's first big population wave washed in on the tides of a Mississippi flood — a flood that obliterated a developer's plan to design a great western metropolis just eight miles above Hannibal, a metropolis that would extend outward and consume Hannibal in its massive grid of mills and railroads and churches and colleges and opera houses. The metropolis was to be named Marion City; its founding genius was a successful prospector in the local salt springs named William Muldrow. Muldrow managed to sell more than $150,000 worth of Marion City lots to East Coast investors on the strength of his great vision, and people began settling on the land in 1835. A tent city was in place by the spring of 1836 — when the Mississippi, swollen by runoffs from heavy snows in the north, rose steadily and turned the flatland site into a vast lake. Some five hundred refugees fled southward to the smaller settlement nestled among the limestone bluffs and sloping uplands. Thus did the Mississippi enrich Hannibal upon the ruined hopes of its first rival developer. The river would not spread its full weight upon Hannibal itself for several more decades.

St. Mary's Avenue forms one segment of a looping boomerang-shaped thoroughfare belt that encircles most of the Hannibal that has stood for a century, and some of the town's most gloriously hilly topography. The present city limits engulf the boomerang by a wide perimeter, and yet most of the population still lives within it. Franklin Roosevelt and his motorcade of twenty automobiles passed along this belt (Broadway to St. Mary's to old McMasters Avenue, now Highway 61, north to Hannibal-LaGrange College, and then back east over Palmyra Road and its extensions to the riverfront and the base of Cardiff Hill) in September of 1936, the year Roosevelt came to dedicate the new Mark Twain Bridge. ("Fine!" the president boomed when fourteen-year-old Louisa

McMein, winner of the Souvenir Bridge Ticket Campaign, presented him with the first ticket. "And can I go across without paying?") The year my father claimed to have appeared in the newspaper photograph along with FDR.

Most of Hannibal's retail business is inside this belt, and all the historic district, including the Boyhood Home and museum. The pharmacy is inside the belt, and Skylands, and the Hannibal Country Club — last redoubt of the old aristocracy — and most of the schools, and the old courthouse, and the chlorine-scented YMCA building with its green institutional walls and its Ping-Pong tables and its pool where Milton Failor had pitched us, the boys of his swimming class, naked and howling into the chemical brine ("Let's give 'im the old *ha-ha!*"); and, next door to the now-vacant Y on Center Street, facing Central Park with its long-empty bandshell, the redbricked building that housed Doc Porter's osteopathic office.

Doc Porter was a Hannibal High Pirates booster in the high-top-gym-shoe years before my attendance there. His office walls were famous for their permanent collection of black-and-white team photos — strangely formal-looking, hair-oiled basketball elevens and football fives.

During my high-school years, the Doctor had fallen into reduced athletic circumstances — he served as a volunteer, the unofficial coach of our tennis team (Duly was the golden number one player; I vacillated between number five and third doubles). Doc may have been the only adult in Hannibal who knew or cared that the tennis team existed.

I wanted to see him. It made no particular sense that Doc Porter was the first of my boyhood acquaintances that I would seek out in this inaugural pilgrimage. It wasn't as if the two of us had had an exceptionally close coach-and-athlete bond. ("You've got no *shoulders,* Powers!" was the only advice he'd ever offered me that stuck in my memory.)

But they had named the high-school football field after him. He was probably the closest thing the town had to a living legend. I parked my car in a vacant space on the slanting street directly in front of his office building, and walked through the door — into a frosted-glass, ointment-scented universe that had not changed in my lifetime.

I told the matronly receptionist that I was an old friend who wanted to surprise the Doctor. She showed no trace of curiosity or amusement — neither did the two women in pantsuits who saw their appointments being usurped — but she pressed a button and spoke into a small intercom. A moment later Doc Porter came through his rear-office door, wiping his hands on his blue smock.

His flattop had turned white. That was the only change in him. He peered at me through his horn-rims and nodded curtly, as if confirming something to himself, and motioned me back through the door. I had the feeling that I was a few minutes late for a rubdown.

There was no question that he remembered me through my beard, my thickening middle. "Where's Duly?" he demanded once he was seated behind his desk, his fingertips pressed together. Then he inquired about the other members of the tennis team — the 1959 tennis team — ticking them off according to their singles ranking. I half expected him to call a practice session at his farm, where he used to drill us on his private court — having collected each of us in his battered station wagon.

We gossiped a few minutes, talked some Notre Dame football — he still maintained his season tickets — and we looked together at some of the old team photographs on his office wall. And then I shook Doc Porter's hand and left. He had been pleased to see me, but it was nothing special — a drop-in from one of his kids. I got back into my rented car feeling, again, not so much that I had come back to Hannibal as that my senses were clearing after some glazed distraction that had lasted twenty-five years.

A locomotive whistle briefly blotted out all other noises in the town. A diesel engine, all silvery and aloof, was easing its hundred-car freight southward along the riverfront tracks four blocks to the east. The train's appearance offered a deceptively animated image of town commerce. It falsely suggested that freights were a routine feature of Hannibal life. That was no longer true. This click-clacking behemoth was just passing through; it could not have stopped in Hannibal if the engineer had wished — the freight yards were gone now. I was looking at a vestigial scene from an epoch that had been launched partly by Mark Twain's father.

The arrival of Judge John Marshall Clemens's family from the hamlet Florida in 1839 guaranteed Hannibal something more than a place in American literary history. Judge Clemens himself helped steer the town toward its long age of wealth and influence in commerce, transportation, and civic graciousness.

John Clemens never enjoyed any of the rewards of that age. His curious fate in Hannibal, during the eight years before pneumonia killed him, was to command personal respect even as his failing enterprises — he was a justice of the peace, a lawyer, and a shopkeeper as well as holder of those seventy thousand Tennessee acres — thrust him ever more deeply into poverty. This flinty unsmiling man died bankrupt in diaspora in 1847, having admonished his twelve-year-old son to "cling to the land and wait; let nothing beguile it away from you."

But while he lived, John Clemens enriched Hannibal. He helped organize the town's first lending library in 1844. He was chairman of the Committee on Roads, which established plank thoroughfares linking Hannibal with smaller settlements. And in 1846, in the judge's office in the Union Hotel at Hill and Main streets, a group of twelve civic leaders met and resolved to put Hannibal into the railroad business. The state legislature granted this group a charter in the following year, and the voting on bonds began.

The Hannibal–St. Joseph Railroad was not completed until 1858, long after John Marshall Clemens was dead and five years after his son had left Hannibal. But its inception marked a turning point in the national commerce. The railroad provided a western overland conduit for goods floated by steamboat on the Mississippi, and it determined Hannibal's preeminence as a lumber center for logs floated downriver from the northern forests. The line was also the first link to the horseback mail route known as the Pony Express.

The railroad generated an economy that actually survived the town's logging bonanza, an economy that was just playing itself out in those boxcar-coupling nights of my boyhood, when the train yards on the riverfront below Lover's Leap still throbbed with the passage of rolling stock. The world's first railroad mail car was built in Hannibal; so was the first locomotive constructed west of the Mississippi. At the century's turn, Hannibal was the hub of four principal rail systems and five trunk lines, accounting for a total mileage of 13,868.

A glorious turreted old castle, Union Depot, survived into my lifetime. It points its spires to the night sky in an early memory of mine, dwarfing the silhouette of my arriving aunt Opal, who stands below the steps of a hissing passenger train, a suitcase in each hand, her movie-star hat tilted down over one eye. Off behind Union Depot, several dozen yards past the last honky-tonk, the Mississippi flows, invisible as evil. It is half past ten on a winter night — my first visit to the station. I have come with my father to meet Aunt Opal, who has traveled down on the Burlington line, down along the Mississippi, from the town of Aurora, near Chicago, for a visit. My aunt Opal is glamorous, like the name of her town.

Now my aunt Opal confers her glamour on the darkened railroad yards; she lends a little edge of drama to the great old station that once received Mark Twain on his last visit. My father, my aunt, and I are players for a moment in the last act of an old town saga — the railroads are nearly gone by now — last-act actors under an Orpheum moon. My father stoops to pick up my aunt Opal's suitcases; she lights a cigarette, and I feel sleepily caught up in the sweet sadness of Union Depot; uncomprehending but in love with this newly revealed enclave within the imploding Hannibal night.

Union Depot was torn down in 1953 and a small featureless brick hut with aluminum awnings was erected in its place. The new edifice now served as a printer's shop.

I had driven all the way downtown to visit Doc Porter at his office — I could see a hyphen of Mississippi four blocks to the east, framed by buildings at the foot of Center Street — but I wasn't ready to walk around the business district just yet. I felt exposed, out in the open. Suppose someone recognized me — a relative, an old classmate, a former teacher. A giddy sort of wish took hold: I wanted to be the spotter, not the spotted. I wanted to burst in on the people I knew; I didn't want them making the approach to me. I needed a sense of the initiative, the upper hand, to cancel out my uneasiness at being where perhaps I really did not belong.

I drove a block south to the main thoroughfare, Broadway, then headed the car back west. I drove until I was nearly as far from downtown as I could possibly be within the city limits. I drove to the point where Route 61, the old McMasters Avenue, intersected with the limited-access dagger of 36 — the new Junction.

I had made a mental list of places to inspect — stores, shops, bakeries, movie houses, the ballpark, the riverfront — all the connective tissue of Hannibal's public life as I remembered it. If the surface textures of the neighborhoods were still intact, perhaps other vital signs of the old infrastructure were functioning as well. I needed to find out.

When I left Hannibal in 1959, three railroad companies still served the town that had once received fifty-four passenger stops a day. Three bus lines came through. There were seven full-scale hotels and nine motels. Five taxi companies stood ready to move visitors around town. There were thirty-one restaurants (including my favorite, based not so much on its country-style fried chicken as on its loopily lewd name, the Moon Wink Cafe), eight ice-cream parlors, twenty-five beauty shops, nineteen registered nurses, twenty-seven clergymen who were willing to have their names listed in the Yellow Pages, and forty-two bars, taverns, and honky-tonks, including the Elite, the Friendly, the Alibi, the Square Bar, and the F. J. Yohn Wonder Bar.

I pulled into a small motel called the Tom 'n' Huck. I remembered it as Beam's Motel, modest and dignified, without the reflexive belaboring of the Mark Twain angle. A woman's face appeared on the other side of a locked screen window — a symptom of darker transition. But when I asked the woman whether I could borrow a telephone directory, she immediately offered me a copy to keep. This was more in line with Hannibal tradition as I preferred to remember it — and would have been utterly in line, had the kindly woman not been Iranian.

Back in the driver's seat, parked in the motel lot, I began tallying data from the current Yellow Pages.

Present-day Hannibal had no hotels. I counted listings for seven motels, one of them a bed-and-breakfast. But this was the sesquicentennial year. *Two million visitors in seven motels?* Even if they didn't all arrive at once? It seemed unlikely somehow.

I looked for railroads. The nearest passenger station seemed to be in West Quincy, about twenty miles up the river. Bus lines? There was a Trailways number. The only other bus company was listed in Monroe City. The two million would have to drive, I supposed. Where would they park? Not in garages. There were none.

The Yellow Pages showed one taxi company.

I turned to the restaurant section. Here the list seemed to have expanded, but on closer reading most of the restaurants, and nearly all the ambitious ones, were in surrounding towns. Hannibal's listing totaled twenty-four — including the three Hardees, the Cassano's Pizza, a Holiday Inn, a Lum's, a Long John Silver's, a McDonald's, and a Ponderosa Steak House. For some reason neither the Wendy's nor the Kentucky Fried Chicken was listed. Possibly they did not accept reservations.

There was one ice cream parlor. It doubled as a Mexican restaurant.

Four clergymen advertised themselves. Not one of them was situated in Hannibal. There were twenty-three churches — including five Baptist, one Southern Baptist, one Catholic, four Disciples of Christ (my old outfit was the one at 1101 Broadway), three United Methodist, a Nazarene, a Pentecostal, and a Seventh Day Adventist. No synagogues or temples were listed.

The really shocking attrition was in the taverns — only fourteen remained in Hannibal, according to the Yellow Pages, very few with interesting names. Gone were the Elite and the Square Bar and the Alibi. The Friendly had moved to a new location (if it was the same Friendly) and opened a branch in Shelbina. The F. J. Yohn Wonder Bar, now simply the Wonder Bar, seemed to have moved across the street.

Once again I put the car in motion. I got back on St. Mary's and followed its curving length toward downtown. Beyond the pharmacy, St. Mary's becomes Broadway and eventually widens out of the neighborhoods and into the town's main business-district boulevard, tilting downhill at Fifth Street toward its terminus at the Mississippi levee.

This time I was after firsthand evidence. The March afternoon had grown late; the sun had dropped below the cloud line to throw a little picture-postcard tint on the old white and sandstone buildings. At a few minutes after four o'clock in late winter, Broadway was nearly empty of the present tense — walkers, automobile traffic — as close to pure archaeology as it ever would be. Ghosts might be on the street now: my grandfather driving his black Packard with both hands; the boy Dulany in his chauffeured Pierce-Arrow; my tilt-hatted father on his rounds in his Nash.

I had to hurry now before darkness came. There were sites I needed to examine personally, the ruins of my boyhood.

My first stop was at 1221 Market Street, half a block from where Market joins Broadway in a Y-shaped confluence known in my boyhood as the Wedge. The Wedge had once been a miniature black community — not "ghetto" so much as compressed universe — only a block long on either stem of the Y. But what a yeasty block! — a jumble of ancient woodframe storefronts, two or three stories high; the Little Egypt tavern and some adjoining pool halls at street level and cheap rented rooms above. Anchoring these frail structures were the Negro Masonic Temple and the prosperous Robinson Mortuary. I always felt a demimonde rush whenever I would whisk past this inviting, forbidding enclave in the family car, this triangle of opaque Negritude smack in the middle of the white town: a momentary blur of low blue neon and a note from a jukebox, a whiff of stale beer on open-door summer nights, a suggestion of dark men sitting on tilt-back chairs in their undershirts, the whites of their eyes impossible to avoid; my eyes meeting theirs for just long enough. Once as we sped through the Wedge on our way to a movie, my brother, Jim, in the backseat, said he believed that Negroes looked especially good in uniform. We all nodded solemnly; a sort of emancipatory glow took hold in the car. Jim's remark was almost Lincolnesque in the context of the times. I never saw an incident of racial violence in Hannibal — the public schools were quietly desegregated just a couple of years before I entered high school — but that was partly because blacks were few and mostly invisible in the town. Those who lived there knew, as the saying had it, their place. Their place was mostly in the fetid floodplain of Bear Creek, an area known as the Bottoms.

A more accurate gauge of prevailing racial sensibilities than Jim's remark lay in a thing my high-school circle of friends and I would do tooling through the Wedge in a crowded car when we were feeling especially witty: we would hang our heads out the window, stretch our mouths wide with our fingers, and make loud guttural noises deep in our white, inviolate throats.

The Wedge shanties were gone now. A triangular patch of grass, oddly small and mundane, lay where those exposed, yet impenetrable old firetraps had sheltered their society. An electric traffic-signal system, all left-turn arrows and synchronized greens, kept watch over the triangle from yellow beams above.

Where had they gone, the people of the Wedge?

Some vestiges of the period did remain. A row of woodframe storefronts, their green paint curling, still stood at the address where I now idled the car, 1221 Market. They were of the same turn-of-the-century vintage as the razed Wedge buildings, and in fact had faced the Wedge from the far side of the street. And yet this row had belonged to a totally separate universe — Hannibal's white working class.

At this address had once stood the Dann Dee Bakery.

My great-uncle Jesse Toalson had opened the Dann Dee when he and his brothers, Jasper and Harvey, moved to Hannibal in the 1920s from Mexico, Missouri. (Jasper, my grandfather, joined

Zimmerman's.) I recalled Saturday mornings in the place when the essence of hot sweet dough was almost like humidity; when Uncle Jesse filled the window with tilted racks of piping doughnuts like rows of coins in a March of Dimes display. Now the window yielded only blackness and the smell of must from inside. On the glass pane of the front door were the remains, in chipped paint, of a taxicab company's telephone number.

I turned the car around and rejoined Broadway, heading east toward the river.

I passed my old church, the First Christian, built of graystone in 1890 with Dulany money — Duly's family line. Beyond the church I had a sense, perhaps deceptive, of vacancies, of empty stretches where buildings had once stood. Four blocks farther down on my left, at Broadway and Eighth, I saw the place that had once been Zimmerman's Bakery.

Zimmerman's. My God, I remembered it as being enormous, a munitions plant of a bakery, blocks long, with half-naked Vulcans inside tipping giant cauldrons of dough like molten steel. Zimmerman's commanded a fleet of black delivery trucks that, parked in a chevron row, spanned the width of the levee. My grandfather was part of a combine, I used to imagine, that supplied bread and sweet rolls for the Allied Forces overseas.

There was still a bakery on the premises — a small storefront called the Pastry Box. On the lettering above its front door the *t* and the *y* were missing from "Pastry," the *o* from "Box."

Near Sixth Street the old blue-framed Rialto marquee, which had heralded Western Double Bill! backed up by Six Cartoons and Serial on the Saturday afternoons of my youth, now advertised

ROBINSON PAINT & WALLPAPER
DECORATING HEADQUARTERS
GLASS-WINDSHIELDS-STOREFRONTS

and the former Mary Ann Sweet Shop next door, where we would repair to let our eyes unspiral over Cherry Cokes served up from the fountain by Jerry Haag's father, now bore a banner that advised

IT'S TIME! COME IN AND TEST DRIVE OUR
CONCERT-READY PEAVY AMPS.

Silverburg Dry Goods, a classy department store at 525 Broadway, had been torn down. At 519 stood a boarded-up thrift store; on its door was a hand-lettered sign: WE NEED VOLUNTEERS.

Silverburg's, gone? (And Sonnenberg's, and the Emporium, and the Missouri Brokerage and the Mitzi Shop and Bowles Clothiers — what had happened to these places?)

And something had happened to the place my grandmother called the Pitcher Show.

At Fifth and Broadway, diagonally across the street from Central Park and anchoring the intersection that crowned Broadway's majestic descent to the riverfront, stood the building that was once the epicenter of Hannibal's cultural life — the Tom Sawyer (formerly the Orpheum) Theater. The Orpheum was the movies — not horse operas but Gable, Cagney, Rock Hudson and Doris Day, the class stuff. It had a lighted arcade and an enclosed ticket booth inhabited in my time by my cousin LeRoy, large and dignified in a wine-colored tunic, and barely deigning to recognize me. With its gracefully curving, upholstered balcony, the theater could seat thirteen hundred people, about one-sixteenth of the town.

Hannibalians had gone to the Orpheum in 1925 to hear the broadcast of Calvin Coolidge's inauguration, free of charge. Ziegfeld brought his Follies there, and the Marx Brothers came, and Sinclair Lewis, and Duke Ellington and Louis Armstrong, and Tom Mix and his horse, Tony. I went there with my grandparents — it was the Tom Sawyer by then — to see every *Pa 'n' Ma Kettle* and *Francis the Talking Mule*. Later, when I went with my friends, the unexpected image of the Frankenstein monster in preview one night frightened me so profoundly that for years afterward, the very utterance of "Frankenstein," or even the word in print (it looked and sounded like dried bones), was enough to trigger spasms of terror.

And once, still later, I went there with my father. It was the only time he ever took me to a movie. We saw *The House of Wax,* for some reason, starring Vincent Price, in 3-D. We sat there in the darkness looking straight ahead through our Polaroid glasses, each of us in his own dimension, each of us clenched and alone. We didn't talk much about it on the night drive home.

The white art-deco marquee still curved over the entrance, but it no longer announced first-run movies. The few burgundy-colored letters that remained seemed to spell out the shreds of some religious prophecy.

The Rialto and the Tom Sawyer — gone. Where did Hannibal people go when they wanted to see a movie?

I eased the car a little farther down Broadway.

Kline's, at 302 Broadway, where my mother ventured to buy a dress once every four or five years, was now something called the Golden Ruler Inc. Its logo was a giant ruler painted in lurid yellow across the front of the building. In the display window, posters announced RED TAG SALE and HONG KONG SWEEPSTAKES.

Next to the Golden Ruler was a narrow doorway and a window — Mr. Nick's Cut & Style Shop. The logo here was a hand-lettered sign; a note, really, Scotch-taped to the window. Behind the note announcing Mr. Nick's was displayed a vacuum cleaner; it was for sale.

Main Street intersected Broadway two blocks from the Mississippi, running parallel to the river. Here was the humming heart of Hannibal's commercial district when I lived in the town. The Fall Festival's brightest lights and scariest rides were laid out here every October; all the guy ropes and the sandbags, the smell of cooking sugar and the grinding Tilt-a-Whirl gears.

But no ride could produce a giddier sensation for me then than simply *standing in the middle of the street* — that traffic-wild thoroughfare domesticated for a few days by orange-lighted shooting galleries and cotton-candy stands. As I stood in the bright-winking street, looking back through the ambling crowds to the closed stores and cafes that lined the sidewalks, a wave of dizzying sadness would always well up in me, muting the calliope pleasure of the night. It was like looking into a glass that revealed the future.

In December, Santa's Workshop went up on the eastern side of the intersection, toward the levee; there was always a gigantic painted candy cane, and Santa kept office hours inside. In the spring, two smashed automobiles would be towed over to where the Workshop had been: a frieze of collision, all mangled doors and flung-open hoods. A dummy's head would be thrust through one smashed front windshield, its skull smeared with red paint to simulate blood — all a friendly reminder to observe the Chamber of Commerce's safe-driving campaign.

But the heart of this heart of the town was the dime store.

Officially known as S. S. Kresge's (gold-leaf letters on a strip of red field), it anchored the northwest corner of Broadway and Main, the premier commercial site downtown. The dime store was cheap-toy headquarters for every child of the working class; it was ribbons and buttons for moms, and cash-register bells and cries of "Thank *yew,* naow!" I would regularly get separated from my mother in the aisles of the dime store, bellowing in panic as the realization took hold that I would never see a familiar face again; I would be an orphan and live in the Orphans' Home. Then a familiar pair of square-heeled shoes would round the corner and I'd rejoin the known universe. Outside, on the corner at noon, the forbiddingly famous Genial Gene Hoenes, KHMO radio's Man on the Street, would prowl suavely amongst the straw-hatted shoppers with his Question of the Day, while two blocks to the east, great barges of grain and coal would churn their way up and down the middle of America, nosing their way between the stanchions of the Mark Twain Bridge.

No longer. The dime store — which had been completely rebuilt in an optimistic curve of art-deco brick three years before I left town, was gone. The building was vacant.

The dime store — vacant?

And still the changes, the absences, unfolded. Half a block south on the far side of Main Street, the marbled arcade of the old Yates & Hagan store (*"shirts 'n' shoes 'n' ties 'n' slacks . . ."*) billboarded a schedule that announced Thursday-evening Bible study. Farther south, the elegant Mark Twain Hotel stood gutted, stripped of its chandeliers and moldings. A demolition notice had been affixed to its northernmost facade.

Still farther south on Main, toward the scraped remains of Union Station and the railroad yards, the hard cowboy bars began.

I turned my gaze from South Main back east, toward the riverfront. Here the worst horrors of Hannibal's transformation lay in my line of sight.

A redbrick levee, the easternmost extension of Broadway, dipped gently into the Mississippi. The levee had been built in the nineteenth century for the unloading of steamboats. In the old days it had formed part of a riverfront vista that included Nipper Park, adjoining it to the south, with its fountains lit at night by colored beams, and grassy promenades. On summer evenings in my childhood, families would stroll to the levee from the shops on Main Street, and listen to the calliope music that floated from the decks of the yellow-lighted excursion boats, and look out upon a deepening river panorama of the sort that had caught the imagination of Mark Twain.

"And then you have the shining river," Twain wrote in *Life on the Mississippi,* "winding here and there and yonder, its sweep interrupted at intervals by clusters of wooded islands threaded by silver channels. . . . And it is all as tranquil and reposeful as dreamland, and has nothing this-worldly about it — nothing to hang a fret or a worry upon."

No longer, at least on the Hannibal levee. Now the river's sweep was disrupted by a large, L-shaped arm of earth and cement that crooked around a small-boat marina. The speedboaters and the power-yachters and the houseboaters of Hannibal stored their vehicles there; it was a liquid gasoline alley. At the point of Nipper Park that thrust out into the river, a Phillips 66 shield crowned the view.

But the marina was not the worst violation of Hannibal's riverfront. That distinction belonged to a towering mass of greenish cylinders that hugged the shoreline a few blocks to the north, beyond the crumbling skeleton of the old power plant, not far from the foot of the Mark Twain Bridge. This was the Hannibal Grain Terminal, a joined agglutination of ten hulking silos — its storage capacity was one million bushels — that brooded more than two hundred feet over the low skyline, throwing the entire town out of scale. Construction on the grain terminal had begun before my family left town in the 1950s. In addition to being a monumental eyesore, the grain terminal had proved to be a significant civic embarrassment: its lease with the city had been written in such a way as to impose an unamortized balance on Hannibal virtually in perpetuity.

A marina, a crumbling power plant, a usurpacious grain terminal: Hannibal's grand riverfront (not unlike hundreds of other riverfronts in America) had degenerated into a kind of municipal storage bin.

The town was getting dark now. The streetlights were flickering on. I had not yet checked into my motel room. I was staying at a Holiday Inn out on the western rim of the town.

I turned my car's headlights on and headed there. I suddenly wanted nothing more than anonymous walls, an institutional mattress, perhaps a franchised drink served up with a digitally coded bill.

I turned on the car radio to KHMO — Gene Hoenes's old station. A female voice, all country-western, said, "*Hello,* Mark Twain Country. . . ."

CHAPTER IV

THE idea for staging a Mark Twain Sesquicentennial Celebration on a national scale did not originate with anyone in Hannibal. The idea originated in the mind, and in the data-card file, of a New York–based consultant, a specialist in commemorations and special events named Alfred Stern.

"I wrote one of my magic letters to John Lyng, the Boy Mayor of Hannibal," recalled Stern, blowing a thin reed of smoke upward from his cigarette, as I talked to him over delicatessen sandwiches a few blocks from his Manhattan office. "This was in nineteen eighty-three. I told him that he should form a commission, that I had twenty useful ideas, and that I should come out and talk to him."

A few of Alfred Stern's "useful ideas" were in the modest category of what Stern himself called "little grace notes" — the consigned development of a special white Mark Twain rose, to be presented to distinguished visitors; an invitation to the Smithsonian Institution to open its traveling Mark Twain exhibit in Hannibal; the staging of an art fair featuring works inspired by the Mississippi River; the construction of a permanent theme stage to be used for demonstrations by musical groups, Boy Scouts, and other local performers.

A somewhat larger share of Stern's ideas might have triggered warning signals in the mind of a prudent person who was familiar with Hannibal's civic temperament. These ideas included the staging of a Mark Twain film festival featuring a bus specially equipped to project up to sixteen Mark Twain–oriented films onto screens arranged in a circle (patrons could choose earplugs carrying the soundtrack of their choice).

The ideas also included a massive riverboat regatta that would call to Hannibal every steamboat or steamboat replica that existed in the country (no one knew how many existed, or where they might be found); the complete restoration of the Mark Twain Hotel; the retaining of the movie actor and gourmet Vincent Price to reproduce a famous dinner at the Lotos Club in New York in 1894, at which Mark Twain had been the honored guest; and the world premiere, in Hannibal, of a Broadway musical play based on *Huckleberry Finn* that was being developed by Joshua Logan.

Finally, somewhere in the center of town, a clock tower would be constructed, modeled on the steeples of European cathedrals, in which miniature replicas of saints clattered out to mark the striking of each hour. In the Hannibal version, characters from Mark Twain's novels would replace the saints.

"That one was a little rich for their blood," admitted Stern dryly.

But the second of these ideas truly pierced to the heart of Hannibal's aspirations for itself as a shrine to Mark Twain. Stern suggested that on November 30, 1985 — the closing date of his proposed festival and the exact night of the great author's one hundred fiftieth birthday — Hal Holbrook himself would appear on a Hannibal stage to re-create his famous role as *Mark Twain Tonight.*

Beyond the celebrity value, there would be a certain symmetry in a commemorative Hannibal performance by Hal Holbrook. Nearly thirty years before, when Holbrook was an unknown actor still researching the subject of his celebrated one-man show, he had come to Hannibal in search of clues to Twain's personality. John Winkler, Dulany's father, had invited Holbrook to study an heirloom film clip — possibly taken by Thomas Edison — showing Clemens, for a few blurred and oddly tender seconds, seated at a veranda table with his daughter Clara, and then waddling, Chaplin-like, toward the camera, trailing cigar smoke. The film was shot at the Clemens home in Hartford in the last year of Mark Twain's life.

John Winkler also possessed a brief transcription of a wire recording of Clemens's voice, and Holbrook had been allowed access to this as well. These two fleeting vestiges of Twain — one visual, one aural — became the basis of Holbrook's stunning impersonation. Thus the notion of Holbrook returning to the very wellspring of his greatest dramatic fame, on the occasion of his subject's sesquicentennial, had the aura of inspiration.

On the basis of this "useful idea" alone, Alfred Stern signaled that he was a potentially valuable resource to Hannibal's city fathers. His letter also hinted that the right kind of sesquicentennial celebration, staged and financed and promoted in the right way, might leave Hannibal rather rich.

Alfred Stern made it his business to keep abreast of what the mayors of various towns and cities should be doing in regard to celebrating, and incidentally exploiting, their local histories. At age sixty-nine, Stern had been masterminding centennials, exhibitions, fairs, and pageants for nearly half a century, starting with his apprenticeship at the New York World's Fair of 1939. After an interval of fulfilling his patriotic obligations — he handled public relations for General George S. Patton's Third Army in World War II — Stern began to market himself around the country as an expert in the field of municipal backward-harkening.

The Winston-Salem Centennial of 1948 had Alfred Stern's stamp on it, as did the Detroit Automotive Golden Jubilee. Stern was the brains behind the Maine Event in 1952 and the Man and the Polar Regions Theme Exhibit at Montreal Expo '67. When the Camp Fire Girls needed someone to put together a Golden Jubilee, Stern was there, as he was there for the Clairol Pavilion and the Borden Company Show at the 1964 New York World's Fair.

By then, Stern, a tiny and dapper man who presented himself in neatly pressed blazers and horn-rimmed glasses, had perfected a formula, an idiom, for saluting the American past that touched the heartstrings of booster-minded businessmen.

Stern's formula — as he explained it to *Newsweek* in 1956 while designing St. Louis's Mid-America Jubilee — was to kick out pomposity and overweening reverence for strict historical detail. "Powdered-wig pageantry," he sneered. "Eight galoots in long drawers standing around a scroll." Stern's answer to this sort of stodginess was to design commemorations with a contemporary twist. "Pour on brandy and light it" was his happy motto.

The 1970s saw Alfred Stern weave his smart marketing gimmick deeply into the nation's ever more brandified vision of its past. This was the United States Bicentennial era, the post-Vietnam, post-Watergate renaissance of American good feelings, and Stern was everywhere with his chipper ideas, his lists of possible tie-ins and theme centers and logos. He consulted for the national Bicentennial Commission itself. He had a hand in designing the 1982 Knoxville World's Fair, the televised Night of a Hundred Stars, the Twenty-fifth Anniversary of Alaska's Statehood — and still Alfred Stern had time to check his data file and write one of his "magic letters" to John Lyng, the mayor of Hannibal.

The boy mayor. Stern could not have known it, but his blind letter reached perhaps the one citizen in Hannibal public life who possessed the necessary brazenness to consider its "twenty useful suggestions" without reeling backward in horror. (The clock-tower idea was an exception.)

John Lyng was thirty-three years old in 1981, when he defeated Hannibal's incumbent mayor, a former city clerk named Lillian Herman, to earn his first term. He would win reelection in April 1983. Before his first bid for mayor, Lyng had held two other elective offices — prosecuting attorney for Marion County, and, before that, at age twenty-seven, eastern district judge of the Marion County Court.

Lyng's political patron was his law partner in Hannibal, a powerful Democratic state representative, later a United States congressman, named Harold L. Volkmer. Volkmer held the keys to John Lyng's political future. If Lyng could earn any sort of reputation for himself as Hannibal's mayor, and if he could content himself with getting reelected a few times until the older Volkmer decided to retire, then John Lyng would inherit the conduits to a national office, having bypassed the obscurity of state politics entirely.

The trick was to earn any sort of reputation as Hannibal's mayor. For decades, the office had been a bad joke in the town, if not the state — a haven for amateurs, eccentrics (one recent mayor had prided himself on personally running the municipal snowplow), part-timers, and other well-meaning citizens hopelessly at sea in the theoretical requirements of city government. Some of these make-believe mayors had been easy prey for corporate lawyers eager to strike usurious contracts with the city; at the same time they had been oblivious of emerging federal acts creating low-interest loans and grants for civic improvements. A caustic witticism had it that a farmer once spotted a tornado funnel headed for Hannibal; when he rushed into town to report it, the people waved him aside: "The mayor would never let anything that big in here."

Into this vacuum strode John Lyng. John Lyng let the tornadoes in. John Lyng governed Hannibal with a preemptive force and shrewdness that was utterly without precedent in the town's political history.

In some aspects, he bore the markings of the town. He spoke in the same midland accents as everyone else; the *r*'s rich in their turnings, the flattened-out vowels betraying a trace of the old southern diaspora — but those vowels could turn steely if Lyng felt himself challenged or pushed. He sported the same dry goods as the other fellows — democratic light-toned suits with service-club pins in the lapels, worn over short-sleeved dress shirts and ties that ventured just a slash or two of sassy pastel.

But then there was the matter of the beard.

It was a *neatly trimmed* beard, no denying that, and unconnected to his mustache besides — but it was a beard, cultivated for everyday use in a town that regarded beards as marginally acceptable for certain tradesmen, visiting cellists, and city fathers getting ready to participate in Tom Sawyer Days. John Lyng's beard, with its prematurely silver glint, wreathed his roundish face like some sort of tinsel. It struck some people as a rather overtly *liberal* beard. It drew attention. It drew comment.

There were other peculiarities that singled him out. He lacked small talk. He lacked humor, or at least the easy mock-rustic banter that served to get Hannibal males warmed up for serious business talk. John Lyng had a manner you'd almost have to say was brash. He was a real get-to-the-point type of person. You just couldn't kid the man along.

All of this may have been forgivable, even the beard. Hell, not only liberals but normal people had taken to sporting beards around the country; the folks of Hannibal knew that. What they found harder to swallow was the tendency for Lyng's brash style to spill over into flat-out crust — a sort of suck-egg gall that Lyng must have picked up over at the state university, where he had got his good education and his law degree. It was said that there was a slickness to him, a sleight-of-hand way of shuffling facts and figures around, sometimes *deferring* the facts and figures, saying he'd have them later, always later.

They didn't mind it so much when Lyng was *campaigning*. The psychology of the town favored any upstart, any challenge to the decades of unrelieved paralysis. It was a great show to watch that boy talk circles around his opponents — first the incumbent, Lillian Herman, then two years later a challenger named Sue Quattrochi. Lyng told them both a thing or two, and that was fine; the town got a show out of that.

But then here he'd come, as mayor, into these committee meetings and council meetings and planning-and-zoning sessions and so forth, and he'd *do the same thing to the people of Hannibal*. He'd come in demanding that things be done his way; he'd swear he had the facts and figures to back him up; he'd bring them in later — and he'd cajole and explain and list all the points in his favor until everyone just threw up their hands and said, all right, dammit, John, do it your way. And the town's quietly tingling underdog nerve began to throb.

(What most of the good committee members never heard was a

favorite boast of Lyng's, one that he would unlimber only among the members of his closest circle. "Give me thirty minutes' warning on any subject," an acquaintance once quoted him as saying, "and I'll talk my way out of it.")

He worked like a dog at his job; nobody could take that away from him. His eagerness was like a physical appetite. And he understood the mechanics of government, the tie-ins to the bigger federal picture.

The boy mayor knew how to apply for U-DAGs — urban development action grants. He knew how to talk state tax credits for neighborhood assistance projects; he talked enterprise zones. It was Mayor Lyng who finally got the Wedge area of Hannibal cleared out, after several years of civic helplessness, by ramming through a plan to grant a right of condemnation to a private development corporation — a large franchise food-store chain. It was Mayor Lyng who extracted the city from its ruinous leasing arrangement with the huge grain terminal down on the riverfront — a lease written a quarter-century earlier in language that had assured amortization payments from the city *forever*. Mayor Lyng went after industrial job development; he built streets and bridges; he restructured the police department; he kept the city budget balanced.

In the psychology that had taken hold in Hannibal by that time, John Lyng was seen less and less as a progressive reformer; more and more as someone to watch — someone who had something up his sleeve.

"A side-door man," people began to say about Mayor John Lyng. "Too aggressive. Gets out in front of the town on things. Vindictive; you cross him once and he won't rest until he nails you." And the people of Hannibal began waiting for the day when John Lyng would get his.

In a subtle but ineluctable sense, Hannibal began to mark John Lyng as an outsider.

He was an outsider in the town where he was born and raised, the town that had twice elected him its mayor. He was a liberal Democrat in a region sometimes called Little Dixie; a Roman

Catholic among Protestant, even fundamentalist, worshipers; the son of a rural Irish-American railroad fireman now mediating with an aristocracy descended from those who *planned* the railroads and used them to transport their lumber fortunes — an aristocracy whose codes and judgments were muted but absolute.

"I got caught up in John F. Kennedy's campaign for president in nineteen sixty, when I was thirteen," Lyng recalled once as we talked. "In my family, it was as though we had *arrived* when he was elected."

But if Lyng himself cited Kennedy as his model, some other citizens of Hannibal thought they detected a discipleship to one or two other Irish-Catholic politicians of American legend: namely, mayors James Curley of Boston and Richard Daley of Chicago. Like those vanished urban bosses, Lyng liked to govern by the dominating force of his personality; like them, he used that force to render dramatic improvements in the town's infrastructure, often getting ahead of the strictest procedural restraints to do so. Like Curley and Daley, Lyng was a complex blend of genuine proletarian public-spiritedness and consuming personal ambition.

It made for a fierce set of drives. Here was a young and talented politician, happily married (to a handsome, forceful woman named Pamela, the mother of his two sons and two daughters), mayor of perhaps the most famous small town in America if not the Western world, looking ahead to an almost guaranteed future — and meanwhile, searching almost compulsively for the device that would propel him into that future.

When John Lyng opened Alfred Stern's "magic letter" on that day in 1983, the device seemed to have fallen quite fabulously into his grasp.

The device that John Lyng sought for Hannibal (and for his record as Hannibal's mayor) was economic. The town he governed may have enjoyed a worldwide reputation for its charm and its hospitality and its literary history. All these qualities were true of Hannibal — true, and increasingly irrelevant. The psychology had all turned sour. Beneath the pleasant, white-clapboard images lay an old and used-up community, just one of perhaps two dozen gasping river towns up and down the chemicalized Mississippi; one of hundreds of outpost towns everywhere: towns stripped of their participation in the century by the century's rush away from their accidental spots in geography; the rush toward the economies and the technologies and the aesthetics of mass — and by an exodus of these towns' most promising children toward an urban, consumer-based Good Life, as celebrated on the conduits of the mass-broadcast airwaves.

Mayor Lyng presided over a town that was aging (20 percent of its citizens were over sixty-five, compared to the national average of 11.6 percent), shrinking (by 16.5 percent since the peak population of 22,761 in 1930), and short on wealth (83 percent of its households had incomes under twenty-five thousand dollars; its households under nine thousand dollars were double the national average). It was a town that had watched helplessly a generation before as its lifeblood industries, the railroads and the giant shoe factory, packed up and went elsewhere. It was a town that had endured the indignity of playing grateful host to a succession of transient companies that settled in the vicinity for a while, created some jobs and some hopes, then hit the city fathers up for hardball capital improvements and tax considerations, then folded or moved on.

It was a town that in the spring of 1973 had endured a blow to its heart from its ancient benefactor and mythic ally. That spring was the spring of the Mississippi River's five-hundred-year flood. A torrent of late-winter snow, combined with early-spring rains, swelled the river to a semimillennial peak flood stage of more than twenty-eight feet — enough to send it roiling and rioting across Main Street, nearly to Third. The dark water and the thick mud washed out the remnants of the old central business axis along Main and the eastern tip of Broadway. The flood symbolized Hannibal's commercial transition from family-owned shops and stores to franchise discount centers, from downtown shopping to shopping center. The Mark Twain Bridge, once a cornucopia disgorging visitors from half the continent, now became a siphon each weekday morning for Hannibal commuters obliged to earn their living in Quincy.

Mayor Lyng's Hannibal was a town, finally, like so many bypassed towns, that had drifted dangerously close to defeatism, self-loathing, even despair.

"Nearly every change in the United States over the last fifty years has been to Hannibal's disadvantage" was the way Gale Newman, the Chamber of Commerce director, put it. "The town has been stranded and left with the resources of the past. It hasn't been able to find a firm foothold to vault successfully into the prosperity of the twentieth century.

"Hannibal," maintained Newman, "is a town that could have died."

That Hannibal did not die, or lose so much of its population as to reduce its civic life to a kind of gothic dissolution (a fate that had descended on more than one small town along the Mississippi) was a testimony to some inviolate strain that lay within the town's most irreducible character — a testimony to the town's moral coordinates. Hannibal saved itself from dying.

Beginning in the early 1950s, and at fitful intervals during every decade thereafter, Hannibal businessmen organized themselves into a series of industrial councils and development firms. Their purpose was to entice companies to locate plants in Hannibal.

The process was excruciating; it involved capital risk; often the result was frustration, if not humiliation. Sometimes these councils purchased land with the members' own money and then offered it to outside companies as an inducement to locate plants in town. Sometimes they offered low-interest loans so the incoming companies could expand.

These industrial councils were not always sophisticated, and they made mistakes. Sometimes companies accepted the enticements, put up a plant in town and then began escalating their demands for tax breaks, more land, even city-owned buildings. Many companies came, stayed a few years, employed a few dozen local people, then moved on. And the process would begin all over again.

Eighteen companies left Hannibal or went out of business between 1965 and 1984. Sixteen companies — the largest employing 350 people — that had arrived after 1965 still remained. The process of attracting and then trying to retain new employers was unending, a constant drain on the energies of mayors, city councils, and businessmen.

Gradually, however, the process began to achieve a certain momentum. Some of the plant managers attracted by the industrial councils' enticements began to discover in Hannibal itself a compelling quality that could not be measured on quarterly profit sheets.

One of those managers was Gale Newman, who arrived in 1968 from a real-estate career spanning several states. Newman came to establish a beachhead for what he called a "miniconglomerate" of real-estate companies, but decided almost at once to move his wife and daughters to town and put down permanent roots. "We were literally embraced by the town," recalled Newman. A muscular and warm-spirited ex-Marine, Newman was easy enough to like. He caught the local eye, too, with his brisk gait, his close-cropped hair, and his penchant for big cigars and shirts with big aggressive stripes.

With his natural optimism and fondness for detailed planning, Newman found himself gravitating more and more toward a quasi-public career in Hannibal. By the early 1980s he was devoting nearly all his time to the dual executive chairmanships of the Chamber of Commerce and the Hannibal Industrial Council — a resourceful and aggressive ally to Mayor Lyng in the pursuit of economic development.

Still, the old traces of paralysis and frustration were never far beneath the surface. When Newman assumed his position with the Chamber of Commerce in 1984, the first thing he discovered was a drawerful of unpaid bills totaling forty-four thousand dollars. "The chamber would not have survived past August nineteen eighty-four if I didn't correct that situation," he said.

There was little question that Hannibal's irreducible, life-preserving will had coexisted with a long malaise, an ingrained pattern of amateurish municipal government awash in an abyss of factional bickering and truculent standoffs. "There was a problem," one political veteran remembered, "of people running for the City Council in order to stop things. It was a transition time; it was nobody's fault, but the attitude was, we've gotta *find* fault. Those were reactionary times."

Factions arrayed themselves in other areas of town life, too: working people, for instance, tended to brood upon a supposed cabal, a conspiracy of control among the families of the old boomtown aristocracy — or the "country-club crowd," as those people were damningly known. In the most corrosive version of this theory, the country-club crowd acted again and again to secretly block attempts to accommodate new industries or civic improvements — the better to keep its grip over a feudal system of low-wage labor.

At times, during the years of slippage and transition, only one attitude, one common mood, seemed to unite nearly everyone in Hannibal: a weariness bordering on contempt for the name and the likeness of Mark Twain.

"Mark Twain" had long since become a reflexive tic of commerce, a brand name that confronted Hannibalians every day from the backs of produce trucks, and antique-store windows, and roofing-company marquees, and the town mental health center, and the billboard outside a dinette in the historic district (advertising Mark Twain Fried Chicken) and the salutations of local radio announcers, and what seemed like a hundred other demonic sources. Merchants who tried to make a business based on the town's famous heritage (souvenir-shop owners, motel operators) often found themselves lumped into yet another faction: the "few" who skimmed the harvest of Hannibal's tiresome promotionalism, to the long-suffering annoyance of the many.

Nevertheless, the local Twain entrepreneurs slogged doggedly on: across from the Mark Twain Home and Museum on Hill Street stood a commercial "Haunted House" that charged people money to stare at wax likenesses of Clemens's characters, and displayed a pair of mechanized vultures in its upstairs window. At Mark Twain Cave two miles downriver from town — which in my boyhood had charged a twenty-five-cent admission fee and loaned out denim jackets against the chill inside — a souvenir shop had been umbilically joined to the entrance, making it impossible for visitors to tour the cave without running a gauntlet of rubber crocodiles, picture postcards, cardboard hillbilly hats, and a compulsory slide show.

John Lyng, aided by a new middle class of arriving business and professional talent, had slashed away at the hopelessness, the paralysis. Even Lyng's enemies gave him that. But there were only so many action grants and enterprise zones; there was only so much conciliating to be accomplished in a town that had watched the century slide away from it, and whose citizens needed someone to blame. There were only so many new jobs to be hustled from small industries; and the large companies, like automobile plants, that could truly invigorate a community for generations were clustering around the cities.

What Hannibal needed was a miracle. What John Lyng needed in his quest for a national reputation was a miracle.

Alfred Stern's letter promised just such a miracle: a civic renaissance based on the town's great heritage; a seven-month-long festival in honor of Mark Twain in his sesquicentennial year; a festival that could, with the right investment and promotion and administration — the right *engineering* — serve as the genesis for a permanent economic development tool.

John Lyng did not grasp the implications of Stern's letter immediately. It was only January; Lyng had a reelection campaign ahead of him and potholes in the streets to worry about. He remembers slipping the letter into one of his desk drawers at City Hall, in his small mayoral office decorated mainly by a large charcoal sketch of himself and his wife, the sketch rendered by a local artist.

"I was aware that Hannibal had had a Mark Twain Centennial in nineteen thirty-five," Lyng recalled later, "and I always just assumed we'd do something similar to it — something modest and local."

But as the months went on, Lyng could not get Stern's letter completely out of his mind. He found himself rummaging for it in the drawer, taking it out, and reading it from time to time.

And one day in April of 1983, dapper Alfred Stern found himself flying from New York City to Missouri. Arriving in Hannibal, he was the guest of honor at the Holiday Inn Twain Land ("The *beautiful* Holiday Inn Twain Land," as he dryly recalled it) before a consortium headed by Mayor John Lyng — a consortium that was ready to talk turkey about proceeding with a full-scale, big-league, world-class, national-outreach Mark Twain Sesquicentennial.

Lyng's group — the nucleus of the Sesquicentennial Commission — offered Stern the position of official consultant. Stern accepted.

A few days after Stern's visit, Lyng extended another key invitation — this time to the young general manager of the *Hannibal Courier-Post,* a heavyset, chain-smoking newcomer to the town named Larry Weil.

John Lyng and Larry Weil then embarked upon an alliance that, with the best of intentions and no question of personal enrichment, would plunge the town into the most traumatic period of its civic history. Stern, the conceptual architect of that period, would be disassociated from it long before its fullest effects took hold.

"*My* mistake" was the way Alfred Stern summed up his experience with Hannibal that day in the New York delicatessen. "They're all very nice people, but they can't produce a wet mouse.

"I had thought that this was the one opportunity for them to have an orgasm. One time when they *might* rise to the occasion.

"Well, I read that wrong."

CHAPTER V

IT is the Jubilee Chorus that sings in my mind's ear when I try to imagine a time before my time: the sopranos and altos and tenors and bass. The Jubilee Chorus is singing from the program. Its members are singing "Ye Banks and Braes o' Bonny Doon," and "Come Where My Love Lies Dreaming," and "Flow Gently Sweet Afton," and "Annie Laurie," and "Swanee River." There are specialty acts, dancers, a fourteen-piece orchestra. Twelve hundred people have come to watch and listen. They have gathered at the new Hannibal High School's auditorium. It is a Wednesday evening in 1935, a cold February night in Missouri in the centennial year of the birth of Mark Twain, and the Jubilee Chorus is presenting a program of Songs and Music of Tom Sawyer Days. The program was arranged by the Jubilee Committee. Its members include Miss Helen Graves, librarian (music); Mr. D. C. Hanly, science teacher (dances); and Miss Mary Wiehe, art teacher (stage). Teachers of mine, all of them, at Hannibal High School a generation later, in the late 1950s. I remember them as old men and women, pale; semicomic figures in their remote, incomprehensible dignity and their outdated marcelled hairdos and their fingers to their lips — trying to hush out the century, we amiable visigoths supposed, if we thought about it at all, clanging along the corridors of the old school building.

It would have been beyond me, then, to imagine these people

as gay and vital, as members of a Jubilee Committee on a night in February six years before my birth, having pooled their specialized interests in music and dance and staging to create this Jubilee pageant deep in the still-sleeping continent just a generation after Mark Twain's death. It would have been beyond me to imagine, or care, then, in my ptolemaic trance at the center of time and the universe, how the building must have spilled its pale orange light out into the town darkness on that night, or how the voices must have sounded to any old Fuller man who might have been passing outside the school building in the absolute winter silence; a muffled rising and ebbing like voices on a low radio; or the orchestra's flourishes; or the curtain calls, the bows and the locked hands and the applause (the audience quickened perhaps by the vaguely illicit pleasure of being inside school premises at night) on this Jubilee that drew Hannibal into its first great commemoration of the man who so blessed and cursed the town.

It would have been beyond me then. But now it is the Jubilee Chorus that sings in my mind's ear when I try to imagine a time before a time.

The connectives were so unimportant in my boyhood; Hannibal was Eden enough without them. But it was the connectives that prefigured Eden; it was the past on which my happy genesis depended. Dulany Winkler — Duly — was my friend. Our friendship needed no history, no context; it was infinite from the moment we sized one another up in Miss Prince's first-grade classroom at Mark Twain School. He is my friend still.

It scarcely mattered to me then how Dulany had come to live in the glorious house called Rose Hill, a great cluster of striated brick wings in shades of deep yellow and orange that commanded a high meadow several hundred feet above my plumb-bungalow neighborhood on St. Mary's. It only mattered that the house existed, with its balustraded staircases and its shinnying-down drainpipes, its dumbwaiters and its secret passageways, its toy-clogged closets and its garage crowded with great silent automobiles, all of them shined, one of them bearing a silver bell on the hood, with a string attached so that the driver might ring the bell.

It did not matter to me that Dulany's family was rich — a fact that seemed remote and abstract to my boyish reckoning, especially since Duly wore the same metal-tipped cowboy belts as the rest of us, and tucked in his shirt in the accepted manner of plain kids — with a careless swipe down inside the front of his pants, leaving the tail and sides to billow out. What mattered more was Duly's fierce disheveled gladness, his indifferent gallantry as a friend. Duly had the strongest sense of justice of any rich kid I knew. He was simply better than life required him to be. He did unnecessary good things; he flowed through Hannibal like a golden river of boyhood; nickels cascaded out of his pockets on behalf of all the kids in his wake. (One famous summer day in our early childhood, Duly showed up at the St. Mary's Pharmacy, bought out all of Melvin Bird's candy on his mother's credit, and began selling it to all the kids in the neighborhood below cost until his mother, alerted by Bird, tracked him down.)

Not that Duly was the sort who bought friendships — it was his Galahad élan that drew followers and, later, girls. He was in all ways strong: even in early boyhood his arms and his squinting blond face were a series of powerful, rapidly sketched circles. But it seemed to me that, in the argot of our pharmacy-bought comic-book mythos, Duly used his strength always for good, never for evil.

And yet Duly's history did bear upon me in ways I could not even dream. He was part of the connectives. In a way that probably not even Dulany understood, he was a prince of the kingdom, a scion of the town's central lineage, and thus a legatee of its destiny.

The Jubilee Chorus might not have sung that night in 1935 had it not been for Dulany's great-grandfather, a titan of Hannibal's aristocracy named George A. Mahan. Mahan was the town's only citizen ever to legitimately claim that classic southern honorific, "Colonel." The governor of Missouri bestowed the title on him to acknowledge George Mahan's overmastering preeminence in the state's civic, financial, and social circles — and possibly out of gratitude that George Mahan never deigned to run for governor himself.

There might have been no particular significance attached to Mark Twain in Hannibal — a town, after all, that the author left when still a boy, and a town that showed no collective signs of rising to champion him in the years of savage criticism following his death — had it not been for the Colonel's personal intervention.

Surely there would have been no Rose Hill, nor its forerunner, Skylands, the even more grandiose mansion crowning the higher swell of land next door — an alabaster house rendered in the Spanish style, with wrought-iron balconies and flagstone terraces, and approached from Rose Hill by an artless little series of wooden steps set into the bank between the houses. The steps are bordered by a thin wooden handrail cut from a sapling in the adjoining woods — a handrail that still rests lightly on its wooden balusters, gray now, more than half a century old.

George Mahan imposed the Twain blessing and curse upon Hannibal. It was Mahan and his wife who purchased the Mark Twain Boyhood Home in 1911 and then deeded it to the city of Hannibal. It was Mahan, his wife, and his son, Dulany — Duly's grandfather — who presented the city with the statue of Tom Sawyer and Huckleberry Finn that has stood since 1926 at the foot of Cardiff Hill, the first statue ever erected to purely literary characters. It was Mahan who designed and financed twenty-one historical markers that still stand across the state along Highway 36, and six additional markers within the town. (The markers' shape, lettering style, and language have been shrewdly aped, in recent years, and planted as come-ons in front of some of the town's more aggressive souvenir shops.) It was Mahan and his family who established a series of literary and oratorical prizes at several colleges in honor of Clemens.

More important than any of these particular gifts was the Colonel's moral gallantry on behalf of Mark Twain — his insistence, in the face of furious fashion, upon the dead author's genius. (I have witnessed bright traces of the old Mahan chivalry in Duly. I saw the traces in school yards and on the football field, Duly's fists doubled on behalf of others; and later in the privileged great-grandson's enlistment as a marine sharpshooter for service in Vietnam. "Chivalry" is one way of attributing the impulses of the Mahan line. Perhaps "moral coordinates" — some pervading essence of the town itself — is another.)

There is a photograph, a formal portrait, of George A. Mahan, that I have always studied for long moments during visits to Rose Hill. It was taken late in his life. He is wearing a pin-striped business suit and is clutching a pocket watch with his left hand; his wedding ring is visible. His hair, parted in the middle, is snowy and full. His face is handsome, unlined. With its high cheekbones and full lips and eyes set close in a kind of squint, it is almost an Indian face, intense and yet opaque. Sometimes as I gaze at the face, I see the face of my own grandfather, Jasper, the baker who lived on Union Street Hill.

George Mahan's life overlapped with Mark Twain's for forty-nine years, although there is no record that the two men ever met. Mahan was born on a farm just outside Hannibal in 1851, just a year before young Samuel Clemens left the town at seventeen. Mahan fashioned a brilliant collegiate career at Bethel College, Washington and Lee University, and the University of Indiana, where he earned his law degree in 1872. He became Hannibal's attorney at age twenty-four. Ten years later, in 1885, he was elected the county's prosecuting attorney (an office occupied a century later by the young John Lyng), and eleven years after that he was elected to the Missouri legislature. In later years Mahan served as general counsel to a number of railroads, banks, and industries in Hannibal. He built the town's orphanage, raised nearly half the capital stock for the elegant Mark Twain Hotel in 1901, served as president of the Chamber of Commerce and as an elder in the Christian Church.

Mahan's marriage in 1882 to Ida Dulany consolidated two powerful family lines and formed one of the town's enduring fountainheads of civic philanthropy. Ida Dulany was an heiress to the vast Empire Lumber Company, one of twelve such enterprises that generated great wealth for the town between the end of the Civil War and the century's turn. The Colonel then began what, in many ways, was his most important career of all: advocate of the reputation and legacy of Mark Twain.

The 1920s saw an abrupt reversal of Twain's "beloved humorist" status in American letters. On the virulent strength of a critical biography by Van Wyck Brooks (*The Ordeal of Mark Twain*), Clemens was demoted to tragic literary failure, even "irresponsible child." The literary lynch mob grew swiftly: to Theodore Dreiser, Twain was "our simple and almost boobish genius"; to Lewis Mumford, he was afflicted with "fundamental barbarism." In 1924 a pair of critics, emboldened by Brooks's attack, even cited Clemens's premature birth as the basis for proclaiming him "as profound a biological failure as America has produced."

Against this tide of high-minded venom stood almost no one in America — except the Colonel. George Mahan was seventy-five years old in 1926, the year he financed the statue of Tom and Huck. He needed no timely crusade to enhance his status in the community; he was already a giant. His regard for the author stemmed from deeper judgments than boosterism or social *oblige*. Mahan was an amateur historian and an authority on Twain's life and works. When he died at eighty-five, in December of 1936, the *Hannibal Courier-Post* noted that "long before the universal ascendancy of the great humorist to a place among literature's greatest, Mr. Mahan looked upon the writings of this son of Hannibal in the true light of the recognition they were later to achieve."

Thus, when the world was willing once again to look with favor upon the works of Mark Twain, Hannibal, Missouri, stood ready to welcome the world with a Mark Twain shrine. From George Mahan's lifetime onward, Hannibal's identity was fused with Twain's. The blessing and the curse had been cast.

Ida Dulany bore the Colonel one child, Dulany Mahan. The photographs and oil paintings of this man show no trace of the father's imperial serenity. The sharp brows are nearly joined in a stare of fixed anguish. It was Dulany Mahan's unhappy destiny —

his blessing and curse — to carry forth the Colonel's own legacy. The patriarch's ironclad dominion over his only son was the stuff of legend among the household staff — one member of which, a chauffeur named Howard, had been hired by George Mahan as a stableboy; he remained a devoted, gray-haired retainer through my boyhood.

Dulany Mahan joined — or was conscripted into — the family law firm. He took up residence at 1001 Center Street in Hannibal, directly behind his father's residence, at 1000 Broadway. In 1929 Dulany Mahan fled to the crest of what was then a lonely meadow in Hannibal to seek his refuge. He built Skylands there, probably as some grasp at personal autonomy, some claim on an identity of his own. The house was, and is, an architectural marvel: two grand stories of glazed cream-colored stucco topped with a red tiled roof in the style of the Spanish renaissance. With its wrought-iron balconies and its Ionic columns framing the front entrance, its circular driveway surrounding a tortoise fountain, its spiraling interior staircase, and its many sunlit wings, Skylands was a masterpiece, one of Hannibal's authentic treasures and a sublime fortress for a father-hounded man.

His solitude lasted three years. Following Ida's death the Colonel, at age eighty-one, built Rose Hill next door to his son and moved in. George Mahan died in that house four years later, impatiently waving off his family's pleas that he let a doctor examine his chest pains. But Mahan did survive long enough to hear the Jubilee Chorus sweetly present its Songs and Music of Tom Sawyer Days, one of the inaugural events of the Mark Twain Centennial of 1935.

The anxious son suffered his own heart attack less than four years later; Dulany Mahan was dead in 1940 at fifty-five. But he left three children. One of them was Ida Estelle Mahan, Duly's mother.

As Elvadine Toalson dreamed her humble pianist dreams on the crest of Union Street Hill, Ida Estelle grew into society across town, dreaming of a career on the classical stage. She graduated from Smith College at age twenty-two and set off on a grand tour of Europe with some of her classmates. At Stratford-on-Avon, Ida sat in William Shakespeare's chair and wished for fame as an opera soprano. Instead, she returned to Hannibal and married John Winkler, the handsome weight-station officer and athlete who had swum the Mississippi's width from Missouri to Illinois.

John Winkler's proposal must have been delivered with considerably more élan than my father's proposal to Elvadine. The couple's charming and jolly reenactment of it is preserved on a reel of silent black-and-white film somewhere inside the Rose Hill archives. The scene opens on John Winkler's black automobile rounding the fountain in the Skylands drive. The suitor emerges clutching a bouquet, nervously slicking back his hair. He rings the Mahan doorbell. The scene shifts to Ida Estelle's upstairs boudoir, where she is touching up her hair in front of a mirror. Startled, she turns, throwing a hand into the air. She descends the staircase in a silken gown and opens the door; an earnest John Winkler thrusts the flowers toward her. In the living room, hamming it up, he drops to one knee, a perfect 1930s silhouette. There is a take of the ring, then a glowing closeup of Ida Estelle — the culmination of her acting career — and then, spliced onto the reel, there is actual footage of the wedding, which took place at Skylands in June 1936. Four years later my friend Dulany was born.

The years passed, and the westward-sloping meadow thickened with lesser neighborhoods that slanted downward until they joined the bungalow flatland at St. Mary's Avenue, where the Powers family eventually came to live. The first large order of Fuller Brushes my father ever sold in Hannibal was to Ida Estelle Mahan Winkler, just a couple of days after her wedding and a year before his own.

My father never forgot the grandeur of that order — it totaled nearly fifty dollars, he used to brag — nor the experience of standing inside the kitchen at Rose Hill. He would speak of it that way; he would accent the fact, as subtly as he knew how, that he once stood inside the kitchen at Rose Hill.

It never occurred to me in childhood (or perhaps it did, in some forbidden and unacknowledged way) that in gaining the Saturday-morning freedom of Dulany's house I had crossed beyond the limits of my father's possibilities — more than that, I had defined some irreversible, and inexorably widening, boundary between us.

Dulany and I roamed the town and haunted Rose Hill's upper rooms for seven months each year. The other five, he was gone — to the family's winter home in Florida for the three coldest months (his parents enrolled the children in school there) and to the summer estate in Minnesota for the two peak months of summer. Those absences heightened our friendship; invested it with a melancholy sense of transience. We would write to each other — smudgy penciled letters on both sides of lined notebook paper confettied along one edge where it had been ripped from the spiral binder; the letters dense as military code with cryptic references understood only by us (the freighted term "pootwattle," for instance, or the deceptively casual punning on the last names of Confederate generals). Then, near the close of each summer or the beginning of each spring, there would come the telephone call with Duly's shout ringing in the receiver, and I would be at Rose Hill, panting from the uphill dash through shortcuts in the remaining meadows, before the last loads of luggage had been lifted from the car.

He came back for the best seasons in Hannibal, the springs and the autumns. His reappearances seemed to quicken everyone in our school grade. The air tasted better and the azure hours between supper and nightfall held more promise of lilac-scented adventure when Duly was around. On Saturdays, whole flocks of children materialized at Rose Hill for chauffeured expeditions to the Rialto. Concentric circles of friends ringed him; it was his unconscious genius that everyone — perhaps me included — allowed himself the illusion of occupying the tightest orbit. He moved, and a great shuffle of children surged with him. His broad, blond face wreathed in an affable squint, half the front of his shirt dangling outside his trousers, his powerful thick torso tilted forward at churning speed, jolly without being *precisely* a cutup (that was our job, we court jesters, Ward Smith and Warren Wilson and Bill Winn and Mike Sohn and Mike Chehval and me), Dulany would lead our collective charge to the movies, to the pharmacy, to the vaster unmarked caverns around Mark Twain Cave for spelunking — and, at night, through all the playgrounds and the meadows and the shadowy cathedral of the high-school football field, where we organized daredevil sprees of espionage and insurrection. The dwellers in the vulnerable orange-lit houses along Sunnyside and Sunset and Greenway Road had little idea of our encircling menace, nor of the ultimate compassion that stayed the heavy stones in our hands.

Dulany's own house was invulnerable — as indifferent to time as the town, the river, and the bridge. At least I assumed it was. It hummed with history; history hovered in the heavy brocaded curtains and in the dark furniture that seemed as old as history; it lay about the rose garden that the hired men Harry and Howard, historical artifacts themselves, tended just beyond the porte cochere. And history reeked down from the heavy editions of Twain scholarship on the shelves in the central library, where we listened to the radio and drew and wrote down our endless, densely imagined fantasy tales and ghost stories and, later, collaborated on our immensely popular mock-historical epics, using our schoolmates as characters in the featured roles. It was this collaboration, silly and exuberant, that forged my closest bond with Duly: we weren't Tom and Huck so much as co-Clemenses of our crowd, our time. Later, in our teenage years, he acquired a miraculous toy, a Wollensak reel-to-reel tape recorder, and our collaborations became electronic — we improvised comic stories, imitated our friends' voices, and even laboriously edited snatches of 45 rpm hit tunes into our productions. We had an act; we were stars. I began to appreciate something of the power of words, and laughter. I began to understand something of how glorious it must have been to be Mark Twain.

I did not know, in those absorbed days about the house, that the founding patriarch of the Mahan/Winkler aristocracy and one of Twain's redeeming champions had built the place and then died there. The idea would probably have terrified me. But Rose Hill did have for me the aura of lineage; it seemed a spawning place of kings. I comfortably assumed the lineage would go on forever. Perhaps Dulany would live in this house someday. Perhaps someday he would inherit Hannibal and its endless trove of stories, and he and I would be partners in shipping them out like logs along the river to the world.

What I could not know was that the present generation of Winklers at Rose Hill would be the last. Nor could I know that the future of Hannibal was shifting, as imperceptibly and as inexorably as a river channel, from the control of the old lumber aristocracy to the whims of parvenus — outsiders.

CHAPTER VI

If Hannibal had subtly edged its mayor from the epicenter of community life, the town proved virtually impervious to its new newspaper publisher. Larry Weil was an outsider when he hit town in 1981, and an outsider he remained, through all his most dogged efforts to integrate himself into the town's circles of influence.

Weil had arrived at age thirty, his life's timetable right on schedule: he'd wanted to be a newspaper publisher by that age. Of course he was not yet *officially* a publisher — the Stauffer chain, which owned the *Courier-Post,* tended to refer to people in Weil's echelon as "unit managers." But the duties were the same, and besides, there was the autonomy. "They espouse complete autonomy for their unit managers," Larry Weil liked to point out in his soft bass voice. "The thing I like about this job is the autonomy."

Weil also liked to quote from what he called the "credo" of the founder of the Stauffer chain: "Count that day lost when you haven't done something for your community."

There were a lot of those homilies being uttered around Hannibal in the early 1980s. Most of them fell from the lips of men like Larry Weil: newly arrived company managers, in town from somewhere else and determined — resigned, in some cases — to make their career marks here. Weil himself was not married; nor was he conspicuously worshipful by nature, but most of his fellow *arrivistes* fit a fairly uniform mold: barbered, squared-away family men and churchgoers; solid types who liked to lean back in their executive office chairs and gaze over at the color portrait on the wall of the wife and kids, and muse with quiet pride about how "people oriented" and "community oriented" their companies wanted them to be.

These were the newest outriders of Hannibal's reemerging middle class. After years of nearly unrelieved frustration in its efforts to rebuild its old industrial base, Hannibal in the past sixteen years had begun to achieve some modest results. The industrial councils had begun to attract a few manufacturing plants to the town. The plants were hardly large-scale; the largest employed something over three hundred people. And yet they made a difference: they amounted to the difference between a subsistence economy and something approaching desolation.

Moreover, they brought to Hannibal this transplanted root system of young professional managers and their families. These were people who had been around a bit; people with a taste of life in larger cities — Mason City, Iowa; Sacramento; Akron.

Many of these newcomers proceeded to develop strong affinities with Hannibal's tranquility and its congeniality to children. Others, like Weil, were a bit harder to read. Their very readiness to drop homilies about being "people oriented" and about counting days lost and so on — all of this sounded just a little tinny to the ears of long-term citizens who didn't need to invoke any homilies before going out each day and earning a living in the town.

Sometimes the newcomers forgot themselves and blurted out more candid opinions about Hannibal — opinions that bitterly contradicted their own homilies. These candid outbursts tended to occur at night, and not at church socials but inside the town's one or two fashionable saloons. At such times, some of the newcomers would reveal a dark, almost virulent bitterness toward that same community, the same "people," as they professed an "orientation" to in their daytime, public moments.

It wasn't just that Hannibal's population was older and poorer than the national average, the managers confided. *It was puerile.*

Hannibal people were simply not very bright. Something had happened to the gene pool. The town was incapable of generating its own leaders — apart from the rare aberration of a John Lyng. Yes, terrible to say such a thing, but a sort of cretinous substrata had set in over the years. You couldn't count on the community to act in its own best interests or to support any kind of progressive change. If anyone or anything was going to save Hannibal, it was going to be the enlightened new talent that had moved in from out of town. God knew it wasn't a pretty thing to say, but there it was.

Sometimes the new managers barely seemed to hear themselves moving back and forth between the good-booster platitudes and the unguarded sentiments in their hearts.

"Hannibal is a neat town; I like Hannibal," declared Richard Halsor one morning behind his desk at the Buckhorn Rubber Products plant, which he arrived to manage in 1981. "The way we look at things in this company, the type of community we're in is very important to us. We operate our business as *people oriented.* My job as general manager here is to utilize and effectuate all the assets we have. We have brick and mortar and all that stuff that companies traditionally pay attention to." (Here Halsor, a blond, well-barbered man in horn-rimmed glasses, leaned forward.) "But companies don't pay attention to their most important asset — *people!*

"We like to feel," Halsor continued, plopping back again and raising his eyes, "that we can impact the environment in which they live in a positive fashion. So, in recognizing that objective, we say, 'What can we do in the community? . . .' "

A few minutes later, in explaining why he had been drawn into Mayor John Lyng's inner circle of sesquicentennial movers and shakers (he became chairman of the finance commission and, much later, the festival's executive director), Halsor appeared to have forgotten his fanfare for the common man. "The expertise is not available in a town like this," he confided. "The biggest problem in Hannibal today is apathy. A lot of people like to criticize the tourism industry in this town. Well, let me tell you something.

The only thing that differentiates Hannibal from a hundred other ratty-assed river towns up and down the Mississippi is tourism!"

The company plant that Larry Weil came to Hannibal to manage was hardly new. The *Courier-Post* had been publishing since 1838, making it Missouri's oldest continuous newspaper. Its one-story redbrick office and production plant occupied the entire block at 200 North Third, as it had for thirty-three years — a strategic location, placing the newspaper within easy walking range of City Hall, within easier walking range of Fitzgerald's Bar, and directly across the street from the Becky Thatcher Restaurant.

In my time, the Becky Thatcher was known sensibly as the Third Street Lunch. Despite its thematic renaming, its essential lunchhouse soul had mercifully survived.

One pushed through the glass-door entrance ("PUSH for the Pirates!") to enter a narrow universe defined by seating options in three parallel rows: orange vinyl booths, hardtop tables, and a counter with twelve revolving stools. These accommodations extended back toward the kitchen with its swinging wooden doors. The counter, to the left as one entered, caught most of the trade. Here the waitresses stockpiled their rows of napkins weighted by knives and forks for the lunch-hour action. Here a customer could sip coffee and gaze into the naked logic of lunchhouse life: the milkshake mixers and the milk dispensers with their weighted steel hafts like great ball bearings; the coffeemaker and the Nestlé's cocoa machine and the iced-tea machine; the idle toaster oven with its scrap of whole wheat bread; the rows of heavy brown coffee cups and weightless green plastic water glasses; the shelves of Variety-Pak cereals and the cardboard stanchions of pocket combs.

There were two small refrigerator shelves under clear plastic panels where the horseradish and the ReaLemon were stored; and a larger, jukebox-shaped refrigerator back near the kitchen. There was brown shag carpeting under the tables and the booths — the surface under the counter stools was linoleum — and wedged between the near end of the counter and the plate-glass window that offered a view of Mills Auto Parts was the inevitable large circular table where no strangers sat, even at rush hour: this was the privileged domain of the regulars, and no waitress needed to ask who the regulars were.

The place, in fact, was *about* regulars. The Becky Thatcher Restaurant made precious few efforts to ingratiate itself to the whims of anybody likely to be attracted by the name "Becky Thatcher Restaurant" — that is to say, anybody ambling around in sunglasses and shorts that revealed too much marbled white buttock skin; that is to say, tourists. The place was open for breakfast at six in the morning, but you wouldn't know that fact unless you *knew* it — or spotted a small hand-lettered notice Scotch-taped recently, and grudgingly, to the front window. At 10:45 A.M. sharp the luncheon menus came out, to be taken in again at 3:15, no matter how many out-of-state noses were pressed against the windowpane. Fifteen minutes later the Becky Thatcher closed for the day. It did not serve supper. People with any sense ate their supper at home.

The historic district, with its constant influx of back-pocket money, may have been just two blocks away, but the Becky Thatcher remained an enclave for locals. Not that strangers were discourteously served, mind you; it was just that they never penetrated a certain *opacity* suggested by the take-it-or-leave-it witticisms of the plaques up on the walls:

COMPANY RULES
RULE 1: THE BOSS IS ALWAYS RIGHT
RULE 2: IF THE BOSS IS WRONG, SEE
RULE 1

And

TO ERR IS HUMAN
TO BLAME IT ON THE OTHER GUY
IS EVEN MORE HUMAN

Not to mention a less risible notice of the sort that some outsiders might have been startled to encounter in the post-Montgomery era of American life:

WE RESERVE THE RIGHT TO REFUSE SERVICE TO ANYONE

The Becky Thatcher enjoyed one other distinction which it made no particular effort to impress upon outsiders: it served the most righteous pork-tenderloin sandwiches in northeast Missouri.

It would be difficult to produce concrete evidence that the *Hannibal Courier-Post* moved its facilities two blocks to the north in 1952 so that it could be closer to a really first-rank pork tenderloin restaurant. That difficulty does not diminish either the primacy or the glory of the Becky Thatcher, nor the honorable legacy of pork tenderloin in Hannibal life.

The pork-tenderloin sandwich is a vestigial culinary treasure, an artifact of the town's southern diaspora and of its era as a pork-producing center. It is also a rapidly disappearing legacy of the days when families, not corporations, owned restaurants in the town and recipes were stored in the memories of the proprietor, and not in the circuits of some computer.

The Becky Thatcher achieved its pork-tenderloin primacy only through a bit of gustatory hardball that spelled the end of perhaps the greatest tenderloin restaurant ever to exist outside the Deep South — Abe & Higgie's Bar & Grill over on Broadway at Fourth Street. My uncle Aubrey Toalson was the "Abe" in Abe & Higgie's, and it was he who thought up the place's famous slogan, hand-painted on the front window: "IF YOU CAN'T STOP IN — SMILE AS YOU GO BY."

Uncle Abe served up definitive pork tenderloins for more than three decades at his grill: the patties smoking hot inside their golden-brown batter, bulging out like little Floridas on either end of a white bun warmed up in a steam table and meant to be consumed with plenty of raw onions, dill-pickle slices, and cold Griesedieck Brothers beer.

Fifty cents let you eat one of the big-bellied Abe's pork tenderloins. All the money in the Mahan bank account would not buy you the recipe. Uncle Abe's younger, frail brother, Roy, a bartender himself by trade, conjured up the ingredients and the cooking method not long after he got back home from World War II. Roy and Abe swore to one another that neither would ever disclose the recipe to anyone as long as the other was alive. Long after Abe had given up his interest in the Bar & Grill, long after the Hardees and the Wendy's had come to the disjuncted Junction, Uncle Abe met a woman at the shopping center, a loyal old customer, who buttonholed him and insisted that he finally turn loose of that damned pork-tenderloin recipe.

Uncle Abe refused. (I can envision his red grinning cheeks and his blue eyes — a boy's face that never grew old.) Nossir, he told her. Roy was still alive. Small Roy, twenty years widowed and shriveled and nearly blind behind his sunglasses, unable to drive a car and shuffling about on a cane made, he liked to shriek, from a bull's penis — Roy was still alive. The secret was inviolate.

But in 1974, Uncle Abe and his partner abruptly learned that they were about to lose their lease. The sudden action left them no time to seek purchasers for their steam tables or their tables and chairs; all of their belongings were sold at auction, and my uncle was obliged to take work for a few years as a janitor at Hannibal High School before he could gather the means to retire.

I asked my Uncle Abe, during one of my visits back to Hannibal, who the owners of the Abe & Higgie's building had been. "Same people who owned the Becky Thatcher," he said, grinning.

Larry Weil did not take many of his meals at the Becky Thatcher. He preferred Fitzgerald's, a spiffy dim-lighted "Drinking and Eating Establishment," as it announced itself, of polished hardwood and studied cool. Fitzgerald's was owned by one James Lyng, in partnership with his brother, John.

Fitzgerald's had opened in 1981 — the year Weil hit town, the year John Lyng became mayor — on North Third Street, one block up from the *Courier-Post* and virtually in the shadow of the Mark Twain Historic District. It had opened in a shadow of another kind as well: a shadow of suspicion regarding the propriety of the federal loan the Lyng brothers had obtained to build it.

The loan was part of a federal Housing and Urban Development program known as the Section 312. The program made low-interest loans available to applicants for rehabilitation of investor-owned properties. Before his first election as mayor, while he was still the prosecuting attorney for Marion County, John Lyng had sought and received two 312 loans totaling a little more than $70,000; he used them to renovate two buildings he owned. One of the buildings housed Lyng's law office.

A third 312 loan, of $37,800, went to Lyng's brother, James, whose renovation endeavors culminated in Fitzgerald's Eating and Drinking Establishment.

In the minds of certain people in Hannibal, and indeed outside the town as well, the spectacle of more than $100,000 in 3 percent federal loans passing into the hands of a sophisticated lawyer and his brother suggested something a little more complex than mere civic spirit. Black leaders in Hannibal complained that the Lyngs had finessed the loans before low-income and minority residents were fully prepared to file competing claims. An election opponent of John Lyng's patron, Congressman Harold Volkmer, went further: he charged that Volkmer either used his influence to secure 312 loans for his friends and associates, or he knew about abuses of the 312 program and refused to take action.

The complaints prompted an investigation by HUD. No criminal charges arose from the investigation, but enough examples of "poor performance" and "mismanagement" of the 312 program were uncovered that the local administrator of the loans, a man named Harvard F. Ebers, was suspended from his duties for a year. (The HUD investigator's report noted that Ebers was aware that some of the loan certifications were false; the report added the following statement: "In-depth interview with Ebers could not be completed because John Lyng instructed Ebers to terminate the interview process.")

The loans to John and James Lyng were cited as examples in the case against Ebers. The investigator noted that in the Fitzgerald's loan, John Lyng, the owner of 306 North Third, had quit-claimed the property to his brother. James Lyng had then obtained the $37,800 loan to rehabilitate the premises, after which he deeded the property back to brother John.

In his report, the investigator wrote: "It appears that John Lyng went through the above motions in order to obtain another 312 loan under the guise that the property belonged solely to his brother James."

Larry Weil himself had published some stinging editorials demanding answers to these charges shortly after he arrived in town and took over the reins of the *Courier-Post.* But as time went on and none of the complaints led to prosecution, Weil's editorials trailed off. And then Weil began to discover some of the positive aspects of Fitzgerald's Eating and Drinking Establishment, as it beckoned him just a block from his office, there in the shadow of the Mark Twain Historic District.

To get to the district from Fitz's, one needed only to turn right outside the front door, walk half a block north to Hill Street, turn right again at the Mark Twain Dinette featuring Mark Twain Fried Chicken, then walk a few paces downhill to the museum and the Boyhood Home.

One needed do only that, but few people did. Fitzgerald's belonged at the opposite end of Hannibal's epoch. The action crowd came to drink there; City Hall types and reporters and attorneys and some of the new plant managers who liked being around the City Hall people. The only spot in downtown Hannibal that could rival Fitzgerald's for out-and-out worldliness was a restaurant on the premises of a former bordello down at 111 Bird Street, just a block from the Mississippi levee. The restaurant was tricked out in red lights and suggestively worded menus and named the Bordello. A sign on the wall promised, OUR CUSTOMERS COME FIRST. Neither Fitzgerald's nor the Bordello served pork-tenderloin sandwiches. Fitzgerald's became the place where Larry Weil belonged. As for his publishing style, Weil ran the paper with a deaconly sort of moderation, cleaving mainly to the balances, the formulas, that bracketed small-town newspaper performance everywhere.

Perhaps the *Courier-Post* was a little ahead of the curve, if for no other reason than its dignity. The paper did not dress itself out in bright come-on colors the way a lot of its contemporaries were doing. It did not run columns by local people who pretended to be in touch with the Hollywood stars; in fact it did not run much regular celebrity coverage at all, although the paper was always glad to give front-page mention when, for instance, country singer Roger Miller was due in town to film a fishing segment for his Country Sportsman spot on the Nashville Network.

(That story, or any bright front-page feature like it, was almost certain to bear a byline that leapt out at me the first time I spotted it: *Gene Hoenes*. The genial KHMO Man on the Street of my boyhood was still in town, still a media star. He turned out to be a lanky, pale, and sandy-haired man behind plastic-rimmed glasses when he finally became corporeal for me one day in the *Courier-Post* city room — genial indeed, but professional as well: he dropped immediately after our handshake into his swivel chair and began pounding out notes on his video display terminal for a front-page story on why I was in town. Hoenes had become the paper's star reporter, I learned, only after his long broadcasting career ended the way long broadcasting careers usually end: a television station across the river, in Quincy, had dropped him as its anchorman, after years of outstanding service, because he did not fit the station's youthful image.)

Larry Weil's *Courier-Post* was, essentially, a staid paper in a staid town. It was a little like the Sears catalogue — you always knew where to find what you were looking for in it. The front page doggedly recorded the official life of the town — City Council meetings, zoning decisions, the utilities, and the park board — and the big national stories. Page two was local briefs — hospital admissions, arrests, burglaries; unknown subjects entering residences, undetermined amounts of money stolen. Page three was world and national news; page four was opinion — Jack Anderson and William Buckley and Art Buchwald and one locally written editorial, cautiously progressive, usually taking the long view: SIGNS OF HOPE IN THE ECONOMY; GORBACHEV IS WILY NEGOTIATOR. Then came the pages of the Wal-Mart ads and the filler briefs: COUPLE AVOIDS HOT SITUATION; MUSICIANS OPPOSE RATING VIDEOS. Then came the clubs and the weddings and the Ann Landers and the Erma Bombeck.

There was a religion page once a week; there was a readers page featuring verse from the Hannibal Writers Club:

BOY WONDER

Boy Wonder came to earth,
Nine years or so ago.
God gave him at birth
Traits that you must know.

I've known this boy,
For quite a while now.
He can be quiet and coy,
Or full of jump, bump and pow.

His bike has to rest,
From time to time.
To keep up with the zest
Of this wonder boy of mine . . .

There was coverage of cultural events. CELLIST PROVIDES SOLEMN SHOW, ran the headline over a concert review, which began on a note of almost ruthless positivism:

> Music lovers were scattered throughout the junior high school auditorium Thursday night to hear a concert by cellist David Low of Omaha, Neb. Many parents brought children to expose them to the quality of sound produced by a professional cellist and accompanying pianist. . . .
>
> Low, dressed in a black suit that matched the grand piano behind his chair, often closed his eyes in concentration while performing. He appeared to be in a world of his own, weaving slowly back and forth on his chair, with the cello propped in front of him. . . .

> Throughout this dramatic piece, the piano and cello appeared to compete. Each played the melody louder and louder, in co-ordination but not together. Portions of this three-part sonata would make a good musical score for an adventure movie.
>
> The cello's deep tones, although occasionally mournful, were spellbinding and soothing, and lulled a few of the listening children to sleep. . . .

And of course there was the sports page. Not the sports page as I remembered it, edited by Ed O'Neill, who'd been at it since 1929 and who wouldn't quit until 1972. O'Neill wrote every word of local sports copy six nights a week, including a voluminous "Sports Chatter" column laid out smack down the middle of the page. He personally covered every local tilt in every season, looking like William Butler Yeats in unsnapped galoshes on the sidelines of the Pirates football games, this gaunt and ancient bachelor with black brows and wild white hair who was already old when I reverentially strung for him on the school road games, coming back to spill my notes on his littered desk in the fluorescent deep of newspaper night; who pronounced his *s*'s with the sides of his tongue in an old-man sort of way; and who nevertheless had not yet sailed to his Byzantium by the time of the sesquicentennial's opening parade: who was *on hand,* this witness to a thousand opening kickoffs and two visits by Halley's Comet.

Larry Weil published a reasonable newspaper in a reasonable town. No one much questioned that. What remained open to question was Weil's ability to live truly *inside* the town; to gain acceptance with the people and the families who mattered, who ran things from one generation to the next. Perhaps this was not a fair test of his success in Hannibal; no stranger moves into a small community of that size and gets absorbed right away into its inner fabric. Perhaps a newspaper publisher, especially, should not make the attempt: too many subtle obligations come with the privileges, too many words to the wise get whispered under the tinkle of ice cubes in a glass.

And yet it was a test — this ultimate acceptance — that Larry

Weil seemed to impose on himself; a test, perhaps, of his final break with his nomadic past. What Weil perhaps did not realize was that he was being tested by the town as well.

"Hannibal is a warm community, but you have to understand its rules," said a businessman who watched it all happen. "The minute you step into the city limits — well, let's put it this way: *if you have the social graces,* you will enter into a 1950s society. I mean lock, stock, and barrel, with all the graciousness, all the innocence, and all the strong feelings.

"But, dammit, you have to pass a test. In order to get in, you must be appraised like a piece of livestock on the hoof. You are given a grace period to show what you are — not 'who' you are, but what you are. During that grace period, you will be observed as an outsider. You will probably be completely unaware of this, but it's going on.

"If you show any sign of social graces, as defined by the town, you're in. But those who fail that test — those who come to town expecting to blow things over, turn things around — are going to be terribly disappointed."

One of the events by which Hannibal society defined itself was the Big Party.

The Big Party was a social convention that had suffered approximately the same fate in America as the pork-tenderloin sandwich. Its voguish years were behind — perhaps by as much as half a century. But in certain remote American towns — towns more concerned with maintaining their internal continuity and in drill-parading their hierarchy than in keeping up with the drifts of fashion — the Big Party continued to flourish. It served the dual function of ratifying the existing peerage, and providing the occasion for petitioners to matriculate into the inner circle.

In Hannibal, a Big Party might occur as frequently as once every couple of weeks, depending on the season. In good weather it might be held outdoors at the country club or on the adjoining properties of two well-connected neighbors. Japanese lanterns would light the lawns; there would be bunting, or crepe paper. The guest list would encompass three hundred people — five hundred, if it spanned two generations. The occasion might be a wedding, a debut, or a holiday. The more ambitious parties would be built around a theme. Guests would come in costumes, or else in formal dress.

The general structure for these larger parties seldom varied. There would be cocktails and reasonably serious hors d'oeuvres at around half past six. A small orchestra or band would play for dancing, and a sit-down meal would anchor the evening — at the conclusion of which, amidst many embraces and the fraternal slapping of backs, local aspirations might emerge forever consolidated, or dashed.

I never personally witnessed a Big Party in Hannibal — my family's idea of the grand gesture running more toward a barbecue at Uncle Abe's cabin up on the Bay de Charles, with my father entertaining the assemblage with his highly regarded horseshoe pitching technique while exhorting my mother to turn up the Cardinals game on the plug-in radio that someone — possibly my father — had wedged into the cabin's kitchen window. The closest I had ever come to being at a Big Party was on graduation night, when the country club opened its doors to the senior class. I recall very little of this occasion other than the recurring heavy sibilance of a phonograph needle as it narrowly missed a 45 rpm record, my thanking God for wrist corsages, rumors of a fistfight between two friends of mine, being *extremely* sleepy (it was the latest I had ever stayed up since Aunt Opal came to visit on the train), and the oddly debonair-seeming aroma of free bacon and scrambled eggs somewhere around dawn.

The Mahan line was not unfamiliar with the Big Party. When George A. Mahan married Ida Dulany in 1882, the *Courier-Post* treated the event as it might have treated Genesis:

A BRILLIANT WEDDING

(rang the stacked headline)

THE MOST GORGEOUS DISPLAY
EVER SEEN IN HANNIBAL

MUSIC, MIRTH AND HAPPINESS
RULE THE HOUR.

OVER 300 INVITED GUESTS
TAKE PART IN FESTIVITIES

The house and the grounds were one blaze of gorgeous splendor. The exterior was illuminated with festoons of Chinese lanterns, suspended from triumphal arches trimmed with evergreens, and beneath which the guests passed. . . .

At the entrance, two colored gentlemen in party costume, with button hole bouquet attachment and white kids, opened wide the portals as the guests entered. . . . At the top of the second flight was another ebony hued sentinel whose prerogative was to separate the sheep from the goats. . . .

A little farther along in her narrative, mere prose proved inadequate to the correspondent, and she abandoned herself to verse:

The Colonel gazed with a father's pride, on his faithful child, young George's bride; While she, with bright eyes seemed to be The pride of that goodly companie.

Similarly, when John Winkler and Ida Estelle Mahan — Duly's parents — were married at Skylands in 1936, the *Courier-Post* reported it as "a brilliant and fashionable gathering."

About 400 guests gathered for the semigarden nuptial event, which, just as the sun began to descend in the west, was at the most beautiful time of day . . . the elevation of the Mahan house giving an opportunity for the guests to enjoy the perfection and beauty of the scene across the Mississippi River and over the bluffs of Hannibal. . . .

. . . an opportunity that geology, or press-agentry, did not reproduce in my lifetime, as the Mississippi by then — for some mysterious reason — was not visible from the Mahan house.

The Big Party did not prove a conduit into Hannibal society for Larry Weil. To the contrary, a certain climate of opinion began to take hold that Weil had palpably underestimated his new community; that he had, in the bitter words of one Hannibal native, "regarded us as a bunch of dumb country hicks."

Whatever the truth of that appraisal, the alliance that Larry Weil eventually forged in Hannibal was not with its social aristocracy; it was with the town's political leadership — with Mayor John Lyng. That alliance paid dividends almost at once. Shortly after Alfred Stern's visit to Hannibal in the spring of 1983, Mayor Lyng asked Larry Weil if he would be the chairman of the Mark Twain Sesquicentennial Commission — a commission that both men assumed by then would create the superstructure of a dramatic economic revival in the town, perhaps on the scale of a miniature world's fair.

Weil accepted, thereby effectively removing the *Hannibal Courier-Post* as a credibly disinterested journal for covering the most consequential undertaking in Hannibal's twentieth-century history. (Mayor Lyng tendered commission memberships to other local media executives, including those in control of two local radio stations; like Weil, those executives accepted.) Thus, at the very outset, the Sesquicentennial Commission conducted its deliberations with virtual impunity, at least as far as public opinion was concerned: its members knew that they could set the terms of their accountability.

And so the citizens of Hannibal began to hear rumors of bonanza. Not only rumors, but actual projections and plans, reported in the local newspaper.

These plans postulated a bonanza of tourism. Their activating symbol was to be Mark Twain. They would be activated by a vast and grandiose engine of late-twentieth-century marketing. The blueprints had been delivered by an outsider, the New York consultant Alfred Stern. They would be financed by outside capital — donations from companies and corporations around the state, and nation, whose products and brand names would be associated with the festival.

And the sesquicentennial would also be administered by an outsider — by the newly arrived town newspaper publisher whose credo, adopted from an executive of the outside-owned newspaper chain, was "Count that day lost when you haven't done something for your community."

CHAPTER VII

By the early summer of 1984, some outlines portending the dimensions of the Mark Twain Sesquicentennial were beginning to crystallize in the comprehension of Hannibal residents — somewhat as the outlines of a steamboat might emerge from a river fog and reveal its onrushing bulk to the oarsman of a small raft bobbing in its path.

The dimensions were breathtaking. The dimensions beggared any previous reckoning of town scale. They rivaled the claims that were then issuing from the prospective developers of Mark Twain Lake over at Monroe City, although each enterprise steadfastly behaved as though the other did not exist. In a series of crisply issued fact sheets and "operational calendars" and "sponsorship-opportunity" lists (the essence of which were routinely reported in the *Courier-Post*), the Mark Twain Sesquicentennial Commission laid out its vision: a leviathan celebration that would sprawl over seven months, from May through November of 1985, fueled by a budget of $5,075,000.

Five million dollars came to more than half the equivalent of the town's annual operating budget. Five million dollars suggested that the festival's true clientele, and its true supervisors, would be drawn from a range far beyond Hannibal's population with its limited pool of small-business supporters. Five million dollars said *na-*

tional corporate sponsorship, and that is exactly what the commission intended to nail down.

But the budget was hardly the gaudiest figure in the fact sheets and the lists. That honor belonged to the total projection of revenue deriving from the sesquicentennial: $250 million in 1985 alone, and something under half that total in succeeding years.

To be sure, the commission was careful not to imply that Hannibal would have this quarter of a billion dollars all to itself. The profits would ripple outward through "the area" — sometimes specified as "the tri-state area" (Missouri, Iowa, and Illinois) — by virtue of a formula that the commission's press releases explained with cool certitude:

"Current projections," the handouts reported, called for the celebration to attract one million visitors to Hannibal in 1985 (that figure was occasionally doubled). The permanent attractions created by the sesquicentennial, in particular the theme center stage in the historic district, would draw four hundred thousand annual visitors in the years beyond. (Hannibal claimed 250,000 tourists in an average year, a claim not universally accepted.)

The fact sheets continued:

> The average tourist spends $50 per day and an average of five days in a destination area. One million visitors in 1985 to Hannibal, St. Louis, the Ozarks and other area destinations can be expected to add $250 million to the area's economy through spending in hotels, restaurants, shopping centers, department stores, boutiques, service stations and other retail establishments. Each dollar spent on tourism turns over an average of three times, thus adding to the area's economic vitality.

The cardinal point about most of these official-sounding figures — the budget, the projected revenue, the varying estimates of visitors — turned out to be their susceptibility to change. Although the handouts bore the imprimatur of the full Sesquicentennial Commission, an entity created by city ordinance and consisting of around a dozen members (depending on resignations and reappointments), most commissioners acknowledged that their conceptual essence sprang from John Lyng and Larry Weil, augmented by whatever buttressing statistics their various consultants could provide. (Asked to account for his estimation of a million visitors after it had become clear that nothing like a million visitors would come to Hannibal, Lyng replied somewhat testily that he and Weil were operating under "optimum" assumptions in those early days. "I've never had the misconception," he added, "that we *weren't* making it up as we went along.")

Whatever their validity, the projected figures were intended for the appraisal of large potential sponsors — national breweries, airline companies, food manufacturers — with plants located in "the area," most particularly in St. Louis. For the Hannibal City Council, which would be asked to commit $160,000 over two years for the celebration, Lyng offered a narrower enticement: a projected sales tax harvest of $200,000 — four times the figure then being realized. That sort of money, one of Lyng's fact sheets argued, would purchase about one and one-third new fire engines, about three new bridges, about twelve new policemen or firemen, maintenance for about twenty-five miles of streets — "and on and on."

The increase in actual dollar volume of business to Hannibal was estimated, variously, at four million to eight million dollars.

And what sort of attractions would bring these million visitors to the destination area known as Hannibal, Missouri, the "world's most famous small city," as the commission handouts were already calling it? In 1984 the answer to that question was limited only by the week in which one happened to ask it. Among Alfred Stern's "twenty useful ideas," only the town clock tower had been rejected, and that rejection had come only after the proposal was announced in the *Courier-Post,* triggering a public uproar. The permanent theme stage was very much on the agenda then, as were the film festival (upgraded by then to an international film and TV festival); the riverboat regatta; the Smithsonian Institution exhibit of Mark Twain artifacts; the development of the special Mark Twain rose; and the grand finale appearance of Hal Holbrook in *Mark Twain Tonight.*

But even those attractions scarcely began to describe the sesquicentennial's scope. In the summer of 1984, Hannibal residents learned that they could also look forward to a national riverlife music festival — five four-day musical marathons that would draw 400,000 people; a "Good Golly Aunt Polly" show featuring stars from the 1950s and 1960s that would draw 12,000; a "Huck"-sters raft race (15,000 participants); the Fédération Internationale d'Aeronautiques helium balloon championships (50,000 spectators); a railroad reunion week (90,000 buffs in attendance); an American storytellers / Mark Twain humor symposium (70,000 storytelling fans).

Nothing seemed impossible. There would be weekly fireworks displays, forty-one in all — 760,000 spectators. There would be 348 performances from the theme stage — witnessed by 470,000. The Mark Twain writers' conference / literary seminar would draw 30,000 book lovers. Eight hundred fifty thousand people would come to hear 432 stories told in daily sessions by "storytellers of all types" from a specially designed storytellers tree. There would be parades, parades every day; there would be *120 parades,* and a total of 400,000 people would come to watch them.

The world's largest guest book — 425 8-foot fence sections, signed by special guests to the celebration, would be viewed by 850,000 — the same number, as it happened, that would view the traditional arts center operation and the youth stage performances. (The daily Central Park band concerts, by contrast, would draw only 249,600 "individuals" — the commission perhaps felt the need to guard against undue optimism.)

And still the litany of events, along with their projected audiences, poured out of commission headquarters. Classic car races with a special parade and a "Tin Lizzie" concert: 45,000 people. A Hannibal marathon; fitness workshops; junior and senior runs: 25,000. Bicycle races! Two-day sanctioned bicycle events. Hell, *tricycle* races. A pedal power parade: 90,000. More balloon championships — the North Central hot air balloon championships; a parade, a banquet, a "name" concert: 95,000. Hometown America Days; a parade; the world's biggest ice cream social: 60,000. A "jubilation" gospel music festival with a "name" performer: 40,000.

Did somebody say Joshua Logan's *Huck and Jim on the Missis-*

sippi? Why not have *two* musicals in premiere? Book Hauptman and Miller's *Big River,* or at least put it on the "Activities Developed and Budgeted But Not Yet Scheduled" list; put it in the paper: 18,000.

A croquet tournament would draw 20,000 spectators. An exhibit of Mississippi River costumes would draw 50,000. There was no limit. An amateur art show? — 60,000. A prize in short fiction? — 300 entries, an "estimated distribution" of 10,000. One hundred twenty thousand people would come to a ten-day Renaissance festival "recapturing the spirit of 'A Connecticut Yankee in King Arthur's Court.' " Six thousand would show up for a one-act folk opera based on "The Celebrated Jumping Frog of Calaveras County" (spelled "Calaveros" in the commission fact sheet). Two days of highland games, "celebrating the Clemens ancestral heritage," would attract 20,000.

A *third* play, *Hannibal Blues,* about "the cantankerous Becky Thatcher in her golden years," would draw . . . oh . . . say, 12,000.

And on and on.

These and other planned events were set down with the utmost seriousness in the Sesquicentennial Commission handouts of early 1984. Beneath each planned event were listed its projected rankings in several categories of interest to potential sponsors: not only in attendance, but also in "media exposure," "demographic group control," and "product/service linkage." Most often, the rankings were authoritatively listed as "excellent" or "very good," with several others listed as "good," and only a few — the writers' conference / literary seminar, for instance, or the storytellers symposium, or the gospel music festival — were deemed "fair" for product/service linkage.

As John Lyng acknowledged several months after this frenzy of projections had suffered its consequences, it was Alfred Stern's letter that had unleashed it all; it was Stern's letter that had forever buried the notion of a modest, local celebration along the lines of the 1935 centennial. "After Stern," said Lyng, "we got to thinking of it as an economic development tool."

John Lyng subsequently got to thinking of Alfred Stern and his letter as the root causes of the sesquicentennial agonies that Hannibal endured. "We were definitely not ready for what Alfred had in mind," he would admit. "The eastern ideas don't sell well here." In his more bitter and candid moods, Lyng would darken that thought a bit. "I've really learned to distrust people outside our community," he would say. "It's not that they're evil, it's just that they're promoters."

That thought may have been true, as far as it went. But it fell short of explaining why Alfred Stern's letter got translated into municipal policy.

Stern did not live in Hannibal. He had no notion of the town's temperament, its economic or cultural history, its complex, interlocking web of hopes and resentments regarding the Mark Twain legacy — or regarding outsiders, for that matter. What Stern (and later a few other imported consultants) had designed was the skeleton of a professional all-purpose sesquicentennial, a blueprint that with a few adjustments in emphasis and nomenclature could have been imposed upon almost any city or town in America. Its specifications assumed an interchangeable community visited by interchangeable tourists — the object of the entire exercise, after all, was not Hannibal itself (with its distinct balances and rhythms, its idiosyncrasies of architecture and geology, the particular play of light upon its slanting surfaces, its subtle relationship with the river, its pork-tenderloin sandwiches), but rather Hannibal as *venue;* as site, repository, platform, for a transcending, mass-marketed modular package called the Mark Twain Sesquicentennial.

But John Lyng did live in the town. He had been born and raised there, the son of a railroad working man. He knew something about the way Hannibal people behaved and thought — he'd put in five years at the *Courier-Post* himself as a young kid. And as a part-time schoolboy worker at the Becky Thatcher Bookshop, in the employment of John Winkler, Lyng surely had learned a thing or two about the nature of Hannibal tourism.

The fact was that tourism had never done especially well for the town (nor, historically, had the official town done well for tourism) despite a general perception to the contrary. Certain Hannibal businessmen liked to point out that in recent years, tourism had received more city funding than any other effort at economic or industrial development (about one million dollars over a seven-year period), yet its revenues lagged far below those of agriculture or manufacturing.

Moreover, it was harder than John Lyng's fact sheets suggested to establish a precise ratio between total tourists and tourist expenditures.

"We don't really know what tourism actually does for the city in terms of dollars," declared Gale Newman, the executive director of the Chamber of Commerce and the Industrial Council. "But there are certain indicators, and they tend to belie the higher projections for tourist dollars that *automatically* enter the economy through retail sales.

"Towns with lots of revenue from tourists ought to have high retail sales per capita. In nineteen eighty-two Branson [a tourist town in the Ozarks region of southern Missouri] had nineteen thousand seven hundred and one dollars per capita, and Eldon [a similar town] had ten thousand three hundred ninety. Hannibal's was five thousand four hundred ninety-five. Even worse, we trailed some of our neighboring towns with *no* tourist attractions."

But despite this ambiguity, no civic leader, including the thoughtful Gale Newman, was even close to questioning the fundamental value of tourism, or the rightness of continuing to develop it. To the contrary: in the mid-1980s tourism — not just in Hannibal but throughout the "Show-Me State" and in several other American regions as well — was undergoing a crash mobilization.

Advertising budgets for state departments of tourism were leaping into the millions of dollars. (Illinois led the nation with a $10 million budget; Michigan and New York followed at $9 million and $8 million; California, which had *no* tourism advertising budget in 1984, committed $5.6 million for 1985, but still trailed Massachusetts and Alaska, at $7.6 million and $6.9 million.) Several states were retaining research organizations to conduct "focus-group" studies aimed at building detailed data-base collections of tourist preferences and behavior patterns.

Trained interviewers were buttonholing moms and dads at trailer parks and historic seaports and haunted stagecoaches all across the width and breadth of the land, thrusting data-base survey questionnaires into their hands, demanding to know: trip type; number in party; number of trips to the state in last five years; estimated spending per day on trip; what "grade" they would give to "this property."

The impetus for this mobilization varied somewhat from state to state — share-of-market competitiveness had something to do with it in the more prosperous regions — but in Missouri and a few other states hit by the farm crisis and the erosion of assembly-line jobs, the motive was sharply defined: economic necessity. These states bluntly identified tourism as a "quick-response" industry, one that could bring in business dollars in a matter of weeks or months. Viewed from this perspective, the tourist mobilization had an affecting, almost bittersweet aura of goodwill about it: if enough middle-class Americans, inevitably including those who were themselves victims of the tightened economic times, could be coaxed and lured and sloganeered out onto the American highway, to view one another's historic districts and theme parks and public-use areas and restored craft villages, a spontaneous combustion of new wealth, new prosperity, would somehow occur.

There was something almost pioneerish in that premise: an echo of community, of common cause; of covered-dish suppers at the table of the family most in need. In this case, America itself was the covered dish. Its purple mountains' majesties, its Boyhood Home of Twain — all would be wrapped up nicely; put in a package, so to speak, and set out for the American public's consumption.

And if the new wrappings sometimes obfuscated the old authentic touches on the dish — the filigrees and the finishings that betokened a legacy, a tradition — well, it couldn't be helped. The imperatives of the quick response sometimes seemed almost to require that a state or a region destroy a village in order to savor it.

"The image of Missouri was very blah," said Marjorie Beenders. "Not negative, not positive, but *blah*. It was my job to change that."

Marjorie Beenders was beginning her third year, in 1985, as director of the Missouri Division of Tourism. A lean and tanned woman of thirty-nine, with slightly disheveled hair and the nervous good humor of a person who hasn't enough hours in the day for the best job in the world, she was busily implementing an aggressive statewide advertising thrust calculated to increase Missouri's $5-billion-a-year tourism industry by 15 percent. Ms. Beenders's calibrations for statewide benefits were every bit as assured, as precise, as John Lyng's sesquicentennial projections for Hannibal: a 15 percent increase in tourism would generate $750 million in new spending, create twenty-one thousand new full-time jobs, and conjure an additional $120 million in tax revenues. The formulas were all there; the statistics awaited their marching orders. All that Marjorie Beenders needed to make it work was a decent advertising budget.

When I visited her in her office in Jefferson City, in the spring of 1985, Ms. Beenders was scraping by on a shoestring advertising budget: $970,000. Her goal — her *requirement* for any meaningful increase in tourism revenues — was $12 million a year, which would catapult Missouri within range of national leadership in the ever-spiraling budgets for tourist advertising. Ms. Beenders was accustomed to state-of-the-industry resources: she had come to the Missouri job from Illinois, the biggest spender of all the fifty states.

"I am known around the state as a cheerleader," Ms. Beenders allowed, talking rapidly as she tapped the ash from her cigarette into the tab hole of an empty Coca-Cola can in her small office. "I'm a hard one to hold back."

Despite the paucity of her budget, Marjorie Beenders was on the verge of at least one impressive breakthrough in image perception: she had made significant inroads toward discarding Missouri's old and venerable motto — the "Show-Me State" — and replacing it with something more contemporary, more high-concept; something less *blah:* "Wake Up to Missouri."

"We *tested* it before we put it out in the media," Ms. Beenders assured me. "We did telephone surveys. 'Show Me' tested stubborn, headstrong, hardheaded. 'Wake Up to Missouri,' on the other hand, tested friendly, positive. Modern-day tourists want that. They want value. They want things nice."

It seemed not to matter to Ms. Beenders that about three generations of Missourians had cherished the "Show-Me" motto precisely *because* it "tested" stubborn, headstrong, hardheaded — traits that happened to fit a large number of Missourians' image perceptions of themselves, and the hell with any outsiders who felt threatened by it. The full slogan, "I'm from Missouri — you've got to show me," had come into vogue in the 1890s. It was first imported to the media centers of the Northeast by a Missouri congressman named Willard Vandiver. At a speech in Philadelphia in 1899, the congressman felt the urge come upon him to lay a sampling of Ozarkean thunder upon his cummerbunded audience. "I come from a state that raises corn and cotton and cockleburs and Democrats," the congressman declared, "and frothy eloquence neither convinces nor satisfies me. I am from Missouri. You have got to show me!" The audience loved it. It had tested well. An authentic slogan was born.

"Show-Me State" had appeared on Missouri license plates for as long as anyone could remember; no one ever objected; and the state's residents tended even to relish the bewilderment of outsiders at the phrase's essential and vaguely intimidating obscurity.

But these were new and different times, times that required a more high-concept way of defining one's heritage. Thus, in the totemic year of 1984, a new logo began to appear on billboards and on TV commercials and on T-shirts and in travel brochures around the state. It appeared as the title to the fifteen-minute promotional film about the benefits of tourism that some developers were showing to the potential investors in the Mark Twain Heritage Theme Park less than thirty miles to the west, in Monroe City.

Against a rising sun, rendered in vivid orange bleeding upward toward yellow in a pattern that somehow suggested the uniform shirts of the Houston Astros, and struck in a purposeful-looking typeface that might be described as italicized digital, was the ascendant slogan: "Wake Up to Missouri."

A couple of newspapers bestirred themselves to editorialize in defense of "Show Me." Several traditionalists pointed out that the new slogan had nothing in particular to *do* with Missouri — it could easily be adapted to "Wake Up to (fill in the blank)." A Wendy's in Hannibal was quick to prove the point on its marquee.

Nevertheless, "Wake Up to Missouri" took its place in the bumper-sticker *ur*-language. Frothy eloquence, it appeared, was finally about to get its due in the state. Like hotel art, the new slogan seemed vaguely applicable in any context, or without context. Whatever.

A hotel, in fact, is where "Wake Up to Missouri" was conceived. "The whole idea came to me by accident," Marjorie Beenders admitted. "It was in New Orleans in nineteen eighty-three, at the American Bus Association convention — the people who do the bus tours, you know? We went down there to promote Missouri. I hit on a gimmick — serving breakfast in bed to all the delegates, using cups and things that said, 'Wake Up to Missouri.' Then it struck me that we had a pretty good state slogan going. But we tested it before we put it out to the media. We did the telephone surveys."

Even without the benefits of a $12 million advertising budget, Marjorie Beenders had pretty much managed to get most of Missouri's 44.2 million acres lined up into one kind of promotional package or another. She had devised pamphlets exhorting people to wake up to the cities of Missouri, the festivals of Missouri, the seasons of Missouri, the lakes of Missouri, the country music of Missouri, the caves of Missouri, the rivers of Missouri, and the hospitality of Missouri; not to mention the arts, sports, canoeing, hunting, fishing, history, wineries, regions, state parks, state historic sites, good times, campsites, and the facts of Missouri.

She had directed people's attention to sparkling new hotels and shopping areas; she had limned the historic Westports and the elegant Country Club Plazas; she had indicated historic highlights such as the old stables where the Pony Express began and the home — the pamphlet made sure to use the warm-sounding word "home" — where Jesse James died. She had recommended toe-tappin' evenings and accessible shoreline; she had laid out the state's history, state bird, physiography, geology, climate, area, mineral resources, state rock, coal, sand, and gravel; she had laid out *lime* — she had done practically everything for Missouri tourism except go out and grab people by the shoulders and drag them over the state line — and still Marjorie Beenders could not for the life of her fathom exactly what the problem was up in the one area of the state that ought to be an automatic tourist magnet: the northeastern area that included Hannibal.

"A lot of communities would give their right arms to be in Hannibal's position," she remarked to me in her office, tapping another cigarette ash into the Coca-Cola can. "But they have to go out and *manufacture* the tourism business. The world will pass them by if they do not."

We spoke in the spring of 1985, a few weeks before the official opening of the sesquicentennial. Marjorie Beenders was aware of the celebration. She was aware that the original plans for it had been to some extent altered, diminished. Marjorie Beenders was aware of all these dynamics, but she could not think of a reason for them. She was hardly alone. Few people outside the prairies of northeastern Missouri would have been capable of constructing a rationale for this behavior that seemed perversely to assault the very wellsprings of opportunity.

Some of the reasons lay embedded in the immutable psychologies of the town and the communities around it — psychologies that formed an unbroken chain back to the southern diaspora of the 1830s that settled this land.

Other reasons lay within the specific drives and compulsions of people who had no connection whatsoever with Hannibal's lineage — and who therefore had strayed deeply into the town's emotional force field before they quite realized they were no longer on familiar ground.

All Marjorie Beenders could understand was that a tremendous opportunity was going to waste.

"Why *not* take advantage of Hannibal's history?" she wanted to know. "People *like* history. So build on it.

"Look at Disneyland. Look at EPCOT.

"Hannibal could be another Williamsburg!"

CHAPTER VIII

THE impulse to exploit the region's historic legacy for commercial gain was not unique to Hannibal. Even as the town's governing officials schemed with outside consultants to turn the Twain heritage into a tourist bonanza, a parallel — but unrelated — master plan was unfolding just a few miles to the west, in the Salt River region of the great author's birthplace. This project had roots that stretched far back into the area's history, and involved the natural elements as well as marketing ambition. Nevertheless its fate might have provided an important lesson to the planners of the sesquicentennial — had any of those planners been in the mood to observe, and take heed.

One day in October of 1968, a very young man dressed in a white linen suit and wearing false white hair and a false white mustache had stood at the edge of Lover's Leap above Hannibal and thought of a vast shrine beside a lake, a shrine to the glory and the memory of Mark Twain.

The lake would be artificial, not natural; and the shrine would include an airstrip, a resort hotel, and a video arcade. Nevertheless, the young man, who was large-framed and handsome in a blue-eyed, theatrical sort of way, could imagine nothing in this vision that would be inconsistent with his sincere desire to recreate the "mood" of Mark Twain's era in American life.

The artificial lake did not yet exist. No outdoor bulletin boards coated with use regulations would dot its shoreline for another fifteen years. But as it happened, the process leading to its existence was being carried out even as the young man stood on his perch on Lover's Leap. Men with bulldozers, under contract to the United States Army Corps of Engineers, were clearing ground along a riverbed less than thirty miles from where the young man stood; the projected site of an enormous dam. At the same time, the United States government was carrying out condemnation proceedings against the thousand residents of a village a few hundred yards upstream from the damsite — a village that had been established in 1834, the same year that Judge John Marshall Clemens arrived in Florida, Missouri, with his family.

The young man was an actor named Michael Jenkins. He had come to Hannibal on that October day with a television crew to star in a dramatized documentary — a blend of fact and fiction — about Mark Twain's life in Hannibal. Jenkins was twenty-one years old. Thousands of members of his generation were rampaging the streets and college campuses of America — as hippies and Black Panthers, as radical protesters against the war in Vietnam. Jenkins's peers were burning American flags and draft cards, regathering their forces after the Democratic National Convention in Chicago to carry on their revolution against the country's systems and institutions.

Michael Jenkins's priorities in 1968 lay elsewhere. They lay in good, wholesome family entertainment.

"I made a choice in those days," he recalled later. "If there is a line in me that connects Mark Twain to Michael Jenkins, it is that of traditional values."

The author of "The United States of Lyncherdom" and the remark, not published until 1923, that "the Christian's Bible is a drugstore" may have found it curious to hear himself linked with traditional values. But then, Missourians of the late twentieth century, especially those with an entrepreneurial bent, tended to think of Twain within rigidly qualified terms. They thought of him as a kindly, homespun philosopher and humorist; the affectionate chronicler of small boys munching green apples and tricking one another into whitewashing the fence. Jenkins took a slightly longer view. "I have great respect for the works of Mark Twain," he told me in one of our conversations. "I'm only sorry that he became a secular humanist."

Michael Jenkins did unerringly grasp one thing about the white town drowsing below him as he stood on Lover's Leap that fall afternoon: Hannibal and the Mark Twain legend were timeless, universal. At least the town seemed that way to Jenkins. The war in Vietnam, the assassinations, the burnings might as well be happening on Saturn, for all they had to do with this placid little kingdom of haze and sumac and railroad yards.

Jenkins had been playing Mark Twain almost relentlessly for the last year and a half. His fascination with the role had taken hold on the night he found himself face to face with the distinguished Twain interpreter Hal Holbrook, following one of Holbrook's *Mark Twain Tonight* performances at Stephens College in Columbia, Missouri. Holbrook had spoken for a few minutes with Jenkins. He had let the young man in on the details of his three-hour transformation, in makeup, from Hal Holbrook to Mark Twain. And then Holbrook had politely suggested that Michael Jenkins try a Mark Twain routine of his own.

Jenkins developed a routine. He performed it on small college campuses in Missouri and on USO tours of Japan and Korea, shuffling about the stage and drawling Twain homilies between Playboy Bunny routines. Returning to America, Jenkins found a base for the role not far from his home town — at Silver Dollar City, a rustic amusement complex south of Springfield in the Ozark Mountains.

It was at Silver Dollar City that Jenkins received his initiation into big-time show business. He met the cast and crew of "The Beverly Hillbillies," on location at the complex for several episodes in 1967. He worked as an extra in some of the scenes.

Michael Jenkins was getting a rare education along two lines that would later serve him well: both Silver Dollar City and "The Beverly Hillbillies" profited by embracing an ideographic, hyper-wholesome, Parson Weems-ish vision of Americana. And both enterprises displayed a great virtuosity in mass-audience packaging techniques. Jenkins listened and observed. His actor's mind stored tendencies; impressions; formulas.

Entertainment. Wholesomeness. Families; *the whole family*. A place you could take the kids and not be embarrassed. Lovable rustics triumphant, upholding the republic's verities. Tradition in a world swept into chaos by revolution.

When Twain-costumed Michael Jenkins looked down from the Lover's Leap precipice and into the unsuspecting vitals of Mark Twain's boyhood town, vague intimations of opportunity began to stir within him. And when he overheard a cast member gossiping about the imminent ground-breaking for a gigantic dam just thirty miles from Hannibal — a dam that would create a twenty-three-hundred-square-mile artificial lake out on the prairie, *Mark Twain's own prairie* — why, Michael Jenkins knew that fate, if not a Higher Power, had supplied him with the perfect stage. One hundred twenty-four Octobers previously, a group of deists, the followers of a New York City mystic named William Miller, had gathered on Lover's Leap dressed in flowing white robes to await a divine message pertaining to the end of the world. In this particular October, a message came unbidden to Michael Jenkins. This one pertained to theme parks.

"It came to me," was the way he described it later. "It just started being born."

"All human beings go to water," was one of the maxims that Michael Jenkins liked to use on chamber-of-commerce groups when promoting his Mark Twain Heritage Theme Park development scheme for Mark Twain Lake. He was speaking in particular of twentieth-century human beings on vacation, but given the significance of the Salt and, later, the Mississippi rivers in attracting settlers to northeast Missouri, the thought had some historical validity as well.

Among the human beings of the great southern migration who were drawn to the Salt River in the nineteenth century was a young Kentucky immigrant named John J. Lyle. Lyle arrived in the region in 1834 along with his sixteen-year-old Kentucky fiancée, Martha Greathouse. He purchased a land grant from the United States Land Office at Palmyra, Missouri, and opened a post office on the north bank of the Salt, just at the crown of one of the river's graceful, horseshoe-shaped bends, on land thick with maple and oak trees, below limestone bluffs cut through with icy small mineral springs that emptied into the Salt.

Because the river was fordable at Lyle's property site, he named his post office New Portland. John J. Lyle then proceeded to lay out the building lots, in precise rows 65 feet wide and 125 feet deep, for a pristine and tragic little village, its limits never larger than seventy-four acres, that came to be known as New Port and, finally, as Joanna.

It was Joanna's peculiar bad fortune to lie just a few hundred yards upstream from the site where men would one day build an enormous dam for the stated purpose of flood control — the dam that would create Mark Twain Lake, the lake on whose shores Michael Jenkins and his partners would propose their shrine to the mood of the past.

The village's compensation for being sentenced to death was to see its name used to identify the dam project for four decades, until the name was officially changed just before flooding began, to honor Clarence Cannon, a local congressman who was never really sure he wanted to back the dam in the first place.

If the Clarence Cannon Dam was a monument to man's ultimate will to neutralize the inconvenient variables in nature, it was equally a monument to man's lingering ambivalence regarding that will. After all, the dam was not completed until the fall of 1983 — a century and a half after the area's white settlers began to feel themselves unjustly served by the flooding river, and nearly half a century after the United States Congress passed the dam's enabling legislation, the Flood Control Act of 1938.

Perhaps back then the notion of tampering with anything so primal as a river was inhibited by a sense of taboo. Perhaps there was some half-acknowledged understanding that those who choose to stake their fortunes within a river's floodplain are striking a bargain with nature and should be willing to accept the risks — which, after all, are scarcely hidden. Whatever the reasons, it is clear that Americans through the first half of the twentieth century seldom found the concept of "flood control," *in itself,* a decisive impetus for tampering with their rivers.

The years immediately following World War II weakened these inhibitions. Postwar affluence introduced a new and exhilarating ethic to the American middle class — the ethic of *leisure*. And leisure, as Donald Duck, Esther Williams, and other icons of postwar behavior demonstrated, frequently required access to water — tame water.

"Liquid streams of gold," was the way one Missouri newspaper editorial of the 1950s saluted, with just the slightest touch of redundancy, America's new, speculative attitude toward its creeks and brooks and rivers. Stories began to circulate — fantastical stories of small towns that magically boomed into industrial dynamos after the "development" of a nearby lake, or the creation of a new one, attracted a rash of companies seeking leisure-rich sites for their employees.

Thus, in the 1950s, there materialized a second rationale for building dams across the nation's rivers. In addition to *flood control,* these dams would provide *recreation*. No one seemed to notice, or care, that "flood control" and "recreation" frequently required diametrically opposing behavior from water (good fishing requires a clear, flowing stream; flood control requires a stationary table). If some university professor or conservationist did manage to raise this point, the dam-minded businessmen were ready with another, offsetting benefit. Dams would provide "hydropower" — a cheap source of electricity for the community.

Hydropower did not always pan out either. There was the case of the Harry S Truman Dam in Warsaw, Missouri, conceived in 1953 for flood control at a projected cost of $150 million. The town's businessmen, enamored of liquid streams of gold, persuaded Congress to enlarge the project so that the dam would accommodate recreation and hydropower interests as well. The result, by the 1980s, was a $488 million debacle. The Harry S Truman Dam's pool level required the removal of five hundred farm families from their land. Its reversible turbine engines, installed to create "hydropower," caused disastrous fluctuations in the water level that destroyed fish by the tens of thousands. A Missouri senator finally expressed the obvious: he pronounced the dam "a calamity."

But in the 1950s, calamities such as this were as yet unimaginable. Rivers were for damming. There was even a federal bureaucracy designed for exactly that purpose — the world's largest engineering and construction agency, the United States Army Corps of Engineers.

The Corps of Engineers had been poised to strike its imprint upon the Salt River at least since 1938, the year Congress included the river in its comprehensive Flood Control Act for the upper Mississippi basin. The Corps of Engineers got as far in its plans as determining that the optimum site would lie a few hundred yards downstream from Joanna, and that Joanna would therefore have to be obliterated. Then World War II began, and flood-control plans all over America were suspended. But consummation was only a matter of time. The Salt River was now embedded within the Corps of Engineers' institutional memory circuits. Its fate was virtually unalterable.

The first time that the Honorable Clarence Cannon's constituents in the Ninth Congressional District of Missouri heard anything about a dam across the Salt River, a dam that would control floods but wipe out an existing village, they repudiated it out of hand. This was in November 1950. A group called the Monroe County Conservation Club had received information that the Corps of Engineers was working out such a plan.

Most of the club members at the meeting favored their organization's own plan for flood control: a grass-roots system of water management that involved the terracing of farmland and the creation of some six thousand small reservoirs throughout the floodplain. This sort of system would require federal allocations — more than $22 million — but that figure fell considerably short of the $30 million price tag that was quoted, in those days, for a large dam across the Salt River.

Congressman Cannon, as it turned out, could not have agreed more. Notified of the conservation club's position, the congressman responded that the very notion of a large dam was "merely an attempt to bring pressure to bear upon our district in order to justify a huge and useless program all over the nation."

Clarence Cannon was a transitional figure in the politics and the fortunes of northeastern Missouri. He was first elected to federal office in 1922, an era in which many people in his district lived and farmed pretty much as people had lived and farmed a hundred years before. Cannon himself was an active farmer. He would rule the Ninth District until his death in 1964, spanning the eras from Warren Harding's presidency to Lyndon Johnson's. For most of those years he served as chairman of the House Appropriations Committee. A Democrat of the pre–New Deal school of thought, Cannon was staunchly mindful of the national debt. He did not seem a likely convert to the dam-builders' cause.

And yet it was to be Clarence Cannon who opened his district up to the ministrations of those who believed that engineering could correct the shortcomings of natural and economic law: engineering not only of the land, but of the human behavior relative to the land.

In February 1958, a group of men from the region called on the congressman at his home in Elsberry, Missouri. The delegation's leader was a young Monroe City realtor named Warren See. See and his friends urged the congressman to reconsider his opposition to the dormant dam project. The "liquid streams of gold" attitude had taken a deep hold on businessmen's imaginations by that time. The delegation was able to offer Cannon a practical-seeming premise for changing his mind: the Army Corps of Engineers (which in its own quiet way had continued to develop plans and surveys as if the project were quite alive) had radically improved its specifications for the dam.

Cannon, always sensitive to the nuances of voter opinion, assented. The businessmen departed his home, exultant, and immediately organized themselves into the Mark Twain Reservoir Area Development Association. Warren See would be the chairman.

The association's glee did not last long. Soon the congressman shifted his ground again. Cannon had been reading the editorial page of the *Monroe County Appeal*. What he saw there — a string of antidam editorials — made him nervous. It was at about that time that the congressman's thoughts began to shift toward the international communist menace. In a letter to newspaper editors dated March 24, 1958, he framed the Joanna dam issue in the larger context of free-world survival. There was, Cannon pointed out, "a deadly enemy awaiting a favorable opportunity to attack us and wreck our cities, slaughter two-thirds of our people and enslave the rest." In an arabesque of logic that might have brought hearty applause from Mark Twain himself, Cannon concluded that "such heavy expenditures as the amount required to build the Joanna Dam — every penny of which must be borrowed by the Government, further increasing the public debt, reducing the buying power of the dollar and increasing the cost of living — should be deferred."

Cannon may have assumed that the Red Peril card was virtually untrumpable in forestalling a decision on the dam; but he had reckoned without one final card — nature's. In July the Salt did what rivers often do. It overflowed its banks, setting a record for flood crest on the river. In August the Salt flooded again and broke the record. Together, the floods caused more than $1 million in damage to farmers with land in the floodplain. The Mark Twain Reservoir Area Development Association was quick to contend that, had the Joanna dam been in place, all of the flood damage would have been avoided.

Now the tide of progress began to turn in the dam's favor. With the election of John F. Kennedy as president, recreation and fitness became a *part* of national policy. In October 1962 Kennedy himself signed into law a $2.4 billion Public Works Authorization bill that included $63 million for a Joanna dam and reservoir, to be constructed across the grounds of the village that supplied the project's name. A conspicuous champion of the bill was the chairman of the powerful House Appropriations Committee, the Honorable Clarence Cannon, who had taken to boasting in letters that "I was the original pioneer in the construction of Joanna Dam." Cannon died of a heart attack in office in May 1964. Congress voted to rename the Missouri project in his memory.

Ground-breaking for the Clarence Cannon Dam began in 1968. Floods and labor problems caused delays that stretched its construction over fifteen years. In 1983 the Cannon Dam was complete — 450,000 cubic yards of concrete on the Missouri prairie, 3 million cubic yards of embankment, a height of 138 feet, and a length of nearly half a mile.

By late summer of 1984 the dam-created lake had reached its planned capacity: 18,600 acres at normal pool surface, 285 miles of shoreline, a watershed of 2,300 square miles. Its total cost had increased to $320 million — a figure that threw the dam's original motivating premise, "flood control," into some economic question. " 'Flood control' is nonsense," declared Rex Campbell, a professor of rural sociology at the University of Missouri and the state's demographer, in 1985. "You cannot economically justify a dam of this nature on the basis of 'flood control.' The developers had to adopt the 'multiple use' rationale — which reduced the flood control function even further, because recreational use requires that you keep the pool's depth fluctuation to a minimum."

But as the tourists streamed toward the lake in its first summers of existence on the prairie, no one seemed inclined to question that long-ago rationale, or even to consider that it had existed, much less to consider that the alternative scheme for flood control along the Salt River — terracing and the small-reservoir system — had never been given a test. The United States Army Corps of Engineers' institutional memory circuits had not failed. It had taken forty years, but the engineers had struck their imprint across the Salt River.

The site of the John A. Quarles farm, which Mark Twain had recalled so fondly as the center of "a great level prairie which was covered with wild strawberry plants, vividly starred with prairie pinks and walled in on all sides by forests," was itself spared, owing to the chance fact that it had occupied high ground. (The farm buildings themselves have long since vanished from the land.) Likewise the nearly abandoned hamlet of Florida, Mark Twain's birthplace, remained above water level, an odd little peninsula of white frame houses, truck gardens, and a two-lane blacktop road that wandered out of town and abruptly plunged into the lake's bottom.

What did not remain — what was not granted so much as a ceremonial mention on the Corps of Engineers' official map of the lake, with all its denotations of recreation areas named in the memories of local entrepreneurs — was the village of Joanna.

Joanna, which had paid the ultimate price — extinction — for the advent of Mark Twain Lake, was now submerged by history as well as by the Salt River. The town's very name had been blotted from the commemorative records to make way for that of Clarence Cannon.

But Joanna had existed. It had existed on seventy-four acres for a century and a half on the north bank of the Salt River and on the east bank of Cow Creek about twenty-five miles southwest of Hannibal, at the foot of high, timbered hills, affording its thousand citizens a view, to the south, of a great horseshoe bend, the river embracing a fertile valley of oak and maple trees. It had existed as the home ground of five generations of blacksmiths and millers and postmasters and school superintendents and preachers and operators of the River View Store; of farmers and their wives who planted their onions and turnips and beets in the dark of the moon, and their beans and peas and corn in the moon's light, and their flowers in the signs of the zodiac, and who stirred their butter into their molasses instead of spreading the butter on the bread, and who made their cough syrup of the inner bark of the wild cherry tree. It had existed as a community of dancers, of men and women and children who danced hard at the annual town picnic at Lucy Springs, who danced in those lost Missouri prairie afternoons, the fiddlers bearing down on the music, heeding the lost voices of the callers for the dance, calling in their sing-song time.

The dancers' graves are gone from what remains of Joanna near the base of the Clarence Cannon Dam beneath the surface of Mark Twain Lake. The Corps of Engineers dug the graves up and moved them after it condemned the land in 1968, to ensure that none of Joanna's history would float up to disturb the vacation tranquility of the tourists who would contribute two to three million "visitor days" a year on the lake. Thus one might have assumed that the excision of Joanna from the region's official history was complete. And yet a history survives.

In 1975 the Herald Publishing Company of Shelbyville, Missouri, a consignment printing service of the town's weekly newspaper, brought out a sixty-five-page paperback volume titled *The End of a Way of Life — The Fate of the Joanna People on Salt River*. The word "End" and the subtitle were printed in red ink; otherwise, the volume lacked decoration or design, save for a hand-drawn and hand-lettered township grid inside the front and back covers. The author was an eighty-four-year-old Monroe City barber and former Joanna citizen named Dee Paul West. West paid Herald Publishing to print about five hundred copies of the book. His researcher was his lifelong friend, Okle V. Rouse.

Dee West and Okle Rouse are shown in portrait near the beginning of the text — the first of the ninety blurred photographs that were shoehorned into the sixty-five pages, some of them vintage, some recent. About half of the photographs are rather unsuccessful attempts to capture the Salt River in its beauty and in its flooding terror; the rest are studies of Joanna's houses and farms and log cabins, and of its people. West and Rouse appear as two frail, elfin men smiling for someone's flash camera in West's living room. West is seated, his typewriter before him on a small coffee table, wearing suspenders and a belt to support trousers that reach nearly to his breastbone, and an editor's shade around his head. Okle Rouse stands behind and to the right of West, wearing a plaid shirt; his left arm rests across the back of West's stuffed easy chair. Both men are wearing frame glasses. The photograph offers absolutely no hint of the outrage to come in the vernacular pages that follow.

Dee West came to live in Joanna in 1900, when he was nine. His father had moved the family from Monroe City to set up a blacksmith shop. Over the course of many years, C. W. West continued to buy small plots of land in the village until, at his death in 1930, he owned all the original seventy-four acres of the 1820s land grants. Dee West acquired the land after his father died and tried to hold on to it when the United States Army Corps of Engineers came calling in 1968. The Corps tried to purchase the land from West. West would not sell, not at any price. The Corps ordered condemnation proceedings. West and Okle Rouse compiled their book in exile, in Monroe City, even as the Clarence Cannon Dam was rising from the ruins of Joanna.

Dee West lacked the lyric eloquence of Mark Twain in expressing his love of his boyhood land; but he did not lack passion, nor a sense of unity with the past. *The End of a Way of Life* is, for the most part, an attempt to preserve some notion of a culture that existed for the five generations of Joanna's history.

Its pages are a compendium of the weddings, the housewarmings, the drownings, the vocabularies, the notions about planting, the corncob-pipe smoking, the measles and the chicken pox, the struggles with Civil War guerrillas, the floods, the schools and churches and post offices, the harvests and the threshings, and the dancing that made up that culture. A procession of families, a lineage, marches through Dee West's accounting; their names, their dates, their transitions are fixed in his volume.

And then comes the outrage. "We never thought anything like this could ever happen to us and our river," West writes on the final page of his narrative. "We fought as hard as we could, but we lost. I, with all the others, have had to let them have the land, which I would not have sold at any price. To me there are many things worth far more than money."

And: "This so called progress is nothing but destruction, pollution and poison. In a few years this lake will not be fit to drink. Fish will not be able to live in it. Boys won't be able to swim in it as I used to when I was a boy."

And: "We have almost exhausted and wasted all our natural

resources and I am afraid we are going to destroy ourselves. It has destroyed our way of living which was good. When men act like machines with no heart, soul or feelings for others it is bad."

And: "This dam and lake have caused more confusion, worry, heartaches and tears than anything that ever happened to our part of the country."

And: "It seems that I loved this place from the first when we moved to the river. I know that it would never have sold and deserted me and would have stuck to me till the last. I really tried to keep it from being destroyed, but I failed. I feel like a traitor."

By the autumn of 1983 the authentic history of Joanna and of Mark Twain's boyhood prairie lay submerged beneath the engineered waters of the Salt River.

Above the surface, on the new shore, Michael Jenkins and his associates would seek to reorder, to "repackage" that history according to the dictates of marketing studies, mass-consumer tastes, and the exigencies of twentieth-century advertising symbols.

CHAPTER

IX

STATE Route 154 is a fine two-lane blacktop with wide shoulders that rises and dips and curves through some of Missouri's most splendid farmland — prairie swells like green loaves of bread — before it begins to skirt the lower extremities of Mark Twain Lake at the Elk Fork a few miles east of Paris. But in the mid-1980s the hand-hammered hog runs and cattle pens visible from the road were empty of livestock, and the white frame farmhouses, while occupied, gave forth a peeled, oddly vacated look.

The national farm crisis had settled on the region. The family farmers of northeastern Missouri and southern Iowa were among the worst sufferers from the twin plagues of lowered prices for their crops and rising interest rates for their machinery. Missouri's farm income had dropped from more than $1 billion in 1981 to $151 million in 1983. Debts of $100,000 were commonplace among these families.

Hannibal suffered too. The town was a retail center for the region's rural shoppers. Its link with the farm economy was symbolized by its greatest architectural mass, the two-hundred-foot-high grain terminal of ten vertical cylinders that dominated the Mississippi riverfront.

Now Hannibal's merchants sat in their stores and shopping centers and franchise food outlets as their traditional clientele from the countryside diminished. The area's unemployment figure rose to a peak of 11 percent — a figure well above the national average.

But there was an even darker aspect to this economic crisis than the mere fact of shared hard times. For the first time in the history of the region, Hannibal and some of the smaller, outlying towns around it began to challenge one another directly for a revenue source that had been exclusively a windfall for Hannibal before the development of Mark Twain Lake. That revenue source was tourism.

Emboldened by the "recreational" promise of the lake — the irresistible promise of "liquid streams of gold" — the businessmen of these small towns allowed themselves to imagine (with some outside, professional encouragement) that they at last had an exploitable resource that was the equal of Hannibal's national reputation as the Boyhood Home of Mark Twain. Given the right kind of development, promotion, and transportation conduits, a vast new, mobile, trend-conscious market of tourists might be encouraged to bypass Hannibal entirely and concentrate their vacation time on Mark Twain Lake.

This newfound mood of competition was not universal. There were people from both Hannibal and the other towns who felt that cooperation — in the form of a unified tourism plan — was the logical way of serving everyone's interests. These people proposed the promotion of a four-day "circuit" that would encourage visitors to spend time (and money) in Hannibal's historic district and then drive on over to take in the recreational pleasures of Mark Twain Lake.

That plan never really had a chance. The city fathers of Hannibal suspected some sort of hidden trick — a scheme to relieve their town of its greatest asset, the Mark Twain brand name. They refused to have any part in any cooperative tourism scheme.

Their very refusal conferred upon their suspicions the aspects of self-fulfilling prophecy. The investors and promoters of Mark Twain Lake and its attractions began to talk and behave as though "Mark Twain" and "Hannibal" were unrelated concepts: as though marketing expertise alone could transpose Hannibal's mythic essence thirty miles to the southwest — just as engineering expertise had changed the Salt River Valley's topography from earth to water.

In the early months of 1984, the debt-ridden farmers of northeastern Missouri and the strapped families of Hannibal began to hear rumors of an impending bonanza unimaginable in northeastern Missouri throughout its long, penny-wise, family-farm history — a Mark Twain Heritage Theme Park. The theme park would be constructed across 150 acres — about twice the landmass of the lost village of Joanna — in the Indian Creek Recreation Area, a peninsula formed by the confluence of the Salt River and a small creek flowing down from the north near the lake's tapering eastern sector — or just about smack upon the dragon's hindquarters. The Heritage Theme Park would be built in phased increments over five years, at a total cost to its developers of more than $13 million. Its design would serve to re-create the beloved humorist's era, his environment, and his most popular fictional characters in a manner pleasing to the sensibilities of Americans on vacation — Americans who might not have read (or had read to them) more than a couple of Mark Twain's works, but who nonetheless held on to a proprietary sort of affection for the half-remembered images of Tom, Huck, and Aunt Polly, Pap and Injun Joe and — well, yes, even Jim, and their wholesome, pre-secular humanist doin's.

The theme park would actually be but one component of a larger commercial development package covering a total of 475 acres. That package would include an airstrip (a plan that was soon jettisoned); a resort hotel of 250 units; a marina and boat-renting facility for fishing, water-skiing, sailing, pontooning, and houseboating; a nostalgic steamboat excursion and dinner cruise; and a three-thousand-seat amphitheater that would feature celebrity entertainment and an original musical, *Tom, Huck & Twain.*

But the defining glory of that entire project — indeed, its justification for existing — would lie in that 150-acre array of ingenious arcades, attractions, and period-piece curiosities designed to re-create the mood of Mark Twain's era in American life.

To that end, there would be a courthouse and a hanging tree, where mock trials and hangings would entertain the pilgrims. There would be an active nondenominational church suitable for actual tourist weddings and christenings. There would be a Judge Thatcher's Barbecue (named in honor of Becky Thatcher's father in *The Adventures of Tom Sawyer;* Becky herself would be commemorated by a Strawberry 'n' Cream Shop). There would be a Huck's Sandwich Shanty, not to mention a Tom's Ship Shop. There would be a stagecoach depot and an Aunt Polly's Vegetable Garden (food services would include such vegetables as watermelon, apples, and peaches), a Tom 'n' Huck's fishing hole, a primitive-weapons display, and a Halley's Comet mine shaft and planetarium. There would be a haunted riverboat and a shooting gallery video arcade.

But perhaps the most fabulous element in the entire package — the one ingredient without which a Mark Twain Heritage Theme Park would have been unfeasible — was the agreement between its developers and the United States Army Corps of Engineers. The corps had taken the exceptional measure of granting the theme park's developers a thirty-year lease, for a nominal rental fee, for the use of corps land near the shore of Mark Twain Lake. The scope of this concession was ten times the scale of any commercial lease granted in Army Corps history. The agreement required ratification by the corps's national headquarters in Vicksburg, Mississippi, as well as by the federal Office of Management and Budget in Washington. The developer of the Heritage Theme Park was to be the Capital Planning and Development Company, of Springfield, Missouri.

As Capital Planning's Heritage Fact Sheet boasted, "Mark Twain Heritage Park is the first project of its kind in the United States in which private enterprise and the Army Corps of Engineers have joined together for development of a project."

Most people in the area learned about the Heritage Theme Park by reading news items in the local papers. But a few — the civic leaders, the boosters, and the spearheaders of community drives — got the word in more direct and inspirational fashion; they got it from the lips of the Heritage Theme Park movers and shakers themselves. At Chamber of Commerce annual dinners, at the Mark Twain Lake Development Association annual banquet, in Holiday Inn function rooms, and in church-basement meeting rooms, the theme park visionaries made their case.

One spokesman in particular seemed to charm and delight his audiences. Speaking in the controlled cadences of a polished stage actor, his Ozarkean phrasings now and then edging toward a dialect that could not have been too far removed from Sam Clemens's own patterns, his fingertips pressed tightly together and his boyish face frozen in profile, his pale blue eyes cast down, Michael Jenkins, the vice-president of Capital Planning, made the project seem almost like a manifestation of heavenly grace.

"There is not a civilized country in the world," Jenkins told the Monroe City Area Chamber of Commerce, "that doesn't know the name Mark Twain. The name identity is there with Mark Twain, Hannibal, and the Mark Twain Lake. You have a tremendous product.

"Mark Twain himself could not have designed it better. We've got something to sell. Let's package it and go get 'em. We are talking jobs and total area economic development."

"We must work together as a group, as a unit, in developing and promoting this dam," Jenkins told the Mark Twain Lake and Cannon Dam Area Development Association. "We must have proper zoning and planning. We must protect what the Lord gave us.

"Your area, the Mark Twain Region, is mature now that the Mark Twain Lake is completed. Recreational water is available."

Some of Jenkins's evangelical fervor rubbed off on his fellow advocates. "With this project of the dam and the lake, we have altered part of God's universe for the benefit of man," the prominent realtor Warren See told a noontime luncheon of the Hannibal Chamber of Commerce. "And I think a higher power had a hand in the success of this project." Billboards advertising subdivisions for sale by the Warren G. See Agency were currently in evidence just beyond the Corps of Engineers' right-of-way about the lake — along with billboards advertising such future attractions as the Water World of Fun. Warren See had been the leader of the businessmen's delegation that had urged the Honorable Clarence Cannon to reconsider his misgivings about the dam back in 1958, invoking in their argument the prevailing vision of "liquid streams of gold."

There was a third spokesman who made the rounds on behalf of the Heritage Theme Park in early 1984. This was Lewis H. Aytes, the president of Capital Planning and Development of Springfield, Missouri. Aytes was the businessman, the hands-on investment professional, whom Michael Jenkins had selected to implement his theme-park dream. Capital Planning was a corporation that consisted, as it turned out, mainly of Michael Jenkins and Lew Aytes. The corporation also drew on the services of Joe Reynolds, a California-based architect, and Janice England, "of Capital Planning's marketing and promotion staff," as the corporate press releases put it.

In his lease application submitted to the Army Corps, Aytes stated that he had been a partner in a firm called Cypress Investments and that he had compiled eight years' experience in the field of financial planning and development. Since 1976, Aytes reported, he had sponsored "more than" thirty partnerships with "more than" 110 private investors, representing a total development worth "exceeding" $10 million. The application described Aytes as an "associate science degree graduate" from California State University in 1981. The papers stated that Aytes had at one time been the owner of Lew's Music Center in Sacramento.

People who were in the audience when Lew Aytes spoke before local booster groups generally agreed that he could not call down quite the theatrical thunder of Michael Jenkins — who, after all, had dreamed up the Heritage Theme Park in the first place and refined its conception over sixteen years. But the small-business men of Monroe City and Palmyra and Hannibal remembered Aytes as a man of almost hypnotic personal charm, a mysterious stranger who commanded an immediate trust. Lew Aytes was the sort of outsider you wanted to have over for dinner, along with his wife and two small daughters.

"I met Aytes for the first time at my house," recalled Dave Zerrer, a Monroe City lawyer who eventually formed a partnership with Aytes to build a Holiday Inn in the town. "It was after he and Jenkins came to our chamber of commerce dinner; that would have been March of eighty-four. Jenkins was the keynote speaker. I said to my wife, 'Why don't we organize a cocktail party and invite the guest speaker?' Well, then somebody said that the president of Capital Planning was coming also, and we should invite him.

"Jenkins and his wife came — Jenkins was married then — but the fellow I really liked was Lew Aytes. I liked him the first time I met him. He was about thirty-five years old then. He had blond hair and a neat, red beard — he presented a very clean appearance. His diction was excellent. He was blessed with a voice tone that was pleasing to listen to. And his wife was just a fantastic lady.

"We became friends. They had two girls, one of them the same age as mine."

Aytes's and Jenkins's thrall over the local businessmen did not depend entirely upon theatrics, or appeals to boosterism, or invocations of the Deity. Lew Aytes put the word out that there was serious money behind his venture, big California money, maybe up to $40 million in big California money that would easily ignite the first phase of the Mark Twain Heritage Theme Park before the ink was dry on that Corps of Engineers concession lease. But rumors of big money were only a part of the overall sell. The Capital Planners blew into the region armed with hard facts and figures. The facts and figures were attractively packaged in such ready-made visual aids as a fifteen-minute promotional film about the benefits of tourism called *Wake Up to Missouri!* There were other visual aids: maps of the Midwest that showed Mark Twain

Lake at the center of a mammoth shaded circle, a circle whose rim touched Chicago to the north and extended well beyond Kansas City to the west.

The shaded circle defined a three-hundred-mile radius around the lake. Within that radius dwelt 18.4 million potential tourists, Aytes and Jenkins reported. And the good news did not end there. Aytes and Jenkins had done some research into the question of just how far the average tourist was willing to travel in order to see an attraction. It turned out that the average tourist was willing to travel, not just three hundred miles, but *five hundred* miles. It seemed a wonder the area had not already suffered some sort of massive gridlock just from the transient traffic.

Not that a dynamic developer like Lew Aytes was about to just sit back and wait for those 18.4 million tourists to find the Heritage Theme Park on their own. Capital Planning, he revealed, was prepared to advertise a little. In fact, Capital Planning was prepared to advertise to the tune of $35 million — *nearly three times the cost of the theme park itself* — to attract its tourist clientele.

A kind of glazed fascination began to take hold in Monroe City. This unrelenting onslaught of data, this promise of untold Western resources awaiting Lew Aytes's pleasure, this offhand invocation of capital on a scale so vast as to elude any meaningful comparison to local wealth (an advertising budget worth perhaps more than the total assessed valuation of the town itself) — it all began to wear down the resistance, the skepticism, of the local businessmen. Had not these promises, these figures, passed muster with the United States Army Corps of Engineers? Were not these revelations nothing less than the ancient prophecy of "liquid streams of gold" made manifest?

It began to seem to some people that perhaps God had indeed graced the region as a Promised Land; perhaps the Salt River, or what was left of it, should be renamed the Jordan.

If the Duke and the Dauphin themselves had burst into those Holiday Inn function rooms and those church basements, fresh from Huck Finn's own raft, their presence could hardly have spurred a more frenzied stampede of speculation. More than a dozen businessmen from Monroe City and surrounding towns seized the chance to buy into Capital Planning as limited partners. The going price was between $25,000 and $40,000, with a deposit of $10,000 required up front.

But the real action was in land speculation. "When Capital Planning hit, the activity hit," remembered one local businessman who joined the activity himself. "The real estate people said, 'Here's the Promised Land.' They jumped those lots around the lake up to three thousand dollars an acre. Before then, they'd been going for about one thousand. Then the first thing you knew, some of them were going for nine thousand, even fourteen thousand — and I mean on windy little roads back in the middle of nowhere. It all started to look like a development. See, all this action and hoopla got the attention of the big real-estate boys in St. Louis.

"I even got a little property I bought by the foot down on a blacktop road. . . ."

Dave Zerrer threw his cocktail party for Lew Aytes in March of 1984. It was at the party that Zerrer confided to Aytes his dream of building a Holiday Inn in Monroe City, and found, to his great gratification, that Aytes was willing to be a partner in the project. Zerrer's memory of the evening remains warm with the memory of his pride at being there at the center of the beginning; warm with the memory of good fellowship and hope, and of the townsmen, his friends, those shirt-sleeve men in their best sports jackets, standing around in Dave Zerrer's living room and letting the good bourbon roll around in their glasses and talking the unaccustomed good talk of prosperity. And the star guest that evening was the stranger with the neatly trimmed beard and the excellent diction, the voice tone that was pleasing to listen to, the stranger who would consummate God's good plan for the ancient ground of Joanna.

In July of 1984 the plan fell to pieces. Lewis Aytes and Michael Jenkins abruptly stopped coming to Monroe City and Palmyra and Hannibal. There were no more function-room speeches to civic groups; no more visual aids; no more screenings of *Wake Up to Missouri!*

And there would be no Mark Twain Heritage Theme Park. No hanging tree, no active nondenominational church, no haunted riverboat, no shooting gallery nor video arcade. No $35 million advertising budget to lure the 18.4 million people within the three-hundred-mile radius.

Capital Planning and Development, it turned out, lacked an essential resource: it lacked capital. And so there would be no further planning; no development.

In the weeks and months following David Zerrer's cocktail party in March, the local investors began to hear things about certain of Lew Aytes's ventures back in California. "What they heard," Zerrer recalled later, "prompted them to check on some things. For the first time, people started to ask some reasonable, businesslike questions."

Sitting in his Monroe City law office nearly a year later — an office decorated with color photographs of his wife and daughters, by pink wallpaper ornamented with the figures of Tom 'n' Huck, and by a framed illustration titled *Quiet Cove Mallards* (with a cardboard-printed résumé of the illustrator curling from the lower corner of one frame) — David Zerrer refused to discuss the exact nature of those questions, or of the information they elicited. Despite everything that had happened, Dave Zerrer was still fond of Lew Aytes; he found it difficult to summon any truly hostile feelings toward the man.

On the other hand, it was impossible to deny the effects of what the local people had learned. The limited partners came together for a conference among themselves; after the conference they informed Lew Aytes that it would be best for him to desist from trying to sell further partnerships to anyone in northeast Missouri.

"That ended up kicking out the bottom card of the whole house of cards," said an investor who was present at the decisive meeting. "Once that cat was out of the bag, it all spiraled downward from there."

It did not particularly soften the pain or the chagrin of the limited-investment partners to learn that their $10,000 deposits, which many of them had scraped together as an investment against future hard times for themselves and their families, would not be returned, even though the stated objective of the deposits — the Heritage Theme Park — had collapsed. These deposits would be retained by the developers — as compensation and fees for services rendered. The Articles of Incorporation made it all very clear.

The articles (which identified the developers as California Cypress Investments, Inc., and not as Capital Planning and Development of Springfield, the corporate title that Lewis Aytes presented to the people of northeastern Missouri) exempted the partnership from personal liability for the return of any capital contributions to the limited partners. And the articles set forth the following compensation provisions: $90,000 in "supervising costs" to California Cypress Investments, Inc.; $150,000 in architectural fees to Joseph B. Reynolds, Jr.; $60,000 as a "one-time partnership management fee" to California Cypress Investments; and $60,000 to be split evenly by Reynolds and California Cypress as reimbursement for "costs incurred in obtaining a leasehold estate."

These were generous compensations that California Cypress, a.k.a. Capital Planning and Development, thought to provide itself, considering the extent and nature of its services to the area around Mark Twain Lake and to the people who lived there. The compensations were particularly generous — one might almost say forgiving — in light of California Cypress's real-estate record in California, a record contained partly in the files of that state's bankruptcy courts and municipal and superior courts, and in the files of the tax collector's office in Sacramento.

Those files show that among certain decisions rendered against Aytes and California Cypress were two bankruptcy judgments: one, in 1983, involving a forty-unit apartment building in Sacramento, owned by Aytes, and another, extending from 1984 through 1985, involving a limited-partnership attraction in the same city, a waterside attraction called the Steamboater. Further, the files show a succession of Sacramento County claims against Aytes for nonpayment of taxes, encompassing the years 1983–1985.

Apparently, no one in Missouri had checked these records before entering into contracts with Lew Aytes and Capital Planning — not the businessmen of Monroe City and Palmyra and Hannibal before risking their personal capital; not the St. Louis District of the United States Army Corps of Engineers before awarding Aytes the largest concession lease, by a factor of ten, in the corps's history.

In October of 1984 Dave Zerrer got in his car and traveled to Springfield, Missouri, and severed his business ties with Lew Aytes. Still, Zerrer could not bring himself to speak unkindly of the man who had promised his region so much. "He was one hell of a promoter," Zerrer insisted several months later. "It was a matter of small circumstances."

Michael Jenkins, too, separated himself from Capital Planning. But like Dave Zerrer, Jenkins found it hard to let go of the dream. He continued to polish a musical that he had written for production at Mark Twain Lake; a musical he still hoped would be mounted there one day. "It's Tom, Huck, and Twain, told by Twain, with music," he said when I visited him early in 1985, months after his sixteen-year vision had evaporated. (We met, at Jenkins's suggestion, in a Springfield "theme" restaurant called the Kountry Kin, which featured such "theme" selections as *"Kountry Sausage — this here's a big ol' piece a our whole hog sausage that we stir up fresh rite here from Uncle Jim's special seasonin' recipe."*) "Everything," Jenkins went on, "from the banjo and fiddle to some up-tempo stuff that's real exciting with the choreography we envision. There will be sixteen songs. It's the story of man's individual rights to freedom, family, home, and community."

CHAPTER

X

"A MAN must not hold himself aloof," wrote Mark Twain in *A Connecticut Yankee at King Arthur's Court,* "from the things which his friends and his community have at heart if he would be liked."

The first public signal that the Mark Twain Sesquicentennial might be headed for rocky shoals flared up in the early weeks of 1984, several months before the festival's agenda of grandiose plans or its $5 million projected budget were disclosed. It caught the wintry town unawares, and many people were inclined to shrug it off, or treat it as a joke, a minor misunderstanding.

And yet the incident foretold a great deal, for those who cared to analyze it, about the potential for ruination inherent in the festival's most fundamental operating assumption — one that implied a radical aloofness from the community's heart; one that would in time drag the entire enterprise to the brink of disintegration.

This ruinous assumption was encouraged by the New York–based consultant Alfred Stern. But it was embraced by John Lyng, the mayor of Hannibal, and Larry Weil, the Sesquicentennial Commission chairman and the publisher of the town newspaper — perhaps the two men in town most obliged by fiat to affirm those things at the community's heart. What Stern, Lyng, and Weil — and later Dick Halsor — assumed, essentially, was that the people of Hannibal were unwilling and incompetent to conduct their own sesquicentennial celebration, much less elevate it to Lyng's dream of a permanent economic development tool. It followed, in their logic, that every important element of the festival must therefore be entrusted to the expertise of professional, outside talent.

Weil, for one, clung to this conviction long after events had cast serious doubt upon the efficacy of outside, professional talent. The "sesqui" (as it soon came to be charmlessly known) was well under way — as was its long string of disillusionments — when the publisher sat for a conversation in his editorial office. I asked Weil then whether he might, in hindsight, have wished to open the festival up to more grass-roots participation.

Larry Weil inhaled deeply on a cigarette and squinted in concentration before answering. "I guess," he said, finally, in his deep, soft voice, "that I just don't believe in large numbers of volunteers banding together and leading in any one direction. I always thought this thing would be dependent on a damn few."

The first legacy of that assumption was the Fiasco of the Logos.

There exists in Hannibal an artist's community — not a colony so much as a loosely arranged society of nearly a hundred painters, engravers, woodcutters, and sculptors. Many of these people are working professionals, design specialists employed by printing companies, successful free-lance artists. Many others are skilled amateurs — men and women retired from the professions or the military, and free, finally, to pursue as a full-time calling the talents that they had relegated to the status of hobby during their years in the work force.

Late in 1983 a member of the newly formed Sesquicentennial Commission approached one of these artists, a man named Sam Lundquist, with a notion that at once struck Lundquist as splendid for his colleagues and for the town. The commission member (it was Art Francis, then the general manager of KHMO radio) asked Lundquist to recommend a local artist who could design an official logo for the celebration.

Lundquist, who cut a dramatic figure in his black mustache, his neck scarves, and his leather cowboy boots, was in a good position to answer that query. As the proprietor of the Modern Art Shop, an artists' supply store on Broadway, and as a working designer of more than forty years' standing in the community, Lundquist knew just about everyone in town who had ever dipped a number two brush into a jar of India ink.

Sam Lundquist responded with an even better suggestion: why not hold a townwide contest and award a cash prize for the winning logo entry?

Lundquist and his fellow artists were delighted when the Sesquicentennial Commission voted to do exactly that. The contest announcement soon appeared in the *Courier-Post.* The winning entry, it was declared, would grace all official sesquicentennial correspondence and promotional brochures and banners and advertisements. The winning artist would earn a thousand-dollar prize.

By January 1984, the commission had received seventy-three entries, all from Hannibal artists who submitted designs on their own time and at their own expense.

In February the commission voted to purchase a logo on consignment from a graphic artist from an advertising firm in St. Louis for the fee of $634.75.

The commission's reasoning was not detailed in the pages of Larry Weil's *Courier-Post.* But Weil, speaking in his capacity as commission chairman, did offer an explanation to the inquiring *Quincy Herald-Whig* across the Mississippi River.

"We couldn't come up with a consensus on any one entry in the contest," Weil told the newspaper, "so we decided to try this other fellow. Time was becoming an important factor. We had to get going in correspondence and in fund-raising, and we needed to utilize the logo for both of those."

Herman Yokers, the president of the Hannibal Art Club, offered a differing perspective for the Quincy paper. "I'm having a tough time holding them back," Yokers said of his enraged fellow artists. Yokers added that he and his colleagues considered the commission's action a slap in the face. The word got around town that several of the artists were considering lawsuits. And on

March 1, 1984, a letter appeared in the *Courier-Post* over the signature of Sam Lundquist.

"It was pleasing to learn of the decision of the Commission to have a contest for this Sesquicentennial," wrote Lundquist in careful language, "but it has been most embarrassing to learn all of the 70-some entries were judged unsuitable and could not be used, and that a St. Louisan was contracted to design the logo.

"I am sorry," Sam Lundquist concluded, "that I suggested the contest that cost the entrants so much of their valuable time and money. I apologize to them."

There was never a collected showing of the seventy-three failed local entries, and so their merits relative to the imported logo are probably lost to history. But if Larry Weil was looking for a certain typographic austerity, he certainly found it in the creation executed by the Centaur Studio of St. Louis.

The logo was nearly *all* typography, save for a hyperdistilled rendering of a steamboat in silhouette, either advancing toward or receding from the viewer, in the lower half of a crest-shaped field. The steamboat floated on a squiggly line — five squiggles — that accounted for the Mississippi River. Above the steamboat silhouette was the italicized legend *MARK TWAIN'S 150th (tm)*.

A peculiarity of the logo — pounced on gleefully by several Hannibal artists — was the amount of information that spilled *outside* the crest, floating freely in a typographic limbo. Along the crest's left outside border ran the upended word *HANNIBAL*, looking as though someone had grabbed the noun by its L and flipped it on its H. Below the crest, in four stacks of italicized type, was the legend

MARK TWAIN'S
150th BIRTHDAY
CELEBRATION
MAY–NOV. 1985

— a curious redundancy with the legend inside the crest, as the Hannibal artists were only too happy to point out.

Thus Hannibal's sesqui began to take form under a design whose unintended symbolism was perhaps more pertinent than its overt message: a cursory, nonindigenous, and emotionally neutral symbol of adspeak — a local echo of the state's brave new slogan, "Wake Up to Missouri."

But in the grand design taking shape at early-morning commission meetings, and at late-night sessions around the rear tables at Fitzgerald's, the logo was really a small-potatoes consideration; a bit of necessary boilerplate. The big-league promotional action lay in *electronic media.*

That was the very thing! Some kind of bang-bang video presentation for the corporate money people; that was the language those boys understood. Something that would focus their perceptions. Something that said *contemporary,* said *national outreach,* said *state of the art.* That kind of total thrust. Alfred Stern had certainly perceived it right: the sesqui had to give a video sort of feeling to the message it was trying to project.

Nor was the price tag any object. Northeast Missouri may have been in a recession. The average Hannibal workingman may have been strapped for grocery cash. But the Sesquicentennial Commission was flush with the projected yield of a quarter-billion tourist sesquidollars. Early in 1984 the commission, urged on by John Lyng and Larry Weil, went high tech: it voted to pay a St. Louis production house $26,320 to create the sesquicentennial video.

When the finished product arrived back in town, the commission called a special screening at the Holiday Inn just so that the town's leading citizens could experience the total energy of Hannibal's first video-packaged image.

For a little more than ten minutes, the guests saw their town transmogrified to video Valhalla, jumping and pulsing and strutting in the same never-neverland inhabited by Coca-Cola drinkers and McDonald's customers and Friendly Skies passengers and presidential candidates.

"There is really no place in the world like Hannibal, Missouri," intoned a narrator's silken voice over a surging musical score. "Every day is like a chapter in a magical dream."

On the screen, there flashed a kinetic succession of natural-looking color photographs depicting the magical dream: happy Hannibalians. Hannibalians working, looking proud of the town, *getting the town ready for the Mark Twain Sesquicentennial.*

"Mark Twain was, in his own words, the most conspicuous person on the planet," the silken voice continued, without quite dwelling upon what line of work made Mark Twain so conspicuous. More quick photographs — Hannibalians beaming at Hannibal landmarks; smiling Hannibal officials with their sleeves rolled up, cheerfully getting down to brass tacks.

"The comet appeared — by request — at his death," purred the narrator. More flashing photographs. More surging music. "The storybook ending to a magical life . . ."

Larry Weil's matter-of-fact bass replaced the silken voice of the narrator. "We've set a goal of one million visitors in 1985 . . . we feel that is a conservative estimate. . . ."

More uplifting music. More dazzling photographs. More storybook magic, more silkenness; a final burst of upbeat music. Fade to black. Up and over. Over and out. Bango.

If anyone in the Holiday Inn audience happened to reflect on the irony — the sarcasm, Twain would have called it — of all those images suggesting happy local folks working away on "their" sesquicentennial, the thought went unexpressed. The sesqui video became the commission's official version of the town and the celebration, the Word made videotape. A copy of the video accompanied every fund-raising delegation to every corporate executive suite in St. Louis and other cities. In fact, the commission secretaries were under strict instructions to telephone every corporate executive in advance of his or her scheduled meeting with the fund-raisers and stipulate that a videocassette recorder be on hand in the suite and ready to roll. The corporate donors were going to experience the total energy of Hannibal's vision whether they damn well liked it or not — and the uncomfortable perception, to some of the peripheral delegates at least, was frequently "not."

The commission waited until the summer months of 1984 to mount its corporate fund-raising campaign — a bewildering display of nonchalance, in the eyes of many people. And as the weeks wore on, and the delegations returned home time and again with less than firm and enthusiastic pledges, some of the support staff began to gossip privately about a certain amount of fidgeting that went on in many of the corporate chairs. The video was too long to hold a busy executive's attention, these staff members concluded. Plus, what high-ranking company official is likely to be impressed with all that stuff about chapters in magical dreams and storybook endings?

The staff people were partly right. But in the end, it was not the sesquicentennial video that undercut the fund-raising expectations of the commission. The flaws in the delegates' approach derived from far more cold-eyed considerations than any mere excess of boosterism. They derived from a perception — to coin a phrase — that the Mark Twain Sesquicentennial lacked, at its core, a coherent organizing plan.

In June of 1984 the Sesqui Commission gained what seemed at the time to be an almost heaven-sent windfall: it gained a full-time director. Here at last was a day-to-day administrator. Better still, here was a person with professional experience in fields closely related to the approaching festival. He was even from out of town. He seemed almost too good to be true.

His name was Jim Gladwin. He was a young Arkansas native presently doing private-sector/public-sector work in St. Louis, and he blew into Hannibal with his sunglasses propped up on his dark curls and his sweater sleeves tied around his neck and an air of can-do, Rolodex savvy that thrilled the sesqui organizers, while at the same time leaving them just a shade self-conscious about the paper coffee cups around the office, a little edgy about the possibility of price stickers on the soles of their shoes.

"I didn't come here to organize a backyard barbecue," Jim Gladwin informed everybody, and for a while, that remark sounded like a bright promise.

The commission, following Stern's suggestion, had advertised the director's position in newspapers around the state. Several

Hannibal people had applied. But in June 1984 Cathie Whelan, the sesqui's administrative coordinator, had telephoned Gladwin in St. Louis to tell him he had the job.

There was no denying that his résumé looked good. He had been the state director of the Special Olympics in Arkansas and was then employed as a marketer of federal economic programs to private businesses for the St. Louis Regional Commerce and Growth Association. Jim Gladwin hit Hannibal as the missing link between the sesqui video and sesqui fulfillment.

Nearly a year later — long after he had grown overwrought, had feuded with nearly everyone connected with the sesqui, had in turn been insulted by several of its leaders, and had finally accepted a forced resignation (the *Courier-Post* blandly quoted commission chairman Larry Weil to the effect that Gladwin had fulfilled his mandate and "now the rest of it is nailing down details") — Gladwin could find corrosive humor in his motive for accepting the directorship.

"I was a candidate for a doctorate in American literature at Washington University when I saw the notice," Gladwin said, rubbing his eyes, as we sat at a West End coffeehouse in St. Louis. "I thought I could go up there and do my dissertation research.

"Credential-wise and opportunity-wise," he added dryly, "it was interesting to me."

Gladwin was certainly interesting to the sesqui's prime movers — particularly the visiting Alfred Stern, whom Gladwin impressed during an interview. In fact, as Stern now phased out his consultancy involvement in the sesquicentennial, Gladwin soon proved to be the older man's alter ego. If Jim Gladwin differed from Alfred Stern, the difference lay mainly in his fiercer intensity, his larger vision, his remorseless pour-on-the-brandy zeal.

It was Gladwin who first began speaking of the celebration not just as a sesquicentennial but as a "mini-World's Fair." It was Gladwin who seemed to embrace the notion that Hannibal's people, apathetic and incompetent, were generally to be regarded as colonial subjects in this paranational undertaking: in hiring his own staff, he told at least one young woman that she had been selected partly because she was a newcomer to the town. It was Gladwin who encouraged publication of the $5 million budget figure that began appearing in the fall of 1984 (the goal before Gladwin arrived had been around $1.75 million). And it was Gladwin, at his most characteristic, who demonstrated a facility for carrying out what Alfred Stern had referred to as "the little grace notes."

Just before Gladwin arrived on the scene, the Sesqui Commission had become bogged down in an infuriating struggle with the official Mark Twain rose.

"Well, of course it was Alfred Stern who proposed that we should have this Mark Twain rose," recalled the local historian Hurley Hagood, an original commission member. "Something that we could present to visiting dignitaries as a memento of the occasion. Now, we have a lady named Helen Beedle. I don't know if she volunteered, but somehow or other this fell back on her.

"She had a beautiful garden — she has the old Griffin place. But what happened on this thing was, pretty soon everyone realized that the rose wasn't that important. They started putting it down, and Helen along with it. They'd laugh and joke about it at the meetings.

"It didn't help any when she came up with her figures. She found out that the rose would cost ten thousand dollars and take two years to get produced; it was a hybrid, you see. Well, it was about then that the kidding around about that rose turned into a laughing matter. The way I think it ended up, they were going to buy a rose that was already produced."

Jim Gladwin soon demonstrated that he knew a thing or two about roses. He knew how to order them sent to the hotel suites of name people who were going to figure big in the sesqui — name people such as Joshua Logan, whose production of a Huck 'n' Jim musical Alfred Stern had recommended for a pre-Broadway run in Hannibal.

"I had a contact with Logan dating from when he'd done *Mr.*

Roberts in St. Louis a couple of years ago," recalled Gladwin. "I got him to make a pilgrimage to Hannibal, where he had a good look at the town and its facilities."

Gladwin smiled a bitter, private smile.

"Eventually, I got him to reconsider," he went on. "I went out to talk to him in New York. I somehow convinced him that the charm of the town would transfer to his play.

"I got him to agree to a three-week run in Hannibal, at the high-school auditorium. I had the funding lined up. I had a sponsor with upfront money; I'd even gotten an option for a PBS special on the whole concept — a Broadway-comes-to-Main-Street type of thing.

"In October we brought Logan, his composer, and his choreographer back to Hannibal. We all went to lunch at the country club as guests of Larry Weil."

By all accounts, the luncheon was not a triumphant social success — witnesses to it recalled that Weil registered profound horrification at the flamboyance of his show-business guests, and later fretted that the entourage had damn near cost him his membership. Nevertheless, a tentative understanding was reached: Joshua Logan's Huck 'n' Jim musical would open on June 15 at the Hannibal High School auditorium — on the same stage where the Jubilee Chorus had serenaded on a centennial February evening fifty years earlier.

"Now, what I did not know, and what nobody had told me," Jim Gladwin recalled, "was that the Hannibal High School auditorium was not air-conditioned. Finally, a woman from the Arts Council approached me and asked: 'What are you going to do about ventilation? That's a hundred-degree house in the summertime.' "

Gladwin rubbed his eyes again. "Well, the fact is, I *solved* that problem. I got an air-conditioning company to agree to contribute the equipment if we would supply the labor for the installation.

"But then Weil and Lyng axed the whole thing in January. We were probably doomed, really, from the moment of that luncheon at the country club. Larry took that luncheon very hard."

Jim Gladwin gazed off into space for a few moments. He shook his head slowly. "The part that was so amazing," he finally murmured, "was the air-conditioning."

Gladwin encountered a somewhat similar problem in attempting to carry through another Alfred Stern idea: an "Art of the Mississippi" exhibit, encompassing great paintings and drawings of the river, from early diagrams rendered for the Lewis and Clark expeditions through time-present works.

"We had been diligently assembling that exhibit," Gladwin recalled. "I had tracked down twelve or thirteen core pieces: a couple of Binghams, some Alfred Waud sketches of the river, even some vintage pilots' journals. I was anticipating loans from the Historic New Orleans Collection, the Memphis Brooks Museum of Art, the St. Louis Art Museum, the National Gallery of Art. Richard McLanathan, who had been curator of American paintings at the Boston Art Museum, had agreed to write the catalogue. I was anticipating seven to eight million dollars' worth of material.

"The question was, of course, where in Hannibal to put it? I had understood that a historic warehouse at Hill and Main, the Selms Building, was going to be renovated. Lyng and Weil were in lease negotiations with somebody; this group was going to create a three-hundred-thousand-dollar project that would include gallery space for us. High security, the works.

"Well, I never could find out when the renovation was going to take place. Every time I would approach the mayor, he'd say, 'Don't worry, if this falls through we can go to Bob Ayres.' Bob Ayres was the owner of the Holiday Inn."

Eventually, the renovation plans for the Selms Building fell through. The group that had been negotiating for the lease was the Capital Planning and Development Company of Springfield, Missouri.

The "Art of the Mississippi" exhibit was never mounted. In July 1984 the city of Hannibal began tearing the Selms Building down.

Then there arose the matter of the theme stage.

Along with the Opening Weekend ceremonies featuring a performance by the famous singing group Up With People, the construction of a concert amphitheater, and the grand finale evening built around the appearance by Hal Holbrook as Mark Twain, the theme stage formed the irreducible, bedrock center of the sesquicentennial. In Alfred Stern's organizing vision, it would be the venue for the festival's daily continuity: the Boy Scout demonstrations and the band concerts and the gospel sing-alongs and the puppet shows that would keep the tourists diverted between the larger rock concerts and the fireworks and the daily parades. (Until the idea was hooted down by the commission and the people of Hannibal, the theme stage was to have been the site of Stern's mechanized clock tower.)

More significant still, the pavilion stage was to be the festival's lasting bequest to the town. It would be the sesqui's answer to the 1935 centennial's monument, the memorial lighthouse atop Cardiff Hill. But unlike the lighthouse, the theme stage was to remain functional. It would serve as a permanent site for public entertainments in the town; it would be the anchoring site for Hannibal's annual Tom Sawyer Days in July and its Folklife Festival in October.

Other plans, other events on the sesqui calendar — even the budget itself — these were mutable. It was inevitable that some ideas would have to be scrapped or reduced; John Lyng, for one, understood that truth from the outset (or so he later insisted). But the theme stage was inviolate. The theme stage was to be the palpable essense of the sesqui, whatever the sesqui itself might prove to be.

The fundamental problem, it soon developed, was similar to the problem of the Mississippi art exhibit: where to put it?

The commission had chosen a site near the riverfront, just a block south of the elevated approach to the Mark Twain Bridge. The land lay between North and Hill streets, two blocks east of the Mark Twain Home itself at 208 Hill. Its most conspicuous use in recent years was as the site of the YMCA's mud volleyball tournaments during Tom Sawyer Days. All that was needed to secure the site was a flash of Mayor Lyng's strong suit: some lawyerly negotiating, to settle on a price for the land with the YMCA.

What no one had anticipated was the YMCA's own hard-boiled negotiating stance. Figures as high as $200,000 for the block of land began to leak out. The city explored alternate sites. Price figures for these sites remained strangely elusive. Weeks passed, and then months. There were no agreements. The possibility began to take hold that the sesqui might have to open before its theme stage was entirely in place.

Suddenly, a seamless and triumphant Mark Twain Sesquicentennial was beginning to look a shade more elusive than Alfred Stern's "magic letter" had made it appear. The reversals, the delays, the cancellations, the abandonments involving the clock tower, the logo, the rose, the Joshua Logan play, the Mississippi art collection, the theme stage — all these began to form a fairly dispiriting list.

But none of these problems implied quite the same level of crisis as did the problems encountered in raising money.

Jim Gladwin arrived in Hannibal in June 1984. In August, Gladwin, Mayor Lyng, and Larry Weil (armed with the sesqui video) finally began to make their fund-raising pilgrimages to St. Louis–area corporations. In September the $5 million budget figure began to appear around town.

This sequence of events might well have been interpreted as evidence of an ascending curve in the financial fortunes of the sesquicentennial. In fact it implied no such thing. In fact the corporate sponsorship campaign was proving to be a journey of discovery for the festival's organizers — a journey of discovery far less redemptive than Huckleberry Finn's fictional voyage of a hundred years before. This journey was a gathering drift toward catastrophe.

The sesqui organizers had pinned most of their hopes for a miniature World's Fair on corporate sponsorships. Big companies, Lyng,

Weil, and Gladwin had hoped, would underwrite special events, concerts, stage facilities, and property acquisition. In return, the companies would enjoy nationwide product/service linkage of their brand names with the festival, particularly as the festival received the ongoing regional and national television coverage that Lyng, Weil, and Gladwin imagined it would attract.

At their most optimistic, the organizers allowed themselves to believe that corporations would contribute more than $2 million in sponsorships. (The rest of the money would come from local fund-raising and city-allocated revenues, together with projected profits from the sesqui and commercial reinvestments around Hannibal's historic district.)

But as Lyng, Weil, and Gladwin, along with members of their support staff, began to make their case in the offices of corporate executives, the likelihood of any such total began quickly to evaporate.

Long after it was over, John Lyng and Larry Weil remained reluctant to talk in detail about the disillusionments they encountered. Gladwin's recollections of the experience were specific and acid.

"They had a frightening disregard for the realities beyond Marion County," he said, referring to Lyng and Weil, and implicitly excluding himself. "They naively believed that the importance of the occasion would compensate for any lack of preparation on their part.

"They showed the video and they made their pitch. But the corporate people hit them with the same questions, again and again: Where are your demographic figures? What about parking? What about hotel space? What are your promotional plans? Your advertising? What is your insurance coverage? Who is your accountant? Who's producing this event?

"And the answer would always come back: We'll take care of all those questions. We'll get it all nailed down. Trust us."

Gladwin offered an example of the fund-raising misadventures. It involved the theme stage.

"I was able to get Pet, Incorporated, in St. Louis interested in a matching grant for the stage," Gladwin said. "It had become a functional reality, by the way, for me to raise money, although that was not part of the job description. Anyway, I penetrated the corporate level of Pet. I got them interested. They voiced a positive response. Then they strung us along for several months; we never saw the money.

"Finally, in sifting the situation out, we found the problem: Pet has a subsidiary plant in Hannibal, an Underwood food plant. The local operating head of that plant felt slighted. We had not apprised him of any of our plans. We'd been working through the corporate level. When they asked their local guy about the theme stage proposal, he couldn't tell them anything; he hadn't been contacted. So the corporate people pulled back."

If Jim Gladwin regarded that episode as an object lesson in the pitfalls of bypassing the local community, he did not choose to dwell on it.

The local community, however, had begun to sense that something was awry.

"The sesqui had been an event that the community had really looked forward to," recalled a businessman from the town. "Hannibal had really thought, at the outset, that this was going to be a local community event, like the centennial had been.

"But then it started to become apparent that there were two or three people putting this thing together. Two or three people, and *not* the Sesquicentennial Commission. Don't *ever* be confused about that.

"And then this wild series of announcements started appearing in the paper; these inflated notions of what the sesqui was going to be. It wasn't long before the people of Hannibal began to catch on that the sesqui was digging an enormous hole for itself."

Perhaps it was the episode of the motorized trolleys that finally moved Gale Newman to confront Mayor Lyng.

"The commission got the idea that we'd be needing some kind of transportation system to shuttle tourists from their hotels to the festival," said the Chamber of Commerce director as he puffed reflectively on a cigar. "Now, of course Hannibal doesn't have an airport that handles commercial flights, and we only have the one big motel, the Holiday Inn. So the thinking was that the chamber would contact Burlington Trailways, the bus line, and arrange with them to provide some sort of motorized trolleys to get people from the airport over in Quincy into downtown Hannibal."

Newman sighed and gazed at his cigar.

"Well," he said, "of course they sent a representative down to find out exactly how many people we expected, and when, and so on. And of course we had to tell him that we *thought* we could expect a hundred thousand people traveling here by air — I believe that was the figure we used — but we couldn't offer them a shred of evidence."

Newman pressed his cigar into an ashtray, rubbing out the flame. "We looked like a bunch of fools," he said. " 'We don't know.' 'We don't know.' 'No evidence.' Well, as soon as businesspeople hear this, they immediately assume they're dealing with a bunch of crazies."

It was in September of 1984 that Gale Newman telephoned John Lyng and said that if the mayor was not too busy, he, Newman, would like to have a visit.

When he arrived at City Hall, Newman recalled, he suggested that the two men go outdoors and across Fourth Street to sit on a bench in Central Park. "You may not want anyone to hear this," the Chamber of Commerce director remembered telling Lyng. "I'm going to tell you what I think is the truth."

The truth, Gale Newman told Lyng, was that Lyng seemed overwhelmed by the sesquicentennial, and Newman was not sure that Lyng appreciated the implications of that problem.

"You have a horse-and-mule festival in the making," Newman told the mayor. Newman added that he understood how difficult it might be for Lyng to accept this, given his deep involvement in the celebration. The problem was compounded, Newman pressed on, by the reluctance of most Hannibal civic leaders to point out the growing anxiety to Lyng; they feared Lyng's well-advertised taste for retribution.

The mayor sat coldly and silently on the bench, Newman remembered, as Newman's monologue, stiffly delivered by now, continued.

"I told him that I wanted to preserve our relationship and continue to make things happen for Hannibal," Newman recollected. "I recounted for him all the disasters: the logo, the theme stage, all the absurd, idiotic things that the community didn't like at all. I told him, finally, that the sesqui was being perceived as a we're-gonna-do-this-without-you type of thing."

Gale Newman had built up to that revelation carefully; it was intended as his clincher, his *coup de grace*. As he reconstructed the conversation, he recalled that Lyng responded for the first time — saying in a low, even voice that that was *exactly* the case.

Newman pressed on. Where was the logic? Where was the common sense? He cited a recent Jim Gladwin proclamation — a regatta on the Mississippi of two hundred paddlewheel steamboats. *There aren't two hundred paddlewheelers in the country,* Newman declared to Lyng. *Maybe not in the world!*

Newman turned to the matter of the parades. A hundred and twenty parades? he asked the mayor. One every day? Who in the hell is going to parade? *Who in the hell is going to watch?*

Think of the town's credibility, Gale Newman urged Mayor Lyng. People are laughing behind our backs . . . the lack of a single thread of evidence. . . . Your enemies are rubbing their hands, Newman told Lyng. Your friends are shaking their heads. The planning is a year behind schedule. *Don't make this mistake,* Newman recalled pleading with Lyng. *Get this thing back to the community while you can. Scale it back.*

"When I was finished, he was as mad as hell," Newman remembered. "His face was flushed, his voice was shaking. He said I had no idea of the apathy in this community. He said the commission didn't need the community's support. He said they were going to do without it."

The sesquicentennial fantasy boiled onward.

By the end of 1984, some people in Hannibal were beginning to wonder about the state of the sesqui's finances. No financial details had been reported in the *Courier-Post,* but neither had any stories of major corporate contributions, at least on a scale that might justify hopes for a $2 million total.

By a beguiling irony, most of the solid pledges received by the sesqui through 1984 had come from local sources: $35,000 from the City of Hannibal, $40,000 from the Hannibal Tourism Commission, $50,000 from the Mark Twain Home board (a private organization created in 1936, with Dulany Mahan as a founding vice-president), $35,000 from the local Southwestern Bell telephone company office. Even the Haunted House on Hill Street, the ineffable tourist attraction near the Boyhood Home with its mechanized vultures and its wax statues, had seen fit to boost the sesquicentennial. The Haunted House had kicked in $250.

Other local companies had made pledges in the range of $15,000 to $20,000. The total amount pledged as of March 31, 1984, was $247,000. A welcome sum, but hardly adequate to the $5 million budget declared by Jim Gladwin. By the year's end, people were beginning to wonder just how much money the sesqui did have, and would have. And people were beginning to hear some disturbing rumors.

Although the *Courier-Post* remained studiously oblivious to any financial questions, the local media were not completely muzzled — at least not for a time. Not with Mary Griffith around.

Mary Griffith was a neophyte reporter for KHMO radio. She had joined the station in 1982 at age twenty-two, less than a year after her graduation from journalism school. She was local, having grown up across the river in Quincy and attended high school there. A smallish and terribly earnest woman who took pains to present a correct, businesslike appearance — she wore dark, tailored A-line dresses and heels, and kept her carrot-colored hair in a neat coif — Mary Griffith was hardly the sort one would consider likely to challenge the power establishment of an entire town. (Her close friends, who knew that Griffith owned a Black Belt in karate, had a somewhat deeper respect for her mettle.)

In the fall of 1984, to the flabbergastation of everyone remotely connected with the sesquicentennial, not to mention the mortification of most of those who were covering it, Mary Griffith suddenly challenged the power establishment of an entire town. She launched her own investigation into the Mark Twain Sesquicentennial's finances.

She did so partly by methods that were as exotic to northeastern Missouri press circles as, say, injecting truth serum into interview sources might have been. She attended meetings — not only the regular Sesqui Commission meetings but the smaller committee gatherings. She considered her intuitive sense that certain things were not adding up. And, in her daily rounds of Hannibal city officials, Mary Griffith began to ask questions.

One person of whom she asked questions was Jim Gladwin. She asked him whether she could see the festival's accounting books. She recalled that Gladwin facetiously demanded, in reply, that Mary Griffith show him KHMO's books.

Mary Griffith was startled by that response — and so she turned to the most admired and most agreeable of her sources within sesqui circles, Mayor John Lyng.

"John always extended great cordiality to me," Mary Griffith remembered later. "He gave me fifteen minutes every day; he always returned my telephone calls. And I thought he was great — I worshiped him. I thought he walked on water."

But as time went on, Mary Griffith concluded that the answers John Lyng was giving her did not necessarily add up to the complete picture of the sesqui's finances. And so during one full meeting of the Sesquicentennial Commission, Mary Griffith fortified herself to do something she had refrained, until that moment, from doing: she arose and questioned Lyng in an open session, in the presence of his peers.

"I was kind of a little bit scared," she remembered. "At that point I wasn't getting any support from anyone — not other reporters, not any citizens. I was tense and uptight. I'd written down a list of questions because I knew how good he was at outtalking people; he was a lawyer and could do that — and I wanted to have all my ducks in a row.

"I read my questions from the list, and I think I sounded pretty officious — I wasn't terribly mature then. I kept calling him 'Sir,' and 'Mr. Mayor,' and it seemed to upset him. I think he was embarrassed that I was questioning him in front of the whole group. He got pretty rough with me."

So rough, in fact, that Mary Griffith fled to the women's restroom sobbing. And yet her painful persistence proved not to be in vain. As the result of her careful reporting and her questioning, Mary Griffith managed to establish that:

— The Sesqui Commission was at least $20,000 in debt, contrary to Larry Weil's and John Lyng's offhand assurances that no debt existed.

— The sesqui's fund-raising efforts technically placed the donors in violation of the state attorney general's ruling that prohibited contributions to not-for-profit organizations without a specific contract delineating the terms. The sesqui organizers had neglected to apply for such a contract.

— Most significant of all, the sesqui had secretly established an independent fund-raising corporation — which Mary Griffith dubbed "The Inc." — that collected pledges, donations, and loans outside the purview of accountability to the city or the commission.

This last revelation was to shed light upon an even more deeply muddled layer of financial record-keeping. Although no evidence of personal enrichment was ever uncovered, nor even hinted at, it became inescapably clear that the sesqui's organizers had sought a device for controlling the festival's budget with total autonomy.

Mary Griffith was not able to break these developments on KHMO radio. She learned indirectly that the station's elderly general manager, Art Francis — a Sesqui Commission member — was not interested in hearing the story on his airwaves. The station decreased Griffith's reporting responsibilities, she said later, until she had virtually nothing to do. She left KHMO in the spring of 1985 for another local station, which increased her salary and her on-air presence — while stopping short of encouraging her to be a sesquicentennial gadfly.

But her KHMO investigation was not in vain. A city councilman named Bob Chriscinske took up Mary Griffith's inquiry. He demanded to see the financial record books. Chriscinske was one of the new young company managers in town; he had grown up in Michigan, and had arrived in Hannibal in 1979 as a foreman at the American Cyanimid Company, the town's largest employer. He was a softspoken, studious-seeming man with a bristly blond mustache, but raw-boned and level-eyed behind his wireless glasses.

"Until Mary Griffith brought it to light, I had not even known there *was* a fund-raising corporation," Chriscinske recalled. "After that, I decided it was time to see the books. Previously, anyone asking to see the books was told the city, or the commission, was under no obligation to show them. But now it was pretty clear they had to open 'em up."

One of the first things Chriscinske noticed was that the Sesquicentennial Commission had borrowed $54,000 from the Commerce Bank of Hannibal, using nothing more as collateral than the as yet unfulfilled pledges of certain corporations. Further checking revealed that the sesqui was using city money budgeted toward industrial development as a "cushion" for sesqui payrolls and expenses.

"That money was supposed to have been reimbursed," said Chriscinske, "but the records showed we were still eleven thousand dollars in arrears."

Bob Chriscinske presented his findings at a meeting of the town's finance committee. "John Lyng was very smooth about it," he remembered. "He agreed we had a problem: we had been dealing with some incompetents. He said, you're right, Bob, we'll correct all that."

The revelations by Mary Griffith and, later, Bob Chriscinske, took on an odd half-life in the town. They were not reported in any of the local media, compromised as the media were through interlocking ties to the Sesquicentennial Commission. Rather than neutralize the embarrassing details, however, this blackout only conferred on them the ghostly authority of rumor. In a town of

Hannibal's size, there is virtually no such thing as a secret, particularly regarding the behavior of public officials. The details, and the exaggerations, of deficits and secret funding vehicles and coverups of collapsing plans made for delicious gossip at the church-fellowship dinners and in Hannibal's households. A climate of opinion regarding the sesqui more corrosive than anyone at Fitzgerald's could imagine was taking hold. If indeed there had been apathy toward the festival before, there was little apathy now. It had been replaced by a sense of violation, a mood that patiently awaited its opportunity for expression.

Meanwhile, Jim Gladwin ushered in Mark Twain's Sesquicentennial year with yet another grandiose scheme. A dinner! A dinner re-creating the menu of a famous banquet in Twain's honor at the Lotos Club in New York in 1894! The honored guests? Potential corporate donors! A celebrity chef to serve it up — Vincent Price! The site? Not Hannibal, of course; Hannibal wasn't right, somehow. Not New York; too far away . . . St. Louis! A Lotos Club commemorative dinner in St. Louis, bringing together the cream of corporate sponsors and the cream of the sesqui organizing elite! But how to transport the organizing elite to St. Louis? Did someone say a motorcade of vans, loaned by the local Ford dealer? Perfect! Get the vans! Rent the hall! Order the roses! Call Vincent Price . . .

The Lotos Club dinner never happened. There were delays, misunderstandings. But the garishness of it all, and the baleful fate that it implied for Hannibal, left one young woman of the town, a wife and mother and a tireless volunteer, in a mood approaching despair.

"They don't know what they already have here," the woman said, an unlovely smile on her lips. "They don't know what they're destroying. People come to Hannibal from everywhere just to touch the way we live, and . . ."

She shrugged and did not finish.

CHAPTER XI

I IMAGINE my father listening to the radio on the night of January 15, 1935, the night that Hannibal came on the air.

It was the night that the president of the United States, Franklin Delano Roosevelt, touched a gold key in the White House and sent out an electric signal that flashed halfway across the continent until it sparked a wire inside the new Mark Twain Memorial lighthouse on Cardiff Hill in Hannibal, igniting the beacon that officially inaugurated the Mark Twain Centennial Year.

Perhaps my father tuned in on the special broadcast on some orange-glowing radio down in Nebo, in southern Illinois, where he grew up on his father's farm. Or perhaps by then he had already left the farm to work on one of President Roosevelt's WPA projects out in the state of Washington, where he strained the muscle in his throwing arm doing heavy roadwork — an injury that kept him from a possible major-league baseball career. (He was known as Peg Powers around the ballfields of southern Illinois because of his throwing arm; his brother, Carl, told me that at my father's funeral.)

Perhaps, perhaps. My father seldom discussed his past. His past seemed to embarrass him. Not any particular event in his past; it was the mere fact of having a past that rendered him uncomfortable.

He had made his own diaspora up from the South to Hannibal; it was the shock waves of the Depression that broke up his family farm and sent the Powers boys scrambling out into the world, in search of better times. Perhaps the farm was my father's Eden, and leaving it caused more upheaval in him than he knew how to articulate. At any rate, his past was revealed to me only in his fleeting, flawed memories — imagining himself in the photograph with Roosevelt when the president cut the ribbon to open the Mark Twain Bridge — or in snapshots from family albums: my young father holding up a chevron string of fish in front of some pine trees, a dented felt hat tilted sideways on his head; or squinting, arms folded, into the camera alongside a skinny Abe, my mother's brother, with somebody's Dodge in the background, one of its doors hanging open.

Perhaps, perhaps. I am free to imagine my father's past; his lifelong reticence freed me. Perhaps he heard Hannibal go on the air up in the state of Washington that January night, listening to some rooming-house radio and rubbing the tenderness in his arm inflicted by a heavy stone that he tried to lift from one of President Roosevelt's WPA roads. My father was a radio fan; Hannibal was on a coast-to-coast hookup that night. The people of Hannibal had sent thousands of postcards around the country to alert radio owners to the broadcast. Perhaps a card reached the rooming house where my father stayed. He might have listened.

He would have heard Gene Rouse describe the scene from the foot of Cardiff Hill — Gene Rouse, the popular announcer for the NBC Blue Network, who had come down to Hannibal on the train from Chicago along with Gerry DeVleige, "NBC's technical expert," as the admiring *Courier-Post* article reported it. The radio program would have begun at 9:00 P.M., Hannibal time, with a short interlude of orchestral music from the NBC studios in New York, followed by a few words from an announcer. At 9:05, the audio feed would have shifted to the White House for the president's greetings and his ceremonial touching of the gold key.

Then at 9:10, Gene Rouse in Hannibal would have taken it

away, sending the nation a vivid account of the crowd reaction at the foot of Cardiff Hill as the beacon pierced the night, touching off the Mark Twain Centennial Year.

The Mark Twain Memorial lighthouse was visible from Cardiff Hill all the way across Hannibal to the South Side. It framed the upstream vista of the Mississippi River from the vantage point of Jasper Toalson's front porch on the crest of Union Street Hill, where Fuller man Paul Powers came with the greatest of aids to meet young Elvadine in 1937.

Perhaps my father listened to Gene Rouse's voice from Hannibal and imagined Roosevelt on the opposite rim of the continent; imagined the midcontinent beacon, the crowds, the glowing centennial town. Perhaps the touch of Roosevelt's finger upon the gold key ignited something in my father, and he prevailed on Bill Helm to assign him the Hannibal territory. All of this is possible to imagine, but my father never mentioned hearing such a broadcast. Of course, I never asked him.

What neither my father nor I would ever have been capable of imagining was the Mark Twain Centennial Broadcast Dinner that preceded the ceremonies. The dinner commenced at 6:30 P.M. at the Mark Twain Hotel. The governor was present, and a senator, and several ministers, and even one woman, a professor from the University of Missouri. Among the local dignitaries in attendance was the eighty-three-year-old first citizen of Hannibal, George A. Mahan.

The guests dined on a menu of Huckleberry Finn cocktail, Mysterious Stranger olives, Breast of Innocent Chicken Abroad, Tramp Potatoes Abroad, St. Petersburg peas, Pudd'nhead Sawyer of Arc salad, Following the Equator bread, Life on the Mississippi beverage, and Gilded Age pie with Roughing It cream. The coffee was named in honor of Nigger Jim.

At a few minutes before 9:00 P.M. the guests, the men with their lighted cigars, grouped around a radio receiver that had been set up in the dining room to hear Gene Rouse put their town on the national radio airwaves. George Mahan and the governor repaired to the broadcast site to offer some remarks. There was orchestra music, and then President Roosevelt touched the gold key. The Mark Twain Centennial had begun.

"Schools of the entire state will be asked to give special attention to Missouri's famous author during the year," the centennial people announced late in 1934. They alluded to "a comprehensive plan of publicity, expected to attract the attention of the entire nation."

The town would create a museum, containing a display of Mark Twain relics and mementos. In May there would be a Tom Sawyer Day, "a day of organized boyish pleasure for the modern Tom Sawyers of the world." In June there would be a Mark Twain Centennial Pageant — "a gigantic outdoor pageant depicting scenes and incidents in the life of Mark Twain and the history of Hannibal."

No events were scheduled for July or August. In September there would be a Mark Twain Homecoming — including parades, exhibits, a Boy Scout Day, and the showing of a replica of the world's first railroad mail car, the original of which had been built in Hannibal.

On November 15, the Mark Twain literary contest prizes would be awarded "to the boy or girl under 16 years of age from each State submitting what, in the opinion of the committee, will be judged the best essay of not more than 300 words on Mark Twain."

The celebration would climax on November 30, 1935 — Mark Twain's hundredth birthday — with a banquet attended by "some of the nation's most prominent literary figures."

The June pageant would be the centennial's centerpiece. Its projected costs filled the bulk of the celebration's budget. On December 3, 1934, the Hannibal City Council voted to appropriate $5,000 for the centennial.

That appropriation was not idly made. The town's budget for 1934 totaled only $150,725; of that amount, $17,000 had been set aside for relief to the poor. The Depression had come to Hannibal. Three local banks had closed. A fourth bank, the Farmers and Merchants, had suffered from an incident endemic to the 1930s: masked gunmen had robbed it of $42,000 in October 1931.

A soup house went up on South Main Street, near Union Depot. The government sent four hundred barrels of flour for the needy. The NRA set up a program in town, and the CWA, the CCC, the WPA, the PWA and the NYA. Many of Hannibal's public edifices and monuments and streets and druidic woodland comfort areas bear the rounded, sturdy imprint of those projects. The Works Progress Administration built the armory and the permanent Mark Twain Museum in 1937; it was the National Youth Administration that put the most recent coat of paint on the Clemens Field grandstand.

These were days and nights of suffering in the middle of the continent. The dust-bowl drought reached Hannibal. In July 1934 the temperature hit 108 degrees. The Mississippi set a record for low water; the ghostly hull of a sunken pleasure boat, submerged since 1903, pierced the river's surface.

The Mark Twain Centennial, bravely conceived, was to be Hannibal's symbolic emergence from this season of despair. The Centennial Committee retained the services of the John B. Rogers Company of Cincinnati, Ohio, a famous theatrical production firm, to create and direct the June pageant, which was to be called *Mark Twain's First One Hundred Years*. More than a thousand local people would put on costumes to sing and dance in the event.

During the spring of 1935 the town hung on every new centennial development. On April 19 it was disclosed that Mark Twain's own writing desk was being shipped to Hannibal from Elmira, New York, where the author spent his final days. The desk would be exhibited in the temporary museum that would open the following week in the Hannibal Trust building.

The museum was dedicated April 26. Among the guests was Mrs. Clara Clemens Gabrilowitsch, Twain's daughter, who arrived dramatically at Union Depot in a special train dispatched by the Burlington line. It was to be her last visit to Hannibal.

Tom Sawyer Day was approaching. The committee sought boys for the parade (the best Tom Sawyer impersonation would win a $50 prize). The pageant committee, meanwhile, announced the nomination rules for the contest that would crown a Miss Hannibal and a Miss Columbia, along with several attendants.

Four thousand children marched in the Tom Sawyer Day parade. The day's events included a two-hour boat excursion in the morning; a free street act, the Flying Beckmans, at noon; another boat excursion at 2:00 P.M.; the street parade at 3:15; another excursion at 4:00; another free street act — the Flying Beckmans again — at 5:00; a moonlight excursion at 8:30, and, finally, at 9:30, yet another free street performance by the Flying Beckmans.

On May 17 the rehearsals for the pageant began. On the night of May 18, at the annual Junior-Senior Banquet in the Hannibal High School cafeteria, there were skits and speeches portraying places and incidents referred to in Twain's works. Principal Harvey V. Mason (my principal twenty years later, a gray and cautious man who lived into the sesquicentennial summer) was moved to offer his thoughts on the subject of the home. I imagine him young but somehow gray; a combed man, gray of voice, holding aloft his characteristic cautionary forefinger. Harvey Mason concluded his address, the *Courier-Post* reported, by saying that the brotherhood of life is the greatest thing to strive for and that he hoped the seniors had profited greatly from not only their home life but their student years at Hannibal High School.

I feel as though I were there for all of it. I know the way that spring comes to Hannibal: the ice surface cracking on Bear Creek in March, and the lengthening light of day, and the first wire-service dispatches from spring training on Ed O'Neill's sports page; the Brooklyn Dodgers cooking up a five-player swap with the Cards. I know the flight patterns of the geese and when to look for the first appearance of green crocus and then redbud, and I know the feeling of hard late-winter sunlight on one's face as one rides, shivering in shirt sleeves, three weeks too soon in an open-top Chevrolet. I know the subtle ways in which a mother's cooking changes as winter gives way, and I know the chill stillness of a town at night in the last cold week of the season.

And then I know what it is like, in Missouri, to walk out of one's house on the first warm morning of spring, and to be stunned by the winy suddenness of it; to be nearly buckled at the knees by the absolute presence of spring. All chill gone; the air warm and still, and spring pushing up through the sidewalk cracks and all the green edges where pavement gives way to nature, and the smell of the river with all its incipient biology from clear across the hilly greening town. I know the onslaught of melancholy, the quickening awareness of the body; the twining urges of comradeship and lust. "The short season," Bobby Schweitzer would say, and he was not commenting on the duration of days, but on what the girls were soon likely to wear.

I can imagine that centennial spring. I can see the red-white-and-blue bunting that festooned the windows of the Hannibal Trust building, which had lain vacant since 1930, following the stock market crash, but which was opened up as the site of the temporary museum. At three stories, the Trust was the tallest office building in Hannibal; it still is the handsomest, all right-angled neoclassical granite anchoring the northeast corner of Third and Broadway. In my childhood it bustled again with business and profession; it was the only building in town (save Dulany's house) with an elevator, a clanking bronze cage that lifted my mother and me to the top-floor office of my childhood doctor, Dr. Landau, who gravely listened to my request for a pill that would make me "tough and strong" — I had been tormented by a mean kid who lived up on the hill. White-smocked Dr. Landau listened, and informed me that I was a worrywart. Generally, though, Dr. Landau understood my childhood medical needs.

I can imagine the Saturday-morning trombone swagger of the Tom Sawyer Day parade, family faces squinting from the sidewalks, some of the children feeling the faintest intimations of future military marches in the air, faraway Hitler staging his own parades. I can conjure the sweaty dash of the Flying Beckmans — I imagine short men in wrinkled tights, drab green.

And I can imagine the preparations for the pageant.

The pageant would be held on the new high-school athletic field. A two-hundred-foot stage would accommodate it. Its aim would be nothing less than to portray all the natural activities of a small town in 1839. A certain sensibility that would not have been completely foreign to Michael Jenkins half a century later seemed to inform the pageant's vision.

"Little 4-year-old Sam Clemens, who grew up to become the world-famed author Mark Twain, will be shown as he joins his family in giving thanks for their safe arrival in Hannibal," the publicity releases promised. "Villagers going about their daily shopping, and pausing to greet the new arrivals, will be portrayed by the large cast."

There would be a thirty-piece band. Two hundred fifty "girl dancers" rehearsed daily at Central School. (And here Hannibal's endless loops, its infinite connectives, rise and pull me without warning into the personal and universal past. I am sitting at the farmhouse kitchen of an elegant, graying woman who was one of the "girl dancers." I have asked her to remember the centennial for me. She places beside my coffee cup a black-and-white photograph of three dozen young women in sailor suits, one of the pageant's dance ensembles. The woman, as an intense girl of seventeen, peers at me from the back row. I let my eyes wander over the faces and find myself staring into the dark eyes of my aunt Gertrude: Gertrude, my mother's younger sister, dead a year later on her high-school graduation day of rheumatic fever; the second sibling of my mother's to die in childhood and the second of three catastrophic deaths in Elvadine's lifetime: Gertrude was a "girl dancer" in the centennial. I had not known that.)

The stage property committee, headed by Mary Wiehe, scoured the farms of Missouri and Illinois for carts and buckboards and carriages and brass cuspidors and carpet bags and an automobile of 1905 vintage and eighty flare torches.

A stagecoach was rumored to be en route from Springfield, Illinois. A "resplendent brouche" for Mark Twain's wedding scene was on its way from Quincy.

Construction for the pageant stage began on June 5, two weeks from its scheduled three-night run. A "trained chorus of 75 colored singers" began rehearsing. "The Pageant," reported the *Courier-Post,* "will be one of the greatest entertainment features ever presented in Missouri. On the gigantic stage it will be possible to present scenes of such large size as to be impossible from an ordinary stage."

The pageant would unfold in seven episodes comprising thirteen scenes. A total of five actors would portray Mark Twain at various stages of his life. There would be a Masque of Nations. The cast total had increased to eleven hundred. There would be 750 costumes depicting periods from the year 1500 to 1902 — the temporal scope of Twain's literary themes. The stage property committee looked for an ox cart, a western bar, a rail fence.

An audience of five thousand was expected for each of the three performances, producing a revenue that would offset the $5,000 cost.

On June 12, a week before the opening, the centennial queen, Miss Hannibal, was announced — a high-school senior named Marian Rupp. Virginia Leighton was crowned Miss Columbia. All was in readiness for the Tuesday night of June 18 — the Opening Night of the greatest entertainment feature ever presented in Missouri, Hannibal's symbolic emergence from the Depression, from the season of hard times.

It rained.

Opening Night was postponed. On June 19 it rained again. "Cold, wind, and wet grounds," reported the *Courier-Post* ruefully. Now the pageant was set back to Thursday, Friday, and Sunday.

On Thursday night it rained again. The opening was postponed until Friday. On Friday it rained again. The date was set back until the following Monday.

THREE THOUSAND AT OPENING, trumpeted the *Courier-Post* in its Tuesday edition — reducing that figure, deep in the story, to 2,241 "by actual ticket count." The second night drew 1,800. The paper noted that "threatening rainclouds hung over the amphitheater during the entire performance."

The third night drew about the same.

The *Courier-Post* was as positive as the existing laws of hyperbole allowed. "Building thrill on thrill as the finale continued," the paper reported in its review, "the Pageant ended in a roar of applause as the entire cast assembled on the stage, with the Masque of Nations dance groups in drill formation and the curtains rolled back to reveal the tableau of Mark Twain and his literary characters. The bursting of sky bombs fired from behind the scene gave a dazzling ending to the performance."

On Thursday, June 21, the pageant staged a fourth performance at reduced ticket prices. The four-day attendance was about 7,000 — less than half of what had been expected.

"Opinion was unanimous among audiences and Pageant officials that the Pageant was a complete success," insisted the *Courier-Post*. But the paper's boosterish efforts could hardly mask the disaster. The pageant chairman admitted that receipts fell far short of paying the pageant's expenses.

The Masque of Nations, the costumed singers and dancers, the trained choruses, Miss Columbia — none of it could hold back the curse of the elements. The Mark Twain Centennial, its centerpiece drenched in bad fortune, had lost its momentum. It moved on in a desultory way toward its conclusion.

A fourteen-year-old boy from Bloomington, Indiana, won the Mark Twain essay-writing contest. The granddaughter of the real-life model for Becky Thatcher showed up for the November 30 banquet ending the centennial; she cut the Mark Twain birthday cake. Of the promised "nation's most prominent literary figures," a Missouri novelist named Homer Croy appeared. Mrs. Dulany Mahan — Duly's grandmother — presented a program of music played on a rare electronic instrument called the theremin.

And thus the Mark Twain Centennial ended, its aspirations partly realized, partly dashed. And Hannibal settled into its long, almost imperceptible period of decline, the white town drowsing through all the summer mornings of my boyhood, toward its next anniversary reckoning with the blessing and the curse of its most famous son.

CHAPTER XII

People come to touch the way we live . . .

I HAD that knowledge as a boy in Hannibal, and took it as a given. The knowledge was part of my Ptolemaic sense of the town as center of the universe. Most townspeople I knew shared that awareness to some extent. No one really dwelt on it; it was a sort of quotidian presence on the edge of people's vision, like the lighthouse on Cardiff Hill. For me, the sense was closer to active consciousness, a living force — a given, a cryptic form of entitlement, but no less thrilling on the skin, in the nostrils, in the blood for all its mystery.

The river nourished this sense, of course, especially when viewed in diorama from my grandfather's front porch near the crest of Union Street Hill. It was the most splendid vision in the state, in the nation, in God's universe — who would not want to come and see it? But my deeper convictions derived from my friendship with Dulany and his family; from my proximity to these guardians of the town's great myth.

They derived from my ambling Saturdays with Duly down the river-slanting block of Hill Street where the Boyhood Home and the museum stood—and the Becky Thatcher House and Book Shop across the street. The Becky Thatcher House was the headquarters of Dulany's father, John Winkler. Annie Laurie Hawkins had lived in this two-story frame house — she was the "lovely little blue-eyed creature with yellow hair plaited into two long tails, white summer frock and embroidered pantalettes" whom Clemens converted into Becky. John Winkler had rescued the house from destruction in 1952 by turning it into a museum. He had restored the upstairs parlor and bedroom. Downstairs he had created a small bookstore, a treasury of Clemens's work and of works about Clemens, and a gift shop. Here gaunt John spent his days, mysteriously managing Mark Twain's posthumous career from a cramped and book-littered little office in the rear.

Outside, on Hill Street, I could examine the clues to my Ptolemaic sense of the town: the license plates on the Oldsmobiles and Pontiacs parked diagonally in the sunlight. Tourists' cars. The cars of the people who drove long distances to touch the way we lived, and to buy postcards of the town. The oddly colored plates under the heavy chrome bumpers read "Ohio" and "Michigan" and "Indiana," and occasionally, like a rare bubble-gum baseball card, "New York" or (rarer) "California." The people who owned these cars lived in places that were abstractions to us; dim images from movies and magazines. California was endless horizon, all sagebrush and Sierra in my Rialto reckoning; an Elysian VistaVision Field floating free in time and space, or bordered only by right and wrong; the titles in white knotty-pine lettering, the title song sung by Frankie Laine. New York was vertical, and black-and-white: slanting venetian-blind shadows on somebody's office wall, and a pencil-mustached man in a pin-striped suit promising someone, by telephone, something that we in tiny Hannibal could hardly avoid fulfilling: *"I'll be there in twenty minutes!"*

And yet they were coming to us, these sunglassed sightseers from those sumptuous geographies and geometries — not we to them. We accepted their pilgrimages with easy grace, we children, secure in our fame, innocents at home.

There was something authentically famous about Duly, as it happened. Duly was *on* the postcards. Duly, my blond and blocky chum with his shirt unbuttoned absently at the navel, could be plucked off the rack for a dime, like an Archie comic book at the

St. Mary's Pharmacy, by any lunch-hungry tourist foraging in the museum or the Becky Thatcher Home. His likeness was impressed on the postcards in Ektachrome, along with his brothers, Chris and John: the Winkler boys as stand-ins for Tom and Huck and Joe Harper, exploring Mark Twain Cave, or lounging in straw hats beside the whitewashed fence, or gazing out upon the Mississippi at a passing steamboat. Dulany's father, John, the state trooper turned rich man, had seen to it that his boys were imprinted on the postcards.

Those postcards are selling still, the Winkler boys preserved on them, gods of the town, almost Grecian in their posed attitudes. I drew one of these cards from its rack during a visit to the museum in the sesquicentennial summer. The three boys are posing in a passageway of Mark Twain Cave. Two are dressed vaguely in "period" costume — jeans and plaid shirts. Young John, the eldest, is in the lead. He holds forth the lantern toward some off-camera cache of cave-buried treasure; his arms are extended heroically and his rear foot trails like a dancer's. Chris, the youngest, is in the middle, bracing himself hands on knees. For some reason he alone has elected to dress out of "period," in a green fringed cowboy shirt, white kerchief, and natty yachtsman's cap.

Duly, a solemn Rubens with one shirttail dangling free, brings up the rear. His pose is at once the least self-conscious and the most curious of all. His head is canted forward and to the right as he stares off-camera with his brothers. But a trick of perspective has aligned the edge of a large outcropping precisely with the rear of his skull. The effect is of Duly, transfixed by riches, about to be buried by a slow-motion cave-in.

Hannibal's connectives keep looping back; the town implodes into an infinity of sequence. The small and sable-eyed woman behind the counter who accepts my change for the postcard is Mrs. Hornback. Edie's mother. My God, it is *Edie Hornback's mother* I am paying for a picture postcard of Duly. Edie, the tiny gamine with Indian skin and panther grace whom I spotted squatting on her haunches, ready to pounce, outside the schoolhouse door in second grade and loved, unrequitingly, for ten years thereafter. I wooed her with cartoons and watercolors and with ardent drawings of her oval and berry-brown face — which gifts she squirreled sensibly away somewhere against the time when I might become famous and establish for them a market value.

I would have surrendered my moral coordinates for Edie (but not my inhibitions); I would have leapt off Lover's Leap for her Indian grace; but in the event, I don't recall a single instance of ever physically touching her. I am not sure that even Duly, growing into his gallant adolescence (and his white Chevy convertible), ever captured her heart, even after his nights of shatter-armed glory on the dim-glowing football field, where the Masque of Nations had been drenched, where Moses Bates had run his trading post. She spurned us both, her artist and her tackle. Edie was a dreamer, I think, after distant men, more distant even than Quincy; men who would come helling into town in cashmere and tragic hot rods; men with names, perhaps, on the order of Johnny Dark. For us, Edie would offer limited adoration — squeals and cheerleader tears at Duly's pondering gridiron prowess, teethy chuckles at my witticisms, little notes written in backhand curlicue and passed to both of us in Mrs. Crawford's history or old Doc Hanley's chemistry.

We were friends, the three of us, apart from the hierarchies of our desires and spurnings. Edie lived in a tidy white house on the corner of a street not very far from Rose Hill and Skylands. In fact Dr. and Mrs. Hornback were social peers of the Winklers. I'd see them often at Rose Hill as I prowled its precincts with Duly, adults playing canasta.

Edie was a school star in her own right, in the terms that defined stardom for young females in those days: homecoming queen attendant, Miss Olympia to the track and field men. The most intense phase of my relationship with Edie ensued in our junior year, when she went off to a girls' boarding school in Minnesota and I became her pen pal. Even then, I had to share her — with the fashion correspondent of the school newspaper. ("*Dear Edie, To classes girls wear tweed skirts, tailored blouses, and heavy sweaters, sometimes topped with a scarf at the neck. I wish you could see*

Janice Pilcher in her royal blue sweater and gray plaid wool skirt. . . .") Then she came back, for senior year, and then I never saw her again. She left to live in California and I left to make my way toward New York; we both became people with oddly colored license plates.

And now a quarter-century later, widowed Jane Hornback spent some of her days behind the counter of the Mark Twain Museum that John Winkler had overseen for forty years, pleasantly accepting the small change that people handed her for the souvenir postcards, the people who had come to touch the way Hannibal lived.

There was one person in Hannibal for whom Duly was authentically famous, postcard credits or no, and that was my father. I think that my friendship with Duly marginally improved my standing in my father's eyes. It may have been his first real clue that I might amount to something. I had penetrated, after all, to every floor and the basement and the four-automobile garage at Rose Hill. My Fuller Brush man father had never made it past the kitchen.

Then, too, Duly satisfied some deep hunger my father felt for the larger-than-life — a hunger that he otherwise fed by his consumption of gangster lore, St. Louis Cardinal anecdotes, and his restless dialing of the radio airwaves.

Duly was the rich son my father never had. When he dropped in at our house my dad tended to find excuses to hang around, eavesdropping and shooting sidelong glances in our direction, perhaps on the prayerful hope that Duly might offer to cut me in on some wildcat oil-drilling scheme.

One Saturday morning, probably during grade-school years, I got permission to ask Duly to breakfast. My father transformed himself into a human mass of flourishes. At table, he presented Duly with the serving platter of pancakes. Duly, in his customary serene oblivion, set the platter down on top of his plate and proceeded absently to eat the entire family's flapjack allotment — Dad's, Mom's, mine, Jim's, and baby Joyce's.

I was horrified — terrified. I scarcely dared lift my head to glance at my father, who was known to turn brooding where portions of food were concerned. I need not have worried. My father was fascinated. He never stopped retelling the episode for the rest of his life. It attained the purity of legend for him; of Norse epic. It ranked with his flawed memory of having been in the newspaper photograph with Roosevelt at the Mark Twain Bridge. ("Damn," my father would whisper reverently, "but ol' Duly ate every one of them damn pancakes.") He was grateful, it turned out, to have been on hand for Duly's seizure of the family's Aunt Jemima resources. It confirmed his every private hope regarding the ways of the rich; it was exactly the sort of thing millionaires did on the radio.

How, then, did we live these lives that people wanted to come and touch? Here, memory mixes with desire. I want to think that we lived in relation to the kingdom of the town, and to the land around the town, and to the river. The town depended on land that depended on the seasons, and I want to remember that we derived our purpose from the seasons; that my friends and I were children of the seasons and ran like panthers and Indians through the town days and nights.

There is some truth in this wishful memory. Nature was never more than a few yards, at most, from anyone within the city limits — except perhaps on Broadway, our greatest cascade of pavement. Nature reached into Hannibal with long fingers; it reached down cliffs and ravines and along creekbeds, and it claimed vast weed-blown fields among the thin advancing colonies of postwar neighborhoods, fields where Jon Eddington and Mike Sohn and I would forge subtle arterial paths connecting our various neighborhood streets, fields that were green and tangled with reptilian intrigue in spring and summer, then exploded into great enveloping ululations of golden husks in the blackbird fall — fields that are now themselves neighborhoods.

My grandfather kept a garden in a lot that he owned a couple of blocks down from his house near the top of Union Street Hill. No one stole from it; it was Jasper Toalson's garden, a garden at the top of the world. In summer I would spend hours with him — the river below us, and away — as he pruned back his blackberry vines and weeded the bean rows in his yellow straw hat and faded overalls. I got so that I could smell the vegetables in their vines. I loved to race back to the house with green peas in a bushel basket, which my grandmother in her pantry would empty into her apron and then shell into a colander with a cacophony of clicks and pings.

My father was a man of the seasons. He fished for black crappie and bluegill on the banks of the Bay de Charles in the summer, staring at his cork in the ripples well beyond the point at which the ripples made my own thoughts bob and drift; and he hunted rabbit and pheasant on the corn-stubble prairie near Monroe City in the winter. In the fall he took his shotgun to the Moose Lodge's skeet shoots for Thanksgiving turkeys. A large black-feathered bird would always strut in our backyard for a few days before its plucked carcass turned up on our dining-room table.

And yet we were not children of the seasons. We bowed to the authority of clocks, and we knew our reflections in mirrors. We were town kids, our panther purity compromised by machinery and order and the ever-encroaching blandishments of mass commercial entertainment.

Linda Pryor went to the movies. Her parents must have let her see every change of picture show that occurred at the Tom Sawyer, and a few at the Rialto as well. She came back to the neighborhood on St. Mary's and disgorged plot summaries; she had something like total recall for scenario, even as a grade-school kid. It was Linda — the graceful, aloof bicycle acrobat of my backyard carnivals — who first filled me in on the facts of life: if an outlaw kissed his girlfriend, the girlfriend would have a baby. (This was about the time that *The Outlaw,* starring Jane Russell, was playing in town.) I was deeply shocked, as I gathered I was supposed to be, although I could not shake the feeling that Linda was holding something back from me. Nor could I rid myself of the sensation that something was coming to our town, or had come;

something at the edges of Linda's happy descriptions; something that didn't entirely belong.

I went to the movies, too, but my own conduit to the larger universe, like my father's, was the radio.

We listened to "Our Miss Brooks" and "Meet Corliss Archer" on Friday nights after grocery shopping, my brother, Jim, asleep; we passed around a yellow-and-orange box of Cheez-Its, the three of us, and I lay facedown on the warm carpet with my nose just inches from the console, my face turned away from my parents so that I would not be embarrassed when Dexter Franklin tried to kiss Corliss, as he did every week. My father and I listened to baseball games on the car radio in hot weather, Harry Caray's play-by-play voice the voice of summer itself. (Later in his life my father listened at night at the kitchen table, his head bowed, alone.) On Saturday mornings at Duly's house we lay on sofas staring up at the ceiling and listened to "Let's Pretend" and "Big John and Sparky" ("Plunk your magic twanger, Froggie!" "Hiya, kids, hiya, hiya!").

My favorite radio show of them all came in on the Mutual Network every weeknight just as I rushed into the house and flopped on the floor, fresh from school. How can I explain the exhilaration I felt for Bobby Benson and the B-Bar-B Riders? How can I evoke the sense of majesty, the prideful anticipation of kid justice about to be done upon hearing Bobby's shrill program-opening shout of "B-Bar-*Beeeeeeeeee!*"?

Bobby was (owing to circumstances that now escape me) the boy owner, possibly orphaned, of the B-Bar-B Ranch in the Big Bend country of Texas. He was surrounded by a vivid and doting coterie of grown-up cowboys, all of whom dutifully addressed him as "Li'l Boss" — all of them, that is, except for the massively dignified Tex Mason, the stalwart foreman and Bobby's most dependable ally in dealing with varmints and owlhoots. Besides Tex, there was Wendy Wales (and his wild tales), a nearly mute but utterly redoubtable Indian named Harka, and (unless I am interpolating this character from another show, possibly "Hashknife

Hartley") a chattering Mexican with an arm's length of humorous names, the last two of which were Bustamonte Rafferty.

Bobby was the grandest kid in the history of children, real or imagined. He was Tom Sawyer with spurs and a knack for trick riding. Husky-sopranoed and ferociously chipper, he rode the range as a peer among the big guys. In fact he was the brains of the outfit — although I always felt that Tex Mason was every bit as shrewd as Bobby, and deferred to him only when he was sure that the Li'l Boss was right as rain.

I identified with Bobby, but I worshiped Tex Mason. Tex Mason was virtue in baritone; he was everything that Duly and I would be when we grew up. Tex Mason was slow to anger; you could push him pretty far, but God help the sidewinder who stepped over Tex Mason's line. I remember actually writhing on the floor in excruciating pleasure one episode, as some low-down dog began to egg Tex into putting up his dukes — a situation that Tex always tried his best to avoid. The saddle bum started off by allowing that he didn't like the sound of Tex Mason's voice. Tex answered evenly that he wasn't in any singing contest. The owlhoot waded in deeper: furthermore, he didn't care much for Tex's looks. Tex hesitated a beat — a lethal sign, to anyone who knew him — before replying that he wasn't in any beauty contest, either.

I forget exactly what the last straw was, but the ensuing enfilade of biffs, whaps, thocks, and sidewinder grunts made it unambiguously clear not only that Tex Mason was in charge, but that God's great goodness ruled the prairie and that redemption surely awaited the pure in spirit.

About a year later, when Tex Mason's horse died on the program, I was almost maddened by shock and grief. I cried so hard and grieved so deeply that I could not eat supper for three days. This was my rite of passage into the knowledge of the stunning damp awfulness of death. I carried the knowledge like a weight in my throat to bed, and dreamed sad horse-dreams. I felt that my mourning forged some sort of dolorous bond between me and Tex Mason. In a sense, it moved me closer to him even than Bobby. Bobby didn't have too much to say about the tragedy, I noticed —

within a day or so he was off on another hijink adventure as though Tex's horse had never even turned up sick.

A few more months passed — another year, maybe. Bobby Benson and the B-Bar-B Riders went on riding the range and tracking down owlhoots and laughing it up over Wendy Wales and his wild tales and musing over the infallible sixth sense of Harka. It was as though a family had drawn in after a loss. We all felt closer to one another, somehow.

And then something started to happen on the show that would prove more disturbing, more of a loss, than the death of Tex Mason's horse. An alien tone began to creep in at the program's edges — almost imperceptible at first, but gathering, gaining definition with time.

Bobby's laugh began to change. I hardly noticed it at first, but one night, flopped on the rug, I thought I detected not a wholesome chuckle but a snicker. Bobby's voice had started to change, too: it was lower, more modulated. Not the voice of a grown-up, exactly, but not a kid's voice either.

At the same time, characters started to disappear from the cast for long stretches — Tex, Harka, then even comic old Wendy. And one horrible afternoon, Bobby flubbed his famous opening cry of "B-Bar-Beeeeeeeeeee!" His voice cracked. And then Bobby Benson did something that startled me as much as if he had burst into Chinese: he laughed at his own mistake. He kidded the script a little. Realization hit me: *He didn't care about us, the kids who were listening!* For the first time since I had been tuning in to the show, I had an image of him as he must have been — not riding the range in the Big Bend country of Texas, but standing in front of a microphone in a broadcast studio, a studio with a clock on the wall. In the image, the kid actor turned to the grown men standing at his side and winked.

I felt humiliated — violated — for having grieved over the death of Tex Mason's horse. I never tuned in Bobby Benson and the B-Bar-B Riders again.

Nothing really changed in my life as the result of that decision. There were lots of other westerns on the radio and I listened to all of them. I kept going to the movies — more westerns, more heroes — and even stunned my parents and myself by escorting Linda Pryor by bus one Saturday, although I had a severe change of heart about it halfway through the matinee and bolted from the Rialto, leaving her to get home the best way she could. I continued hanging around with Duly, feeling privileged to be his pal — movies, the radio, the pharmacy, the cavernous layers of his big house, which we prowled restlessly, like ghosts. We had long since decided from the movies and the radio that valor and justice were important, and we made up stories to each other that involved valor and justice. I thought that Duly would someday inherit Hannibal and its trove of stories, and I would be his partner in shipping them out like logs along the river to the world.

But we were only two children in a small town in the middle of the continent at the end of American time, and a seed had been planted in a radio actor's laugh, and the identities we were assembling would do us little good on the far side of the Mark Twain Bridge.

About the only thing that would remain constant in Hannibal over the next thirty years would be the people, the people with oddly colored license plates, the people who came to touch the way we lived.

CHAPTER

XIII

WELL before sunup on January 23, 1985, John and Pam Lyng left Hannibal by car for the St. Louis airport. There, they caught a flight to New York to inaugurate the national publicity campaign for the Mark Twain Sesquicentennial.

John Lyng transported with him one of the eight-foot fence sections of the "World's Largest Guest Book." After a press conference in New York, the Hannibal mayor and his party would fly on to Hartford, Connecticut. It was in Hartford that Mark Twain had first encountered huckleberries, and where in 1873 he built an hysterically overwrought and pretentious mansion, which he was obliged to sell at a loss in 1903. On that site, and without a trace of irony, Lyng would present the commemorative fence section to the Hartford mayor.

The kickoff national press conference was held the morning after Lyng arrived in New York, at the Lotos Club on East Sixty-sixth Street.

I went over to the Lotos Club to watch the press conference. I felt happy over the fact that Hannibal was enjoying some attention in the national limelight, and I wanted to see Lyng again. I had met him during a brief visit to town the previous November, and he impressed me then as a man on the very verge of likability — quick-minded, intense, earnest — but a wary man, finally, whose attention skewed off at a slight angle; a man who found it tempting but somehow inappropriate to throw back his head and laugh.

There was a television crew setting up a camera on a tripod when I arrived in the Lotos Club parlor at about ten o'clock. The room was already harsh with television lighting. Lyng had not arrived yet, but the commemorative fence section was there, propped against a wall, looking like nothing so much as a hellishly forbidding piece of luggage to carry on an airplane trip.

A few men and women with name tags pinned to their lapels were standing around a table at the rear of the room, drinking coffee from china cups and munching on Danishes from a buffet table. These were mostly public-relations people from the New York firm retained by the Sesqui Commission, and some young staff members from the Cigar Association of America, which had a hand in sponsoring the event. I didn't see many reporters. In fact I saw no one whom I recognized for certain as press, and I began to wonder whether the several rows of folding chairs would come close to being filled up by the time the ceremonies began.

I drank some coffee and chatted with a photographer and tried to fight off a farcical, but presently unwelcome memory of the first press conference I ever covered. It was in Chicago. It had been called by Dakin Williams, the brother of Tennessee Williams, to announce his candidacy for a United States Senate seat from Illinois. "Why don't you slide on over there," the city editor had said, handing me a press release.

In the hotel suite where the conference was to take place, I encountered tables piled high with campaign statements, buttons, and glossy photographs of the candidate. There was an elegant silver coffee service; there were rolls and napkins and silverware. There was a microphone; there were folding chairs. There was Dakin Williams, and there was me.

I had the first question. "What," I managed to croak, seized with some insane compulsion to play the situation out, salvage some kind of story — a scoop, by God — for my newspaper, "do you see as the major obstacle facing you in this campaign?"

Dakin Williams had smiled and considered the question, his blue eyes glittering with a strange inner merriment. "Peaking too early," he told me.

Now, awaiting the start of this press conference, I picked up a media package and thumbed through the information sheets. The main press release began with an attention-grabbing anecdote; it explained that Halley's Comet blazed into the night sky when Mark Twain came into the world and, true to his wish that he depart the world when it reappeared, he did. A Twain quote followed: " 'I came in with Halley's Comet in 1835. It is coming again next year in 1910 and I expect to go out with it. . . . The Almighty has said, no doubt, now here are these two unaccountable freaks. They came in together, they must go out together.' "

Having established the jauntiness of Twain's death, the release skimmed the highlights of his life. Few writers, it noted, have found as warm a place in the hearts of millions around the world as Twain. It noted that Twain rubbed elbows with people from all walks of life: beggars and criminals, common folks and great intellectuals, kings, presidents, and men of vast wealth. It noted that he traveled widely and befriended people everywhere and became a widely read journalist and eventual author. It noted that honors bestowed upon Twain confirm the high regard in which he was held by his contemporaries. "It was 'Huckleberry Finn' in 1884 that skyrocketed the Hannibal-bred writer to international fame," said the release. "Written while Twain was living in Hartford, Conn., 'Huckleberry Finn' contained vivid descriptions of life on the Mississippi River."

John Lyng walked into the Lotos Club parlor, wearing a brown suit, accompanied by his wife, Pamela, and by Cathie Whelan, the commission's administrative coordinator, who had flown in the day before. The three seemed flushed and excited by the occasion. Lyng was almost hearty as we shook hands. I asked him whether his reelection campaign would distract him from attending to the May opening of the festival. The April 2 elections would install Hannibal's first four-year mayor. Voters had approved an expansion of the traditional two-year term in 1983 — an expansion, many people assumed, that had been tailored for John Lyng.

"No major candidates have filed against me," Lyng replied. The lone challenger, it seemed, was a photography-store owner who had never before involved himself in civic life. "No mayor of Hannibal has ever run for reelection unopposed," Lyng added — an interesting mark, I thought, of his grasp of the town's political history.

Lyng moved to the front of the parlor, near a miked podium, so that the publicity ceremonies could begin. About half the folding chairs were occupied now, although I still recognized no one as a reporter. The television camera was from the Public Affairs Satellite System, a newsfeed service. A technician flipped on another bank of television lights, and everyone in the room instinctively ducked and squinted. The lights, aimed at the podium, were reflected back into the audience's eyes by a large mirror above a mantel at the front of the room.

There were a few moments of expectant, squinting silence, and then the French doors at the side of the parlor opened and a man wearing a white Mark Twain suit and wig and mustache shuffled in, trailing blue cigar smoke. A few of the people in the audience clapped a little.

The man's name was Roger Durrett. He was thirty-five years old, from North Carolina, and he had been performing a show, *An Evening With Mark Twain,* for the past seven years. His own press release noted that his makeup took three and a half hours to apply. It added that this year Roger Durrett would be traveling throughout the United States as the official spokesperson of the Mark Twain Sesquicentennial Commission and as the ambassador-at-large for the Cigar Association of America.

A press release inside the media package hinted at the direction the publicity people hoped the conference would take. "What would Mark Twain think about women's rights? President Reagan's new cabinet? The fitness craze?" it asked, or prompted.

The mayor of Hannibal and the Mark Twain actor shook hands and toasted one another with champagne for a few minutes, while the satellite-system TV camera recorded it and a photographer hired by the public-relations firm snapped still photos. Then Roger Durrett shuffled to the podium microphone, almost spectrally backlighted by the reflection of the camera lights, and began to field questions in character as the seventy-year-old Mark Twain — prefaced by a few humorous remarks about his love for a good cigar.

Many of the questions were along the lines of "What do you think about women's rights?" "How about President Reagan's new cabinet?" "Have you been following the fitness craze?" I may have been wrong, but I had the impression that the bulk of the questions were being gamely tossed out by the young staff members of the Cigar Association of America.

After about half an hour of this, it was over, and I wished the mayor and his wife and the administrative coordinator a successful time with the fence section ceremonies in Hartford. It was unclear later how much of the national television audience saw excerpts of the Lotos Club event — the publicity people said that it was "available" to 85 percent of the TV outlets in the country — but a still photograph of John Lyng and Roger Durrett as Mark Twain was published in the *Courier-Post.*

A few days later, on February 5, Jim Gladwin's resignation as executive director of the Sesquicentennial Commission was announced in the Hannibal newspaper. The item quoted Larry Weil as saying, "We are grateful to Jim for the hard work he put into the project and now it's just a matter of cleaning up the details and getting ready for the celebration."

On February 17, a Baptist preacher named John Chappell brought still another one-man show, *Mark Twain on Stage,* to the Municipal Auditorium in Moberly, a small town west of Hannibal. It was noted that Chappell used makeup that took three hours to apply and dressed in a tailored white suit carefully replicated from the one Mark Twain wore in his lifetime.

The Sesqui Commission's treasurer, Richard Halsor, announced an operating budget of $560,500. Halsor did not allude to the high-water budget projection of $5 million.

On February 28, a *Courier-Post* article under the byline of Laurie Vincent reported that on the hundredth anniversary of the United States publication of *Huckleberry Finn,* the book was not taught in the Hannibal public-school system — nor had it been taught as long as some of the older teachers could remember.

English teachers in the system, the article said, felt that the book was inappropriate for younger children, and that some older students felt disdain for Mark Twain.

It quoted Rosemary Schneider, chairwoman of the English department at Hannibal Junior High School, who pointed out that the word "nigger" appeared in the novel more than two hundred times. "A younger child may not be able to interpret that usage correctly," Ms. Schneider told the correspondent. "I think high school students could intelligently handle the material."

Ms. Schneider did direct Laurie Vincent's attention to the fact that seventh graders were required to read *The Adventures of Tom Sawyer*. That book's instruction coincided, she said, with an annual promotional contest in which the Chamber of Commerce selected two seventh graders to serve as Tom and Becky, ambassadors for Hannibal.

On March 14, the Sesqui Commission released, through the *Courier-Post,* the names of several entertainment groups for the celebration. They included the Music Box People and Spiritualities, two Hannibal singing groups; the Mark Twain Men's Chorale of Hannibal; the Inspiration Ringers and Celebration Singers from Manhattan (Kansas) Christian College; the Missouri Symphony Trio, String Quartet, and Brass Quartet; and the Air National Guard Jazz Band from St. Peters, Missouri. There was no mention of Up With People, which had been advertised as the main attraction for Opening Weekend, May 4 and 5.

Several paragraphs farther along, the article mentioned that entry forms for the celebration's three parades — on May 4, July 4, and September 2 — were available. There was no explanation as to why the number of parades had diminished to three from the earlier announced figure of 120. It was also announced that Mayor Lyng and Cathie Whelan had met with officials of the American Sternwheelers Association in Marietta, Ohio, and that "at least" nine sternwheelers would be in Hannibal July 11–14 for the American Sternwheeler Association riverboat regatta. In fact, Ms. Whelan disclosed that the association would hold its annual meeting in town at that time. The article did not comment on the earlier projections of two hundred riverboats at the regatta.

The following day, the *Courier-Post* reported that the theme stage would not be ready for the celebration's official opening. The article quoted Mayor Lyng as explaining that the delay was due in part to the withdrawal of the stage's initial corporate sponsor (Pet Milk). Lyng noted that Southwestern Bell Telephone had agreed to assume sponsorship of the stage. Larry Weil was quoted as saying he hoped the stage would be ready by July 1.

On March 31 the Sesqui Commission released a "recalculated financial statement." Under "Assets," the statement showed the following:

Cash in Bank	$00.00
Petty Cash	$00.00
Pledges Receivable	$36,037.70
Pledged, designated for Specific Purposes	$137,700.00

The "pledged, designated for specific purposes" column listed five purposes: the theme stage, the renovation of a historic ice house, a wind symphony concert, the construction of a performance amphitheater, and "specific event sponsors."

Under "Liabilities," the statement showed:

Notes payable	$122,000.00
Contracts payable	$52,094.68
Estimate of lodging expense with contracts ($47 per room)	$1,410.10

Difference between obligations on Sesquicentennial statement and calculations from supporting documents	$3,092.21
Projects to be supported by specific pledges	

(Here the statement listed the same five projects that had been enumerated in the "specific purposes" column on the "Assets" side)

	$137,700.00
Total liabilities	$316,296.00

The small advertisements for John Lyng's mayoral opponent had been appearing in the *Courier-Post* for several weeks by now.

The man's name was Richard Cerretti. He was thirty-eight years old. He and his wife, Dorothy, had lived in the town for fifteen years, although they were unknown to any of the people who went to Fitzgerald's — or anyone who belonged to the country club or attended Hannibal's Big Parties, for that matter.

The Cerrettis had three children. Besides owning a photography store, Richard Cerretti was a former grade-school teacher. In both his paid advertisements and in his interviews with reporters, Cerretti often stressed that he was a devout Christian. He wore a small gold insignia — two bars curved to form the shape of a fish — on the collar of his shirt.

The photograph in his campaign ads showed a placid-looking man in square rimless glasses with a high forehead dusted by wisps of silvery hair. The fish insignia was visible on his collar.

The ad's copy was hardly more insurrectionary than the candidate's appearance. RICHARD CERRETTI WILL LIVE BY THE CITY CHARTER! the headline proclaimed. Below, in small dark print, there followed a list of six or seven charter provisions, each followed by an alleged violation by Mayor Lyng: bidding errors on road projects, laggardly response to a citizen petition to amend the charter, failure to execute a written purchase order for a local architect's services.

VOTE FOR THE MAN WHO WILL OBEY YOUR CITY'S CHARTER, the ads concluded. It did not seem that Richard Cerretti had exactly hit on the sort of clarion theme that would mobilize an emotional groundswell of reform-minded voters.

If there was any hint of sauciness at all in Cerretti's campaign, it surfaced — cautiously — as a single line in a yellow handbill (CITIZENS OF HANNIBAL STAND ON YOUR FEET AND BE COUNTED) that the challenger's supporters began slipping onto the windshields of cars a few weeks before the election. "Give 'Mark Twain' what he deserves," the line read, cryptically, "respect and a burial."

By the end of February, contributions to Richard Cerretti's campaign stood at $495.

I visited Hannibal again late in March. I looked in on John Lyng, who put aside his schedule, ushered me into a pickup truck and took me off on a brief tour of the sesqui preparations near the riverfront. There was no physical evidence yet of a theme stage, but farther south, beyond Nipper Park, on the far bank of Bear Creek at its confluence with the Mississippi, workmen had been grading a fan-shaped expanse of land and making ready the foundations of a small cement stage. Eventually the fan-shaped area would be covered with asphalt, and a few girders would rise above the cement stage to support a stagelight fixture. This was to be the amphitheater, the venue for the sesqui's larger concerts — symphonic, jazz, country, rock.

A strong late-winter breeze off the river tore at John Lyng's necktie and ruffled his silver beard as we hiked over the graded earth. He was in his shirt sleeves, but he didn't seem to notice the cold — or me, particularly. As he gestured and pointed, he could have been speaking to a tour group, or to a vast throng. What had his attention, it struck me, was that graded earth itself — those overturned clods and lumps of Hannibal's oldest soil, here scooped up and reordered at John Lyng's command. I looked at John Lyng striding the bulldozed earth and recalled my father, at peace in winter on the prairie cornfields with a shotgun cradled in his arms.

John Lyng was only a few years younger than I. I had never

known him nor his family as a boy — he was of a different kid generation than I — but now in middle age we were practically contemporaries. I wondered what he saw when he looked east down Broadway toward the river. I wondered how much of the town the two of us saw in common. I wondered what was lost, and gained, by growing up in a town like Hannibal and *not* leaving it — but living on there as an adult, the child's impressions not sealed and preserved, as mine had been, at the end of childhood, but transmuted by an adult's gathering sense of limitations and temporariness — and possibility. I tried to imagine asking John Lyng these questions, and could not. It would have to be at Fitzgerald's, over drinks, at night, not in the light and cold wind of a business day — and the talk at Fitzgerald's tended toward other things.

I took leave of the mayor back at City Hall and walked over to the Becky Thatcher Restaurant, where I treated myself to a pork-tenderloin sandwich. Then, in the early afternoon, I drove out to the northernmost corner of town, to the campus of Hannibal-LaGrange College, to pay a call on its president, Dr. Larry Lewis.

Hannibal-LaGrange had lain just beyond my perimeters in boyhood. My friends and I, who would troop through any nocturnal backyard, prowl any vacant building or orchard or even the country club golf course by the light of the moon, never ventured there. It was not exactly that we avoided the campus — it was simply not exactly real to us; it was not precisely a part of the kingdom.

For starters, the campus was almost like an appendage to the town. It lay out there on the northern rim, bordered by fields and farmland and, at its back, by woods — woods that dropped down along craggy hills to the Bay de Charles. Then, too, the campus was laid out — willfully, it seemed — in a way that pushed its population even farther from contact with the town. Most of its hundred acres lay between the main road and the lecture halls. The squarish redbrick buildings, spartan and formal in their nineteenth-century design, were clumped together in a small huddle almost at the edge of one's vision as one looked through the arched entranceway (HOME OF THE TROJANS) from the road.

Finally, there was that inescapable matter — that mystery — of the college being Baptist. We weren't sure exactly what it meant to be Baptist, my friends and me, but we knew that it was a whole lot more *something* than our grapejuice-and-mighty-fortress Sunday protestations, and possibly contagious as well. We were all properly in awe of the Twainesque God, we Sunday-school comrades, and wary of the Devil, who lived in the middle of the earth, in the hot place whose name it was a sin to mention. (I was not deeply versed in the concept of sin as a boy, either. For quite a while I was under the impression that sins actually collected on the top of one's head as one committed them, like dandruff, and could be eradicated by a vigorous rubbing of the scalp.) Jesus was likewise an enigma — a kindly and vaguely sorrowful man with his head perpetually tilted, who had some sort of interest in sheep, and who was infinitely good and patient and suffering, although touchy about how people used his name.

I suppose that my boyhood theology could be said to rest comfortably on the assumption of an afterlife — heaven for climate, as our distinguished citizen had once put it, and hell for society — and on the metaphorical notion of prayer as a sort of celestial long-distance telephone call. I had a series of dogs named Laddie, each one of which died, after a year or so, of what my father chose to call "distemper," but which may have had to do with my father's disinclination to have the dogs properly inoculated against doghood diseases. After each Laddie's passing, I would go down into the basement of our house on St. Mary's, lie flat upon the cold dust of the cement floor — a position I felt to be reverential — and put in a prayer to God, asking, after a few opening pleasantries, if I might have a word or two with the late dog of the moment. God was an unfailing sport about it, and never once so much as hinted that I put a reciprocal bee in my father's bonnet concerning his tightfistedness with veterinary bills.

My father, for his part, did everything within his mortal power to enrich my appreciation of the Christian life. He made it a personal rule to attend our church every Christmas and every Easter, often unprompted by even the gentlest of threats from my mother; he turned the radio on to the Reverend Johnny Golden every weekday morning; and, when seized by a certain mood of barbed joviality, he would often sing to me a fragment of a hymn possibly learned in his own childhood, the words to which are engraved in my memory: "Jesus, lover of my soul, hang me on a hickory pole. If that hickory pole should bend, hang me on the other end."

Within this general framework, I believe, we were a fairly standard Protestant family in the town.

But these Baptists — they were another kettle of fish entirely. Baptists were reputed to be nondrinkers, nondancers, noncard-players, and fiendishly good at basketball. Beyond that, not much was known about them, except that they had a weird way of stretching out their vowel sounds. (A prominent local Baptist preacher named Calvin Albert was said to be able to convert souls to Jesus simply by pronouncing, at top decibel, his own name.)

And so my friends and I stayed away from the campus.

Its architecture to the contrary, Hannibal-LaGrange College opened up in 1928 — a creation, more or less, of the Hannibal Chamber of Commerce. In 1927 the chamber decided that a college would add a certain tone of respectability and refinement that was missing from the town's prospectus. Fortunately, it was not even necessary to go through the botheration of founding such a citadel. The city fathers imported one — a Baptist institution from the village of LaGrange, about forty miles north of town. The terms were a hundred acres of campus and $175,000 cash — which the chamber secured through a townwide fund-raising campaign, a pre-Depression burst of philanthropy that Hannibal never again equaled.

The first year's enrollment (in 1928) numbered 225 students. In 1985 the enrollment was 720 — an increase of fifty over the previous year, and the first 700-plus enrollment in the college's 126-year history. A glance at the classifications of Hannibal-LaGrange students — by church preference and by areas of academic interest — suggested that the college eluded any of the easy stereotyping that might accrue to a small Baptist institution in the heart of what is frequently called "the Bible Belt." While it was true that the plurality of students listed their church affiliation as Baptist or Southern Baptist (319), the second-largest category was "Unchurched or Unknown" (193), and the third-largest was Catholic (62). Similarly, while the largest academic concentration lay in "religious vocations" (78, including one student who listed "Christian communications"), a far larger grouping was distributed among the allied pursuits of business (46), business administration (25), and computer-related skills (52).

Nor were Hannibal-LaGrange students to be written off as a bunch of Comstockians, ready to call down hellfire and brimstone at the merest thought of a well-turned feminine foot. To be sure, Bible study and door-to-door "witnessing" expeditions were among the most typical extracurricular activities. At the same time, for three years running the college had supplied the winning contestant in the Miss Hannibal pageant, the winner each year going on to contend for Miss Missouri.

Perhaps most tellingly, given the long history of skepticism by conservative churchmen toward Samuel Clemens's work — his "secular humanist" leanings, in Michael Jenkins's phrase — Hannibal-LaGrange College was the only educational institution in Clemens's hometown to confer special emphasis on his writing. Not only was *Huckleberry Finn* taught in classes on American literature; President Lewis explicitly defended the novel as a "spiritually sensitive book." Furthermore, Dr. Lewis was on record with his intention to establish a permanent center for Mark Twain studies.

It was because of such a diverse, not to say unorthodox, stewardship that I wanted to meet Larry Lewis. I had heard that he was an interesting and complex man, a blend of old-fashioned evangelical puritanism and state-of-the-art techno-Christianity (all those computers behind all those severe redbrick facades) — one of the more redoubtable civic leaders in a town not exactly top-heavy with civic leadership. I had heard that Dr. Lewis struggled gallantly but with dismal success to regard jazz music in terms other than the very pipes of Satan; at the same time, he made sure that every service club in Hannibal was represented by at least one Hannibal-LaGrange administration member. He himself was president of the Chamber of Commerce and held a membership (financed by the college) to the Hannibal Country Club — an adventure into the secular life that some of his predecessors would have considered as roughly equivalent to grooving on the sounds of Jelly Roll Morton.

Dr. Lewis received me in his office, which smelled of eucalyptus and which featured a large dramatic oil painting of a sailing ship on a storm-tossed sea. He was a small but strong-featured man; the term "muscular Christian" leapt inevitably to mind. His shock of wheat-colored hair, combed Kennedy-style across his forehead, and his narrow-set blue eyes gave him a boyish look; but everything else about Larry Lewis suggested tight control.

He introduced me to a long-legged fellow in a blue suit and curly black hair, a man whose rumbling voice, at first syllable, called forth a galaxy of Sundays in the pulpit with fried-chicken dinners soon to follow. This was the Reverend Jim Hefley, an Arkansas preacher, the author of more than forty books *(Textbooks on Trial, America: One Nation Under God),* and presently Hannibal-LaGrange's writer-in-residence.

Dr. Hefley seized my hand and unloosed a veritable hallelujah of information helpful to someone who had come to write about Hannibal. He informed me that Hannibal was probably the best-known little town in America; he launched into a heartfelt analysis of Mark Twain's "Calvinist consciousness"; he assured me that none of Twain's writings was risqué; he opined that one of Twain's "guilts" related to his wife, Olivia, "a card-carrying Evangelical," whom Clemens led away from her faith; and he regretted that I could not have been on hand to hear one of his recent sermons, which had covered the topic "What Mark Twain Couldn't Conquer (But Red Foley Did)."

Dr. Hefley glanced at his wristwatch and made his apologies; he had some appointments to get to. Dr. Lewis and I sat down in facing, spacious easy chairs.

"We've made a very, very deliberate effort to bridge the college to the community," Dr. Lewis acknowledged. "It used to be 'that parochial school up on the hill.' We are trying to get back to the idea of a Christian *community* college. After all, the *community* originally provided the land for us. The Chamber of Commerce insisted that every pledge for our foundation here be paid. That sense of *community* is why I see to it that we have one of our administrators on the board of every service club in town."

I asked Dr. Lewis what he thought of the relationship between the Chamber of Commerce, his organization, and the Mark Twain Sesquicentennial Commission. His jawline worked for just a moment before he spoke, and when he did, he sorted his words.

"When the commission was created," Lewis said, "the chamber was circumvented completely. I believe that the leadership was felt not competent to be an adequate catalyst for all the plans.

"The sesqui movement," Lewis went on, warming now to the topic, "has centered in a few people. It has become a dog-and-pony show, put on by professionals; it is not a grass-roots event. There has been a real failure to involve local groups."

But, Dr. Lewis said, the sesqui people had lately shown a sudden resurgence of interest in localism. They had asked the chamber for a sizable donation. The chamber had rebuffed them.

"To *totally* circumvent the chamber," said Larry Lewis, a little heat creeping into his voice now, "and then to come back to the chamber for a meaningful contribution — their first approach to us was for sixty-five hundred dollars, to help them sponsor a weekend. We didn't respond to that. Then they wanted us to solicit a hundred fifty businesses to give at least a hundred dollars apiece, toward a goal of fifteen hundred dollars. We did not agree to it. We said we would support the sesquicentennial, we'd encourage our members to support it, we'd contribute Tom Sawyers and Becky Thatchers for every event, we'd even expand the Frog

Jump — which we've sponsored during Tom Sawyer Days — to an international event." Dr. Lewis sighed and looked away. "But . . . ," he said, and spread his hands.

I nodded. I understood. I was starting to feel an unexpected kinship with Larry Lewis. I had no illusions regarding the limits of that kinship — I liked jazz — but here, at least, seemed to be a local leader who understood the necessary balances, the moral co-ordinates. Here was a man whose instincts matched Mark Twain's regarding the essence of a town's heart, and the price of aloofness from it.

I asked him to summarize his vision of Hannibal's future.

Dr. Lewis did not hesitate. It was clear that he had given the matter a good deal of thought.

"A major renovation of downtown Hannibal should be a major goal," he began. And then it came: "I can see specialty shops, leather goods — folk art is one of the biggest things in America today. We must get the store owners to agree to a facade for their buildings; nineteenth-century. Period sort of design. Nineteenth-century costumes, long skirts . . ."

I fought back a strong impulse to ask Dr. Lewis not to say any more. I did not want to hear this. I did not want to have the illusion dashed so quickly. Michael Jenkins came into my mind. The Mark Twain Heritage Theme Park. The Court House and the Hanging Tree. The Judge Thatcher's Barbecue. The Haunted Riverboat, the Shooting Gallery Video Arcade. People in costumes. Packaged name-identity. Hannibal as a cartoon of its former self, a parody of its past. Hanniballand. Twaintown. Haunted. Step right up.

I phrased my next question to Dr. Lewis as delicately and as mildly as I was able. I asked him what he thought the psychological effect might be upon people who were asked to wear those costumes, to conduct their businesses behind those facades, to present themselves to the gazes of strangers as make-believe characters in a strange and transparent charade.

Dr. Lewis answered in tones of iron. "It's business, okay? It's business! It's making the most pleasing and profitable presentation with the available resources. Is it any different for them," Dr. Lewis wanted to know from me, "to put on nineteenth-century garb than it is for McDonald's girls to put on their costume, or the people at Disneyland?"

I had to admit to him that, as nearly as I could understand, it was not. We shook hands and I left his office, the campus, and the town, heading my rented car out of Hannibal and south to St. Louis. My flight back to New York departed later that afternoon.

In the coffee shop at Lambert–St. Louis Airport, I thought about my conversation with Dr. Lewis — and about Hannibal — as I idly watched a waitress make her rounds. The waitress was dressed in the sort of costume that was standard-issue at airport coffee shops everywhere: a brown silk blouse with slitted sleeves tied loosely at the wrists with bows; sleeves that billowed to reveal her bare arms and shoulders, and a skirt whose hem swung and swirled just above her knees.

The waitress was perhaps sixty years old. The billowing slits in her sleeves exposed flesh that had lost its suppleness and hung loosely from the bone — the points of her elbows caught the eye. The short skirt rendered to any stranger's indifferent gaze the blue veins in her calves.

The truth of the woman's costuming was all in her shoes: they were the kind of shoes that mailmen and security guards wear — shoes with corrugated foam-rubber soles, built to ease the wear and tear on the feet. I wondered whether the waitress had had to fight a battle with the manager to win the right to wear the comfort shoes instead of standard-issue spiked heels.

The waitress's fantasy-uniform had nothing to do with her authentic identity, or nature, or function in the airport coffee shop (nor would it have, for that matter, on a woman thirty-five years younger than she). But the truly grotesque thing about her costume was that it did not work on *anyone's* terms — not hers, not the coffee shop manager's, not the customers', not the absentee consultant's who had recommended the design. It succeeded only in bringing into sharp and obvious relief what it was intended to conceal. It obliged the wearer to become a parody of herself, a walking violation of her own past.

And yet, in the tormented logic of American corporate merchandising — the logic intelligible to all those computers behind all those severe redbrick facades — the outfit did work. By agreeing to wear it, the woman entitled herself to earn an income that she might otherwise not be able to earn. In that scale of necessity, her costume made sense. It was business — hers, and none of mine.

My flight number was called. I left some change on the table, change that would ripple into Missouri's tourist economy, and flew back to New York.

Richard Cerretti did not behave like a dilettante candidate daunted by campaign contributions of $495. On March 18 he wrote a letter to Governor John Ashcroft of Missouri. Cerretti had noticed that in all the frenzy of establishing the festival as a national event, no one on the Sesqui Commission had thought to invite the Missouri governor.

Cerretti's invitation, written on his photography store's letterhead, began:

"To introduce myself, I've been a Christian businessman in Hannibal for ten years. God has been working to put me in a unique position and opened the doors so that I could file for the office of mayor. I've found it exciting. . . ."

CHAPTER XIV

On April 2, Richard Cerretti carried every precinct in every ward in Hannibal to unseat John Lyng as mayor.

The photography-store owner and former grade-school teacher, the "Christian businessman" with no experience in politics, gained the first four-year mayoral term in Hannibal's history — the term that had supposedly been "reserved" for John Lyng. The victory meant that Cerretti would be the presiding mayor for John Lyng's Mark Twain Sesquicentennial.

The incumbent city counselor, an ally of Lyng's, was also voted out of office.

Cerretti received 2,898 of the 4,816 ballots cast — a majority of 60 percent. His victory left many people in the town (excepting, obviously, some of those who did the voting) nearly paralyzed with disbelief.

Almost no one had expected Cerretti to make a serious showing in the race, not even those who had grown disillusioned with the incumbent. John Lyng was ironclad. No man or woman of any prominence in Hannibal had bothered even to file against him.

Furthermore, there had been no opinion polls, no straw votes, no early portents of any kind to indicate that a groundswell was building against Lyng. I had spent three days in town in the last week of March — mostly reading at the public library and visiting with some schoolboy friends who had remained in Hannibal to establish rewarding careers in law and real estate — and I had scarcely heard mention of an election campaign. Lyng and Cerretti had met for two or three low-key public debates, which the *Courier-Post* had routinely covered; but there had been no rallies, no thunderous speeches, no campaign buttons, no sound trucks, no parades. The one indicator of voter sentiment that I noticed — billboards featuring the candidates' names that several people put up in their front yards — seemed to suggest a heavy advantage for Lyng. (Cerretti supporters later said that they had been afraid to advertise their preference for Lyng's opponent.)

In retrospect — from Lyng's point of view — the absence of any visible excitement toward the election was ominous. The town, so pointedly unconsulted during all the preparations for the sesquicentennial, had waited in opaque silence for election day, and then had delivered its opinion in the only language likely to register with those who were running the show. The town had found a way to get involved.

There was no consensus on what it was that defeated John Lyng. That Lyng had "lost" the election, as opposed to Cerretti's "winning" it, was generally undisputed. "Cerretti ran on Lyng's record, and won," was the way one city councilman explained it to me. But what, exactly, did the record reveal?

Whether it had been Lyng's high-handedness with the sesqui plans, or his general bit-in-the-teeth arrogance as mayor (the gist of Cerretti's small, mild newspaper ads), or Hannibal's lingering cussedness regarding anybody who got too far out in front of the town's rhythms, or God's intervention, or some combination of all these, remained a matter of debate.

Shortly after the election, a fashionable theory took hold among the country-club people and the people who hung out at Fitzgerald's: that Cerretti had won out of apathy; that hundreds of people who would have voted for Lyng decided to stay home on Election Day, believing there was no serious chance of an upset. Perhaps some voters did abstain on that assumption; but the general turnout was higher than it had been in either 1983 or 1981.

Not that the country-club crowd was particularly anguished over

John Lyng's loss. "No matter how bad the current mayor turns out to be," said one prosperous businessman a few weeks after the election, "he did the community a service just by running and being elected."

Some members of the old aristocracy chose to regard the whole thing as a joke, another punch line in Hannibal's long dark comedy. The story got around that when Richard Cerretti approached one well-connected townsman after the election, to ask for helpful suggestions, the man's first piece of advice was that Cerretti demand a recount.

John Lyng wasn't laughing. Those who were with Lyng at Fitzgerald's on election night said later that the young mayor wept as the returns came in. The next day, however, Lyng was composed, even tactful. He offered congratulations to Cerretti, refrained from spite, and said that he had no excuses for his defeat.

The *Courier-Post* was less restrained. Sounding the first battle cry of a political trench war that would torment the town for months to come, Larry Weil's newspaper published a long editorial that eulogized Lyng's administration and concluded with a thinly muted challenge to the winner:

> The next month will be a time of transition as Lyng prepares to turn over the reins of city government to Cerretti. . . . During that time, we presume, we will learn some of the details of Cerretti's plans for Hannibal, details which were lacking during the campaign. Hannibalians by now know pretty well what Cerretti is against, but haven't as clear a picture of what he is for.
>
> Throughout a bitter campaign, Cerretti promised "new directions" for City Hall. It's our fervent hope that those "new directions" include "forward."

People who wondered what sort of tone Richard Cerretti's administration would take were not kept wondering very long. On April 5, the Friday after his election victory, Cerretti demanded a meeting with the members of the Sesquicentennial Commission at City Hall. Several broadcast and print reporters from Hannibal and Quincy gathered in the corridor, hoping to coax the mayor-elect into his first press conference (Cerretti had brushed aside all requests for interviews following his victory).

Cerretti's performance at the meeting was brief and, in its way, brutal: abjuring pleasantries and ignoring reporters' questions, the small gray-haired man strode into the council chamber and thrust a single sheet of lined notebook paper toward Chairman Weil. The first line of the hand-lettered message read, without salutation, "I want the following information by Wednesday, April 10."

The information Cerretti wanted involved the anatomy of the Sesquicentennial Commission, its infrastructure, its plans, the state of its financial health. The mayor-elect demanded, among other documents, the sesqui's certificate of incorporation; the contract between the city of Hannibal and the commission (specifically showing who was authorized to sign contracts on behalf of the commission); all signed contracts for entertainment and for consultants; the current schedule of events; and, finally, a broad category of financial disclosure — monies received and expended, pledges made to the commission, and all notes of debts and obligation.

After Cerretti left, Larry Weil granted an interview to the reporters in his capacity as sesqui chairman. Weil declared himself to be "very disappointed" with the meeting, which he called a complete waste of time. In reply to a question, Weil said that he had no intention of resigning from the commission. "This celebration is bigger and more important than Larry Weil, Richard Cerretti, John Lyng, or any other individual," Weil said. "As a consequence of that, we will take every step available to us to make this thing a success."

On April 11, the day after his deadline for the sesqui documents, the mayor-elect unleashed for the first time the full extent of his fury — "arms waving, ranting and raving," as Larry Weil and others later remembered it — regarding the festival and its planning.

The occasion was a joint meeting at the Holiday Inn among the commission, the Chamber of Commerce's executive board, and Cerretti. Once again, the mayor-elect dispensed with any attempts at formal courtesies; he turned, snarling, upon the sesqui finance chairman, Dick Halsor.

Armed with an analysis of the commission's financial reports, Cerretti began an emotional cross-examination of Halsor. Wasn't it true that the festival was in even worse financial shape than the March 31 "recalculated financial statement" indicated? Hadn't the commission been double-counting certain assets — listing some corporate pledges both in the "earmarked" and the "general" columns? Was there not a mammoth difference between corporate pledges "receivable" ($36,000) and pledges actually received (about $5,000)? Where was the accounting for $250,000 in outstanding loans from a local bank?

"He had them," recalled Gale Newman, who watched it all unfold. "He had the goods to blow 'em all out of the water. He *had* them, but when he got into his tirade he lost everything he'd gained. It *was* a tirade, and it was bad. It was bad. I think that at one point even Cerretti realized he'd lost it. He'd been going over an hour, and he finally called a recess. When he came back in, he'd cooled down. But by then, I think he'd lost whatever chance he might have had to work cooperatively with these people, who were, after all, a big part of the Hannibal power structure."

On April 24, less than two weeks before Opening Weekend, the first chilling hint of possibility arose that there would be no sesquicentennial. Mayor-elect Cerretti announced that he would not support any further funding of the celebration by the city. Reading from a prepared statement — and again refusing to answer any direct questions — Cerretti complained that he had not received all the financial statements he had asked for. "The financial records were incomplete," he said, "and I am still discovering more potential liabilities. I do not know whether all the programming or entertainment has been paid for yet and I could not find sufficient pledges listed to cover the debt."

Sesqui chairman Weil had no direct comment, but promised, "We will address this latest lapse of leadership on Cerretti's part at Friday morning's commission meeting."

On Friday morning — April 26 — Larry Weil relinquished his own leadership. He resigned as Sesqui Commission chairman. The previous night, before a special meeting of the City Council, an emotional Weil had launched into his own tirade against Cerretti. Declaring himself tired of the "negative thoughts" that had prevailed over the last three weeks, the *Courier-Post* publisher had gone on to make this charge: "My view is that what we are dealing with is a fanatic, obsessed with carrying out a personal vendetta at the expense of the community. He has resorted to dealing in half-truths, deceit, and misstatement of the facts solely for the purpose of torpedoing our celebration."

Weil concluded his resignation statement the next morning by saying he hoped that Richard Cerretti would make a gesture similar to his own, surrendering his mayoral victory "to the City Council." Cerretti was not heard from in reply.

Weil's resignation may have saved the festival. Following his gesture, ten of the twelve incumbent and incoming council members verbally endorsed the event, and called for a communitywide effort to put the sesqui back in working order.

Thus, at the eleventh hour, Hannibal was finally being invited — implored — to take charge of the greatest civic event in its history. Missing from the controls, on that Friday morning, were every one of the original architects of the Mark Twain Sesquicentennial — the New York–based consultant Alfred Stern, whose "magic letter" had started Mayor John Lyng to thinking about the festival as a "permanent economic development tool"; Lyng himself, who would surrender his office on May 7, the Tuesday after Opening Weekend; Jim Gladwin of St. Louis, the executive director who tried to implement, if not surpass, Stern's grandiose visions; and Weil, the newspaper publisher / sesqui chairman whose *Courier-Post* lost its adversarial distance from the festival story during the very period when some detached reporting and editorializing might have checked the planners' headlong dash to the brink of chaos.

The commission voted to name Dick Halsor, the "people-oriented" manager of the Buckhorn Rubber Products plant, as temporary chairman. In accepting, Halsor declared, "As of now, 'positive' is the key word. We've had too much negative. We're certainly not about to quit. We've paid our price."

In the weeks after Richard Cerretti's election as mayor, it would become more or less reflexive for many Hannibal people (and certainly the *Courier-Post*) to speak of politics as the unwelcome force that descended shroudlike upon the town and its celebration plans — as if the Mark Twain Sesquicentennial might have clicked along just fine had it not gotten enmeshed as a campaign issue between two mayoral candidates.

In a sense, perhaps, politics did color the nature and the fortunes of the celebration. Perhaps John Lyng had an eye to his own political future, as well as to the town's economic hopes, when he accepted Alfred Stern's vision of a grand, highly programmed, professionally run festival. Perhaps Richard Cerretti played on a populist undercurrent — a political sentiment — when he subtly urged the voters to give Mark Twain "respect and a burial."

But politics alone could not account for the bizarre and exotic *nature* of the festival as it was originally presented to the town. Politics had no hand in conceiving the idioms, the symbols, the marketing strategies that comprised those early visions, nor could politics account for the blind, and ultimately wrenching, indifference of the planners to the question of whether Hannibal's particular temperament could or would adjust to such plans.

Just as politics had no primary role in the buildup — and eventual collapse — of similar idioms and symbols and marketing strategies that were clustering at about the same time around Mark Twain Lake near Monroe City, politics was at best a passive conduit for the forces that converged on Hannibal in the sesquicentennial year of Mark Twain's birth. The forces were extrapolitical. They were also ubiquitous: even if Alfred Stern had not written his "magic letter" to Mayor Lyng, it seems almost inescapable that somehow the idiom of sponsorship-opportunity and total-revenue projection and projected media exposure and demographic group control and product/service linkage would have found its way to the sesquicentennial — as would the accompanying symbolism of Good Golly Aunt Polly rock shows and "Huck"-sters raft races and storytellers trees and the world's biggest ice cream social.

These idioms and symbols and marketing assumptions were coating the country. Their traces could be found in the thematic redevelopments of seaport districts in New York and Baltimore and Boston; in thematically restored Williamsburg, Virginia, and the theme battlefield of Gettysburg, Pennsylvania; in theme-park attractions from southern California to Florida; in the detritus of failed World's Fair sites in Knoxville and New Orleans; in all the Old Towns and Historic Districts and Lincolnlands and Olde Mistick Villages and Nostalgic Railroad Rides and the Interpretive Centers with their recorded narrations, and the museum battleships, and all the color-coded, transistorized, molded-plastic, brochured, belogoed, prepackaged venues of America where confused and distracted tourists gathered for a few moments to peer, as across a jagged fissure, at the half-remembered remnants of what once had been a history.

I was not able to get back to Hannibal for Opening Weekend. By all accounts, it was a glorious success. The Mississippi River glittered under sunny skies, and temperatures were in the high seventies. The Mark Twain Sesquicentennial began with a "fun run" in Riverview Park near dawn on Saturday, May 4. At 9:00 A.M. there was an Avenue of Flags ceremony at Broadway and Main, down near the former dime-store building where Gene Hoenes used to prowl with his microphone, where Santa's House went up at Christmastime. The parade lined up at 9:30 at Maple and Broadway, near the point of the old Wedge, and kicked off at 10. Led by the United States Navy Band from Great Lakes, Illinois, sixty-five units marched east toward the river — past the old site of Zimmerman's Bakery, past the old Rialto and Tom Sawyer theaters and the old Mary Ann Sweet Shop, down along the old site of the Fall Festival — and turned left on Main, marching north to the historic district.

There were floats, bands, Cub Scouts, fire engines. Ed O'Neill was in the crowd to watch — and Mary Wiehe, my old art teacher and Jubilee Chorus stager, and Floyd Capp — Officer Capp, to the intact town of my memory. My uncle Abe and aunt Nellie were there, and Doc Porter. So much of the intact town *was* there. The Colonial Fife and Drum Corps of Alton, Illinois, showed up in revolutionary period costume and won three awards. Buckhorn Rubber Products won for best corporate float. John McIlroy of Bowling Green won first prize for fancy dress (western man). His wife, Paula, won a first for fancy dress (western woman).

There were fireworks, dance music in Central Park by Little Ronnie and the Impersonations, some gospel singing, and the antics of a few theme characters, including Hannibal the Frog, a local woman in a green costume and molded-rubber frog's head that featured a transistorized air conditioner on the inside. Hannibal the Frog was to serve as a kind of permanent mascot for the celebration, with various townspeople taking turns under the molded-rubber helmet.

After it was all over, temporary chairman Halsor pronounced himself satisfied except for the rock 'n' roll band in the historic district. "Mark Twain is not identified with rock 'n' roll music," Halsor told the *Courier-Post*.

Hannibal-LaGrange College held its 127th commencement on Opening Day. The speaker, Dr. W. A. Criswell of the Southern Baptist Convention, told the eighty-eight graduates that God would use the trained Christian mind to reach to all parts of the Earth. He said that the world was seeing a wave of materialism.

On Tuesday, May 7, Richard Cerretti was sworn in as the new mayor of Hannibal. Cerretti told the people assembled in the council chambers that it was time to put aside differences and reconcile. The inauguration was otherwise memorable for an appearance by

Mark Twain, as portrayed by a Washington actor named Bill McLinn ("Mark Twain Himself!" proclaimed his press releases, which added that McLinn had performed as Mark Twain more times than all other Twain impersonators put together, except Hal Holbrook). McLinn was at pains to point out to the City Hall reporters that, unlike his counterparts, he dressed for his lectures in *black tails* instead of a white suit. Moreover, Mr. McLinn made it a rule never to smoke a cigar in an indoor lecture hall. McLinn said that the official Mark Twain papers at Berkeley, California, were the source of his adopting these practices.

"I think Twain is saying," McLinn explained to the reporters, "and I agree, that we shouldn't take ourselves too seriously."

On May 9 the Sesquicentennial Commission named John Lyng as its executive director.

My next chance to visit Hannibal came during a week of thundershowers in the middle of May. Spring had taken hold now in Missouri; the wild and fragrant air beside the river was heavy with it, and on this trip I wanted to savor the journey into town as much as I wanted to learn things while I was there. For that reason I made no appointments — not even with the new mayor, whom I badly wanted to meet. This visit, I hoped, would be for reconnoitering old aromas and temperatures and balances of light on blossoming surfaces. The time-present town and its preoccupations, its urgencies, I hoped, could wait.

There are two parallel routes to Hannibal that branch off to the north from westbound Interstate 70 about twenty miles beyond the St. Louis airport. The more efficient route, the one I normally took, is U.S. 61, set back from the Mississippi by fifteen or twenty miles for most of its stretch, until it skims the western edge of Hannibal at the Junction. Sixty-one is the truckers' route to Fern's (and, likely, the route of the old southern diaspora up from Kentucky). A divided-lane highway for about half its length, 61 thins out at the Pike County line, where it continues as a brisk two-lane strip through gently rolling farmland on up to New London — near the site where young Sam Clemens and his fellow

Marion Rangers shot down the shadowy-eyed stranger in *The Private History of a Campaign That Failed.* From there, it widens to ten final miles of divided road.

A slower, narrower, and more lyric highway is State Route 79, which hugs the Mississippi's western floodplain through half a dozen grain-terminal and filling-station hamlets — one is likely to grind one's gears behind a John Deere harvester out of Old Monroe, Winfield, Foley, Elsbery, Amanda, or a few other wide spots — until the old road kisses the great river's shore halfway to Hannibal, at Clarksville, the site of Federal Lock and Dam No. 24. From there on in, the ride is sheer poetry — if one can stand the suspense. The road begins to rise and fall with the humpback hills that brood over the river's Missouri side, as Illinois recedes flatly into the blue-hazed east.

North of Louisiana, a fading but exquisite village of antebellum, colonnaded houses wedged into the steep-dropping hills, 79 starts to zigzag as well as rise and dip: the blacktop surface spins into breathtaking curlicue swoops, then suddenly boosts the car to the peak of a green-skinned hill, the vast Mississippi rising out of nowhere to greet one's fleeting glance.

State 79 was the route I chose for my drive up from St. Louis. The dogwood and the redbud blossoms are lovely along this road in May, and besides, the old highway was full of memories.

This was the route my father liked to drive on those rare and consummately plotted summer Sundays of my boyhood, the once- or twice-a-year splurges to St. Louis in the Nash for a Cardinals baseball doubleheader. As I headed north now in the heavy May air, I recalled how it was to get up early on the appointed Sunday morning and slide cool jeans along my legs instead of church woolens. I recalled the cold fried chicken my mother would pack for lunch, and I recalled the way my father liked to show off along the way — propping the funny papers across the Nash's steering wheel so he could glance down at Skeezix and Gasolene Alley as he drove, achieving his purpose of scaring the hell out of my mother.

I remembered peering out of the car window upon the same landscapes that I was seeing now — the gulleys and the creekbeds and down upon the roofs of barns ("Mail Pouch Tobacco," said their roofs, and "See Seven States from Rock City") — imagining these quickly glimpsed vistas as sites for my private western-movie fantasies, me with my holsters reversed like Wild Bill Elliott's. I remembered the exhilaration I felt — a school's-out giddiness based partly on my anticipation of the great urban ballpark with its pennants and loudspeakers and geometric girders and beer smell and the first shock of white Cardinals uniforms trimmed in red; but based, too, on the derived sense of my parents' rare holiday happiness, their illusion, so seldom indulged, that the day would last forever and money was no object. "Give 'at boy an orange sody pop," my father would instruct the gas-station man in Clarksville. Back on the road, glancing at my Nehi-guzzling face in the rear-view mirror, he would assure my mother that I had attained the workingman's notion of nirvana: "He don't give a dam' 'bout *anything!*"

And then to return home late in the summer Sunday night, me curled in the backseat, faintly headachy and hallucinating on baseball, the glimpsed coil of Stan Musial in the batter's box, while the Nash's headlights played like spilt milk on the blacktop rind of 79. To return in those soft-consonant summers of my boyhood — Nash, Hannibal, night, never. Never grow up.

Awash in these memories, I rounded a limestone bluff and rolled into green Hannibal almost without noticing it. Route 79 approaches town from the South Side, curving below the cluster of rounded loaves that includes Union Street Hill, where my grandfather and grandmother had lived. A big-deal slab of limited-access-pavement now connects 79 with Third Street, the main link with the center of town — the better to shuttle tourists back and forth to Mark Twain Cave with its umbilically attached souvenir shop. The slab obliterated the old grid of local streets that had conveyed my grandfather's Packard across Bear Creek ("So called, perhaps," Twain once dryly observed, "because it was always so particularly bare of bears"). The slab in fact wiped out the small and modest Bear Creek Bridge itself, so low and intimate with the creek, and often submerged by its floodwaters. It also eliminated the need, or the opportunity, to wait in one's car for the passage of a hundred-car freight-train — click-*click,* click-*click,* click-*click.* Now a humped and floodproof causeway launches traffic at projectile speed from 79 toward the traffic signal at Third and Broadway.

I reached the intersection at a red light and used the pause to scan Broadway east and west. Hannibal hardly looked like a town in the throes of a sesquicentennial. I was not sure what I'd expected — throngs on Broadway, perhaps; the street roped off to traffic; sandbags and guy-ropes holding tents up; yellow lights and calliope music; Officer Capp twirling his billy club. What I saw was a small town asleep on Sunday.

The light changed and the driver behind me honked his horn — a taste of New York right here in the heartland. A pickup truck on Broadway accelerated and backfired. I turned right and eased my car down toward the river.

There were no people strolling the streets. No booths, no exhibits. The only evidence of a seven-month celebration was fastened to the streetlight stanchions. On each one flapped a banner that bore the sesqui logo — the commercial logo consigned to St. Louis and wrought in St. Louis. It made a weird sort of symmetry — a sterile and insubstantial design announcing an invisible celebration.

I checked into a gracefully restored guest house on South Fifth, directly across the street from the public library's granite steps and a short block south of what used to be the Tom Sawyer Theater, facing onto Broadway. The Victorian-style lodging stood next door to a somewhat more modest and unrestored two-story wood-frame building with chipped white paint. Its address, I realized, corresponded to a number I had copied into my notebook from a city directory of 1937: the building had been a rooming house then, the first place my father had lived when Bill Helm assigned him the Hannibal territory.

I spent the first two days of the week loafing around Hannibal. My shyness at the prospect of being spotted on the street began to wear off. I began to relax in the spring weather and play at a sort of make-believe. I pretended that I really had reentered the old town, the old coordinates. I experimented with the notion that Hannibal was not *that* remote from my New York life; that air travel had collapsed all distances; that I could afford the fares, maybe indefinitely. I began to live out a sort of recurring dream that people experience sometimes after having visited a remote and enchanting island or seashore: the dream, tinged with a sense of Icarus-like power, of *instant access back;* the ability to step from a crowded city street and into hyacinth-scented paradise.

I would awaken from my antique-washbasin guest-house room in the soft and chilly dawn and stroll the empty downtown streets with my hands in my pockets, heading north up into the steep old neighborhoods where Dulany and I had prowled. The yellowing gothic houses, many with cavernous porches that meandered around a corner to the side, leaned out of plumb under their figured cupolas and cornices; it was as though their muscles had gone flaccid with age. The lace curtains in the windows were drawn; I imagined old women with bird feeders in the backyards and history, framed in ovals, on the wallpapered walls.

After obligatory breakfasts at the Becky Thatcher — the waitresses were beginning to treat me as a regular — I would read histories of the town at the library, where the courteous and helpful librarian, Ann Sundermeyer, piled my desk high with reference volumes I hadn't known existed. Then I would stroll to the historic district and the Mark Twain Museum, bid good morning to Jane Hornback, and climb a narrow stairway to a small, cluttered office on the second floor. There I could usually find an hour or so of the best conversation available in Hannibal, or perhaps anyplace else, in the person of the museum's young curator, a gifted historian and raconteur named Henry H. Sweets III.

Henry Sweets's rotund father had been a landmark character in my boyhood — the head of pathology at Hannibal's two hospitals, a man of healing securely in touch with the ancient verities.

The son now presided over the small jewel of a Twain museum with some of the same deep, formalistic reverence for the past and its riches. Henry Sweets's office was a cameo museum in itself —

chockablock with its yellowing maps of the town and the river, its haphazardly stacked oil paintings and etchings from the nineteenth century, and its sublime clutter of old books and periodicals dealing with some facet of Mark Twain lore.

From the center of this happy dishevelment, Henry Sweets's voice would rise in some mellifluous recitation of town fact or Twain anecdote. It was a voice too big for the room, really; a voice designed for the tenor registers of Protestant hymnsong or for the lectern in an age before lavaliere mikes — a connoisseur's voice piped up from the capacious Sweetsian midsection with plenty of decibels in reserve—a voice of I-Speak-for-America oratorical winners and masters of ceremonies on Fourth of Julys.

I loved listening to him — loved the peculiarly nineteenth-century phrasings of his stories, as if this horn-rimmed young man (I put him at roughly ten years my junior; I had not known him as a child) had managed not only to store the eternal town in his memory but actually, by dint of encyclopedic knowledge, to inhabit it. We were both in love with the same beautiful chimera, Henry Sweets and I; but Sweets had come the closer to possessing her, having become her proprietor.

Besides his day-to-day duties as the museum's curator, Sweets managed several other projects. He edited and published a quarterly newsletter of scholarship and stories regarding Mark Twain, called *The Fence Painter*. He was an original (and surviving) member of the Sesquicentennial Commission — where his role, I gathered, was to be the obligatory pleader, mostly in vain, on behalf of more emphasis upon the historical presence of Twain amidst the raft races and the Good Golly Aunt Polly events. (There was a certain bittersweet price attached to being Hannibal's ranking Twain custodian, at least in the 1980s.)

Henry Sweets's other notable project was almost Faustian in its presumptions. In the hands of any other living person — perhaps save Dulany himself — it could easily be taken as an act of historical ghoulishness. Henry Sweets was cutting into the sacred Boyhood Home itself: fileting it, laying its westernmost wall open for viewing through a series of glass panels.

The rehabilitation, as Sweets described it, was necessary. In the century and a half of the house's existence (Judge Clemens had built it in 1844), the ground level along Hill Street had risen in relation to the foundation. Moisture had seeped in to weaken the old wooden beams in the earth. Meanwhile, the accumulated weight of thousands of visitors a year had placed undreamed-of stress on the judge's domicile; its framework sagged visibly and the floors and walls were alive with creaks.

Under Henry Sweets's guidance — I imagined the shade of his doctor-father looking on with approval at his son's diagnosis and prescription — a two-story "viewing gallery" of brick foundations and wooden beams, artfully concealed from view on Hill Street itself, would be erected in the narrow corridor separating the home from the museum. Ascending a staircase from the museum's rear garden, visitors would be able to look in on Tom's room, the middle bedroom (which had been closed off to visitors trooping through the home itself) and the parents' room. They would then pass through a new doorway in the museum wall and descend a stairway to the first-floor level, where they would view the parlor, the dining room, and the kitchen.

It was an ingenious project, and it filled me with awe. I, who had suffered glaze-eyed through a hundred herded tours through a hundred forgettable "attractions" in varying degrees of tricked-up quaintness, could never shake a feeling of clammy fascination as I set foot inside this leaning old dollhouse with its tangible, almost suffocating aura of occupancy by a suprahistorical force. Perhaps my senses were quickened by personal ghosts: John Winkler's voice was on the coin-activated narration machines. Whatever the reason, the home was the only shrine that ever felt like a shrine to me. I was appalled and yet envious of Henry Sweets's audacity at cutting into it. As long as the motives were provably noble, I would have liked to take a preservationist divot or two from the old homestead myself.

After my morning chin-sessions with Henry, I would cross the redbrick street (the block was sealed off to traffic now; no more oddly colored license plates) to the Becky Thatcher Book Shop, a bell tinkling as I opened the door to John Winkler's old domain. A middle-aged couple named Charles and Ruth Anton presided over the crowded shop now; I would exchange town gossip with them and stare at the tourists who came in, ducking and squinting, to ask about condensed editions of *Huckleberry Finn.*

I pointed my rented car up the steep blacktop lane leading to Lover's Leap. A footpath had risen there in my childhood, skirting the druidic ruins of WPA benches and gazebos fashioned out of fieldstone. More recently the town fathers had turned the bluff into an asphalt parking lot and put up a cyclone fence along the edge, waist-high, giving the primal vista an institutional look, like the grounds of a nuclear reactor. I indulged a vision of Michael Jenkins climbing over the fence, careful of his Mark Twain pants. Still, the view of the town, the river, and the bridge remained magnificent, and I could see, in the foreground below me, the scars of uprooted railroad tracks radiating outward from the circular scab where the roundhouse used to be.

I drove up Union Street Hill and idled in front of the last house on Booker Street, where the neighborhood ended above the down-sloping apple orchard. The trees had grown tall enough to all but obscure the old vista of the Mississippi framed by Lover's Leap and Cardiff Hill, and the house itself looked absurdly tiny — could my parents have fallen in love on that little indentation of a porch? — but otherwise everything was intact, including the imitation brick siding that my grandfather himself had nailed up on the sides of the detached garage, where he stored his Packard.

I made a pilgrimage up the old meadow in the middle of town, along Laclede Street, and I looked again at Rose Hill and Skylands, secret and unobtrusively foreign as embassies behind their bordering hedgerows and fir trees. I didn't stop. Ida Estelle Winkler would not return to town from Florida for another half-month, and I didn't want to explain myself to some unfamiliar, suspicious groundskeeper. The old houses, I could see, had not budged as much as a minute through time.

I drove out to Mark Twain Lake late one afternoon. The spring's woodland blossoming had improved its effect, and the fingers of water sparkled; but I still could not bring myself to regard it as charming. Joanna's small grid lay down there somewhere. I sat on a rock for a while and arced some pebbles into the lake, increasing its pool elevation a little; and then I drove back to town.

I visited friends. One night I went down to the railroad tracks near the riverfront, beneath the great hulking cylinders of the grain elevator, and ate dinner by myself at the Bordello ("Skirt Steak," smirked the menu). A couple of tables over, a skinny man and a red-faced beefy woman, separated by a pitcher of beer, were having the sort of discussion that often culminates in a knife fight. Moving to the bar, I ran into a cousin of my mother's, a squat flat-topped man who had retired from the railroad. He bought me a drink, and as he talked about the family — now mostly gone; dead, moved — his eyes filled with tears. I left the Bordello sensing and smelling the invisible Mississippi as it sluiced past me in the darkness, a hundred yards away. I felt for the first time the endless emptiness of night in a small town alone. I missed my own family, intact and vital and nine hundred miles distant. It was not true that one could step from a city street into paradise, nor could one step back again. I thought of some lines I'd read not long before; the opening verse of a John Ciardi poem: *I have a country but no town. Home ran away from me. My trees/ripped up their white roots and lay down./Bulldozers cut my lawn. All these/are data toward some sentiment/like money: God knows where it went.*

The next morning I gave up the pretense and got back to following the preoccupations of the time-present town. I went to a meeting of the Sesqui Commission.

CHAPTER XV

THE meeting was at 8:00 A.M. Sesqui headquarters had been moved from City Hall to its own location, behind the plate-glass window of a storefront on North Main Street, in a block of discount stores and knickknack shops and taverns. The space, a former television dealership, had been stripped of all its furnishings: besides a conference table and some chairs set up for the commission members, it now served mainly as an impromptu warehouse for billowing boxloads of sesqui souvenir items; sesqui buttons and bumper stickers and T-shirts and sweatshirts, all in what seemed to be the official sesqui colors of green and white, all featuring what I took to be the official sesqui symbol and slogan (as distinct from the official sesqui logo) — a cartoon drawing of Hannibal the Frog, encircled by the words "Hannibal's Jumpin'!"

The commission members ambled in, each new arrival opening the door to let in a blast from a pneumatic drill out on the street, each pouring out a cup of coffee — paper cups in plastic holders — from the pot brewed by Pamela Lyng. Most of the commissioners sported "Hannibal's Jumpin'!" buttons. I nodded at Gene Hoenes, covering for the *Courier-Post,* and at Henry Sweets in his horn-rims and short sleeves. There was some throat-clearing and some strained talk about last night's thunderstorm. I sensed that commission meetings were not exactly occasions for raucous horsing around.

Dean Eshelman, the financial chairman, read his report: revenues, $252,000; expenses, $277,000. A $25,000 deficit. Some more throat-clearing. Executive director John Lyng, looking the picture of rectitude in a short-sleeved white shirt and necktie, tendered his resignation as a commission member ("I can't be the boss and a member at the same time"). Cathie Whelan, the administrative coordinator, reported that Hannibal Cable TV had donated two hookups for the new headquarters window so that the schedule of events, transmitted on Channel 7, could be displayed. "We need two TV sets from anyone," she noted. Dick Halsor said to contact local TV dealers — "get 'em signs saying 'donated by.' "

Pamela Lyng reported that she had obtained two mannequins "from the waist up" from the Famous, a woman's shop down the street, to be used for promotional window displays. Buckhorn Rubber had lent the chairs. The O'Donnell Funeral Home had supplied Cathie's small desk. Some extra trash cans were still needed.

"We're expecting Aunt Polly today," Cathie Whelan remarked, and I stared at her for a moment before I realized that she was referring to another molded-rubber mask and costume to be worn by a volunteer on weekends. Rhonda Trosen, the young and demure projects supervisor, reported that unfortunately there had been little response on the Youth Hobby Show. "We'll have a kite-building session on Friday night," she informed the commission. "We need word-of-mouth. Mention it to your friends."

Cathie Whelan put a match to a cigarette, waved it out, and said through a puff of blue smoke that an ad hoc committee was needed for tent decoration. Dick Halsor put in that such a committee was also needed for tent repair — there was a hole in one of the tents from the rainstorm of the previous night.

John Lyng gave a report on the theme stage. "We've got more people working on it now than ever before," he said. Regarding the land acquisition, "We're working on it. There is tentative approval of purchase prices. The theme stage remains on track. . . ."

I sat sipping my coffee and listening to these voices eddy and flow, in their familiar rhythms, in this dim and dingy little storefront room in drowsing Hannibal, the pneumatic drill brrrrrping and brrrrrping out on the street. I tried to square the scale of the things they were droning about on this morning with what they must have been talking about a year before. I tried to recall what it had felt like to conjure the sesqui of Alfred Stern's "magic letter"; the imperial sesqui of the fireworks and the daily parades and the musicals in world premiere, the sesqui of a million visitors and a $5 million budget and a $250 million yield in revenues; the sesqui that would thrust Hannibal up from the damnation of twentieth-century river-town blight and usher in a kingdom of marketing on the banks of a liquid stream of gold, forever and ever, amen, sing hallelujah and Wake Up to Missouri!

I tried to weigh all that hypothetical grandiloquence, those world-class ambitions, against the reality of these people sitting half-silhouetted by the morning window light; these people with their cigarettes and coffee and their automobile payment booklets and their service-club pins. Some of these people had been vilified around town for their efforts; most had been ridiculed; one of them had seen his political career dashed. And here they sat, surrounded by souvenir T-shirts, talking of ad hoc committees and the need for extra trash cans.

"We've got a problem with the excitement we've generated," John Lyng was informing his fellow commission members. He raised his hands to tick points off on his fingers. "Number one, maintaining that level of excitement. Number two, when you generate excitement, people come in and give you a list of ten more things to do."

To say the least. Around the table, heads nodded soberly at this shaft of insight. Which was real — the calculating and headstrong boy mayor who unleashed the torrents of "excitement" on his town in the first place? Or this staid and innocent townsman so starchily mindful of outside influences?

Had anyone in this room, Lyng included, understood the exact nature of the alchemy that had been set brewing in Hannibal's name, or the implications of its spreading vapors? Had anyone taken the full measure of what had nearly happened to the town —

of what had in fact happened? Or of what that happening implied for the times, the country, the forces blindly working to separate a culture from its past?

Around the table, the talk had turned to rock concerts. At the end of May, the amphitheater would open its scheduled series of musical events. There were some big names coming to Hannibal: the Ozark Mountain Daredevils, Pat Hazel and Duke Tomato, NBC's Doc Severinsen. There was some wariness expressed regarding the presence of rock bands in Hannibal. The sort of crowds they would draw; the "element." Should the rock concerts be taken off the calendar?

At this suggestion, several heads swiveled toward the rear of the storefront, toward a small, lighted alcove behind Pamela Lyng's coffee machine. I had glimpsed a man moving around back there when I came into the sesqui headquarters for the meeting. I hadn't recognized him. He seemed different from the citizens around the conference table. I'd had a fleeting impression of shoulder-length hair, of someone talking into two telephones at once; I'd had a sense of *total energy*.

I caught Cathie Whelan's glance and raised my eyebrows. Soundlessly, she mouthed two words: "*Mad Dog*."

Aha. I'd heard of him. If Mad Dog was here, it was a lead-pipe cinch that no rock concerts were going to be taken off any calendars. Mad Dog's presence signaled something crucial about the Mark Twain Sesquicentennial, something I had not picked up from the tenor of the meeting itself. It signified that in spite of all the reversals, the humiliations, the broken plans — in spite of all this, the sesqui had not abandoned its dreams of national grandeur. It meant that John Lyng and his ever-shifting cadre of assistants still clung to some vestige of Alfred Stern's original promise. There was still a chance for Hannibal to go big-time with its celebration, and that last chance was embodied now in the person of Mad Dog Manus.

The meeting dawdled on toward its conclusion. I itched for the first decent chance to slip back to the alcove and say my howdies to Mad Dog. At the table, a commissioner was droning about the need for good *marketing* of entertainment, rolling the word around as if it were an exotic curiosity, a new kind of microchip. Someone else wanted to know what to do about railroad noise during a concert — the tracks ran within yards of the amphitheater site. Clearly, this *was* a bit of exotica — no one, apparently, had thought of it. "What are you going to do?" the commission member kept demanding. "The train comes by, and they're playing, and what are you going to do?" No one seemed remotely on the verge of a solution. There were shrugs, some rueful grins.

Someone else changed the subject — the town's largest company, American Cyanimid, had agreed to sponsor Hal Holbrook as Mark Twain.

"Hal Holbrook and Bill McLinn," a commissioner muttered. "We're gonna have dueling Twains."

"I'm in the midst of an interview now," snapped Mad Dog, slapping a hand over the telephone receiver as John Lyng steered me toward the alcove. "We've just announced Air Supply."

I could see at once why Mad Dog might be the answer to John Lyng's prayers for salvation. He gave the impression of being, if possible, even less interested in backyard barbecues than Jim Gladwin had been. Everything about him radiated *major,* radiated *contacts,* radiated *rock and roll.* In fact, I'd heard whispers that he had toured with Canned Heat, toured with the Beach Boys. Bruce, he may have known, and Billy and possibly Tina. Mad Dog was the sort of guy who could have been from anywhere and everywhere — the *road* was where he gave the impression of being from, mainly. I was a bit surprised to learn that he was in fact from Quincy.

"I was in Florida on vacation when I got a call from a KGRC guy up here," said Mad Dog, abruptly dropping the phone on its switchboard cradle and launching our interview without transition — my visible notepad and pencil had obviously caught his interest. "They asked me on advisement on certain projects. I saw certain things that needed shaping up right away, things like — let's say I saw certain things. I came into a situation where I had six weeks where I should have had two and a half years. Okay? I was hired to be a shark. I was hired to be a terminator." A light on the switchboard flickered and Mad Dog jammed it down, snatching up the receiver: "*Manus.*"

This was fun. For all Manus seemed to know, I was a reporter from *Rolling Stone*. I decided to go with it. The flow, the moment. While Manus barked orders into the telephone, I nodded to an imaginary beat, chewed an imaginary stick of gum, and jotted down some descriptive notes. Some perceptions. I wanted to evoke the man's style, his whole essence. I wanted my readers to have a concept of Jack Manus, total personality.

I noticed that despite his powerful shoulders and a certain bear-like way of moving, Manus dressed against type. Very three-piece suit, very collar pin, very pocket watch *and* digital wristwatch — with all this plus the long gold hair, he was pulling several statements together.

"That's very positive stuff," Manus was saying into the receiver, and I decided, *yes,* that was it! Mad Dog Manus was into a whole positive karma.

My perception was confirmed when Mad Dog hung up and turned to me again. "I'm not a normal rock person," he told me. "I don't drink, take drugs. I try to be a respectable type in an unrespectable area. I've been twelve years in the business — I just turned thirty-one. Agent, tour manager. I toured with Canned Heat. Now I've got my own business in Quincy — Mad Dog Productions. I came to the sesqui because there's a certain virginity of trust here. Okay?"

He had been brought on board in April after the previous entertainment consultant, a St. Louisan named John Camie, had begged to be released from his contract. "I can do little to assist you in securing talent," Camie had written in his farewell letter to Dick Halsor, the finance chairman, "because of the lack of funds necessary to hold these groups as well as the tenuous situation of the amphitheater construction." Camie went on to complain that in his last visit to Hannibal he had brought a stack of entertainment contracts to be signed. "It seemed," he wrote, "that there were other things of more pressing importance and the contracts and the ticket sales were never discussed and therefore I felt that it was a total waste of my time and effort. . . . It is my professional opinion," Camie had concluded, "considering present managerial, operational and fiscal handicaps that are the reality of the situation, an extension of our services would not promote the interest of either the Celebration nor of our company."

Camie's sour opinion of the sesqui people had been returned in spades. Dick Halsor, for one, took an exceedingly dim view, to say the least, of the amounts on those entertainment bills the promoter had presented. "He was taking acts, booking them for two times what they actually should have cost us," Halsor had told me several weeks earlier. Then Halsor had added what seemed almost the obligatory coda to any discussion about sesquicentennial expenditures: "Quite honestly, there had been little or no accounting done."

Not that Camie's successor was greeted with olive branches and "Hannibal's Jumpin'!" buttons by everyone concerned. A sizable faction within the commission had approved Camie's general tendency to book "family" types of concert groups instead of rock bands. They agreed with his assessment, often stated, that "Hannibal is not rock 'n' roll. Hannibal is family; Hannibal is children." This same faction was stonily unimpressed by Mad Dog's traveling credentials: they referred to him not as a promoter but as a roadie, and shrank back from his hip, take-charge style.

Nevertheless, one fact seemed inescapable in the changing of concert promoters: in falling back on Mad Dog Manus, the Sesqui Commission had made yet another concession to "local" as opposed to "outside" management of the festival. Once again, it seemed belatedly obvious that the local choice had been the preferable one all along. For all his self-dramatizing and his downtown ways, Jack Manus did have legitimate contacts within the music industry. Moreover, he understood the bottom line: he understood how much was too much to pay, not only for groups but for lighting, sound, amenities. Within days after he had come to the sesquicentennial, Mad Dog Manus had nailed down the first firm commitment from a "name" star — NBC's Doc Severinsen, whom he secured for an impressively modest $10,000. And now, on this morning, Mad Dog had struck again: he was able to "announce" the Australian group Air Supply — not exactly Twisted Sister, maybe, but a band with some Top-Forty cachet among younger teenaged audiences.

"I was student body president in college," Manus was telling me now — moving along to the reflective-history portion of our imaginary *Rolling Stone* interview, perhaps with his community image very much in mind. "I'm very interested in people. My whole life has been related to understanding people. I'm interested in the young people of this area. People think that because this is Mark Twain's home district, there are no problems. Well, they're wrong. Okay? Today's kids are defining themselves a lot quicker. I find, essentially, two cultures of kids here. . . ."

Mad Dog went on like that for a few more minutes, until the small switchboard on his desk began to flicker again, possibly with more positive commitments from more major groups. I wished him well, a genuine wish, and left the sesquicentennial headquarters. Soon it would be time to return, for a while, to my other life in New York.

But no sooner had I stepped onto the rain-washed pavement of North Main Street — where the daily town life unfolded, as it always seemed to, absent any tangible reference to the presence of a summer-long celebration — than I was struck with a thought that branded me irrevocably as a townsman, and not a very contemporary one at that.

What about rock concerts? I asked myself. *Are they — well — right for this particular festival? What about the — well — "element" they might attract? What's wrong,* I asked myself to my own horror, *with a good polka band? What did we elect Richard Cerretti for, anyway?*

CHAPTER XVI

HANNIBAL drifted into the years beyond its centennial with happy dreams for its future. The town had prospered a little from the jubilee, despite the Depression's frugalities and despite the rain-drenched failure of its central event, the pageant, with its soggy Masque of Nations. Some of the organizers totaled things up and figured that two hundred thousand visitors had come to take a squint at Mark Twain's hometown.

Most of those visitors had arrived by passenger train. Automobile travel from the populous east was constricted by the absence of a highway bridge across the Mississippi — motorists crossing from Illinois had to risk the old Wabash bridge, bumping along over wooden ties for the railroad tracks that linked Chicago with Kansas City.

But the year 1936 would mark the end of that era. In 1936, Hannibal would leap boldly into the automobile age. By the fall of that year, the Mark Twain Bridge would be complete. The population stood at its peak — 22,761. It was clearly time to consolidate the town's future and its past, to integrate its mercantile interests with its exploitable Tom 'n' Huck heritage — and thus join Hannibal inextricably to the vital conduits of the nation.

In March it was announced that a Mark Twain Commission would be organized, for the purpose of perpetrating the Twain traditions in Hannibal. Twenty-seven committee members were chosen. Dulany Mahan, the Colonel's son, was elected one of two vice-presidents.

The hometown author's status in the wider world seemed to be underscored in April, when a library in St. Louis unveiled a bust of Clemens that had been executed in 1915 by an Italian sculptor named Vittor. "The bust," reported the *Courier-Post*, "depicts Mark Twain as having beetle brows, windblown hair and a slightly hooked nose. Persons at the unveiling who knew Mark Twain in life commented it appears to be an excellent likeness."

The bust had been purchased largely with a $200 gift from the honorary president of the International Mark Twain Society, the Italian premier Benito Mussolini.

The heritage movement received its first rebuff in June. The City Council voted unanimously to kill a proposed ordinance that would set a $75,000 bond-issue election in August for the construction of a Mark Twain Museum and the purchase of necessary land.

The museum would have enclosed the Boyhood Home on Hill Street, allowing space for the exhibition of Twain relics and related articles.

The *Courier-Post* was furious. "For many years," it fumed in a June 16 editorial,

> Hannibal had the dubious reputation of not fully appreciating the greatness of its world-famous son. Last year the centennial celebration staged here did much to remove this blemish and no less an authority than the official publication of the National Geographic Society, referring to this event, called Hannibal "the best-known small city in the United States." Would the aldermen prefer to revert to the days when visitors openly charged Hannibal with not adequately recognizing the man the world has placed among the greatest in literature?

The editorial of course omitted any reference to the more recent decline in Clemens's literary cachet among such critics as Lewis Mumford and Van Wyck Brooks. In any case, it was almost certainly a sensitivity to Hannibal's Depression-depleted fortunes, and not academic caution, that inhibited the council.

The very day after the *Courier-Post*'s outraged editorial came an announcement from Hollywood that kindled enormous excitement in the town. Selznick International Pictures had purchased film rights for *Tom Sawyer,* and a contingent from the movie colony would arrive in the area to gather data on local scenes to be used in the filming.

The Hannibal newspaper assigned a correspondent to travel with the Selznick people. On July 21 came a somewhat dismaying dispatch — buried as tactfully as possible in the body of the story.

The movie group had paid a visit to Clarksville, thirty-five miles south of Hannibal on the Mississippi, the report began, "and also visited New London and, making a wide swing by automobile, was scheduled to call at Hardin and Hamburg, Ill." Then came the crusher.

"It will not be possible to film the picture in Hannibal," the newspaper quoted the research director, one Eric Stacey, "as the setting requires a town with a riverfront neighborhood having no factories, telephone poles or business buildings.

"This is necessary in order to create the atmosphere of the look, the time of which was the period 1835–1845.

"The setting would be ideal, with all the original scenes of the story located here," Stacey said, "but the growth of Hannibal has created modern industrial scenes which would not fit into the setting of the picture."

Hannibal was too modern to authentically replicate its own past! The notion projected some nice ironies fifty years into the future. And although the town had received something of a custard pie in its face from its first direct brush with the image-engineers of the twentieth century, the *Courier-Post* remained dutifully impressed with the visitors from Lotus Land.

"The research work on the picture will be tremendous," the paper assured its readers, "and thousands of subjects must be checked and verified for accuracy before even the work of writing the dialog [sic] is started."

On July 22 the newspaper reported with commendable sportsmanship on the qualifications of Hannibal's likely cinematic usurper.

> Clarksville, a pleasant, cultured town 35 miles south of Hannibal on the Mississippi, is the most adaptable for the film of any located thus far, Stacey said, but the setting is handicapped somewhat by not having a steamboat wharf or landing of the type used in the old river days. . . .
>
> The motion picture director [sic] said that Hannibal probably will be used as a base of operations if it is decided to use a location in this section. . . .

The next day the paper gave its readers a glimpse into the hell-for-leather pace of a Hollywood research crew:

> The crew drove nearly 400 miles in three states yesterday in search for a possible location. . . . Today they remarked that they had eaten their morning meal in Hannibal, at noon in Hamburg, Ill., and their evening meal in Keokuk, Ia.

The Selznick people went so far as to screen-test a "typical" Tom Sawyer from the area, selected in a contest by none other than Nina Clemens Gabrilowitsch of Detroit, Mark Twain's granddaughter. The typical Tom turned out to be the thirteen-year-old son of Clarksville's mayor. A newspaper photo showed a stolid, placid-faced boy in a straw hat, gripping a paintbrush as if it were a briefcase. He did not make the final auditions. The Selznick people went back to Hollywood, and Hannibal's dreams of playing itself in the movies faded.

In September, President Roosevelt arrived to dedicate the Mark Twain Bridge. On November 30, the Hannibal Chamber of Commerce observed the 101st anniversary of Mark Twain's birth by presenting to the city the property adjacent to the Boyhood Home, for use as a museum. The money had been raised through a popular subscription. The property's first owner had been Moses Bates, the founder of Hannibal, the *Courier-Post* reported, and editorialized,

> It is an encouraging sign to those who are anxious to preserve here those Mark Twain traditions . . . that the reaction [to acquire the building] has been so spontaneously favorable. Hannibal cannot allow a dwindling interest in things relating to Mark Twain when the world is giving him a greater place each year.

George A. Mahan died on December 16. In August 1937, WPA laborers removed the existing building from the land next to the Boyhood Home and constructed the Mark Twain Museum from native stone. In 1938 the Selznick studios released *The Adventures of Tom Sawyer,* with child actors Tommy Kelly and Ann Gillis portraying Tom and Becky. Glossy stills from the movie are still on display at the museum.

Hannibal, its dreams disturbed but not dashed, drowsed onward.

CHAPTER XVII

"I ALWAYS knew that I was going to win," Mayor Richard Cerretti was explaining to me in his office at Hannibal City Hall. "I lost not a minute's sleep worrying about anything. I don't know where you are in your faith, or if you have a faith. But when I was deciding whether to run for mayor, I went to my pastor. He told me that God wants Christians in business, in politics. He wants Christians ruling the world instead of heathens."

The tiny office might have been a temporary hideout for a man on the lam, so stripped was it of ornamentation or even identifying marks. The large charcoal drawing of John and Pamela Lyng was gone, of course — but no depiction of the Cerretti family had replaced it on the wall. The mayor and I sat in facing cushioned chairs. Beside us was a small desk, its polished surface innocent of phone messages, correspondence, any of the usual appurtenances of authority. In fact the only symbol of any kind in the room was the fishpin — two intersecting bars of curved gold — fastened to Richard Cerretti's starched shirt collar; his emblem of Christian faith.

This was several months before anyone knew about the hidden tape recorder.

"Our church is the All Faith Fellowship," Cerretti told me, seeing that I was staring at his pin. "The service is led by the Spirit, and not tradition. There's a freedom in the worship — a freedom to wave your arms, sing and speak in tongues, dance in the Spirit. Five years ago I was too inhibited to let my emotions be a part of my worship. Not anymore. Somebody who was listening to the Spirit came to me and said, 'Roll your cares over on Jesus.' "

He ventured a smile — a wispy little man in rimless glasses who sat with his knees pressed tightly together, who spoke in an inflectionless voice just above a whisper, and who fidgeted almost like a child as we spoke — sometimes leaning forward to peer at me, sometimes smoothing his necktie or patting out the sleeves of his shirt.

He scarcely seemed like the ranting tyrant I'd heard about at the Holiday Inn meeting, the imperious demander of the sesqui's financial records, the spurner of reporters' questions — "the ayatollah," as Larry Weil, for one, had taken to calling him. Cerretti's letter to me in New York, granting my request for an interview, had been almost shy. He would not mind my questions, he had written, and in fact looked forward to my visit. "I'll give you fair warning, though," he added, "that I am not a politician and haven't yet learned how to couch my responses in political rhetoric. If you can tolerate that we'll get along fine. . . ."

That sounded more than tolerable to me, and in the middle of June, back to Hannibal I stole.

I had spent an itchy month in New York, restless for this opportunity. The town and its travails, its intrigues — never mind the past now — had me hooked. At my office, I had pored over each new issue of the *Courier-Post* before I read the *New York Times* or the *Wall Street Journal.* The new mayor and the City Council had declared war on each other almost as soon as Cerretti was sworn in; over budget cuts, over the hiring and dismissal of certain city employees. While the sesquicentennial languished and bled, Richard Cerretti replaced it as the number one issue in Hannibal.

I spent hours on the telephone talking to friends in Hannibal — "sources," as I came to think of them — when I should have been about my daily responsibilities. At night I lay in bed, my wife beside me and my children safe and near in the next room, and I smelled the Mississippi; I saw the minaret of a lighthouse and I heard the rhythms of Missouri voices. It was June, and I was restless to be back in the white town.

June would be a decisive month for the sesquicentennial, or what was left of it: Mad Dog Manus's big-name entertainment acts would start to hit the riverfront amphitheater now. In fact the amphitheater concert season had begun two weeks ago, May 31, with typically dismal results. The inaugural act, the blues singing team of Sam and Dave, whose "Soul Man" had been a hit single in the 1970s, had managed to lure only three hundred spectators, at $5 a ticket, to the fan-shaped asphalt slab that John Lyng had built to accommodate thousands. (Construction had been feverishly completed on the day of the concert.) The attendance was miserable despite a front-page preview piece by Gene Hoenes in the *Courier-Post* clearly calculated to whip up a frenzy of interest: "With their vocals and arrangements of contemporary and original material, the group has a solid rhythm section augmented by horns that create a unique, fiery sound on the stage. . . ."

It didn't work. If Air Supply, the first "major" attraction, failed to significantly surpass that attendance level, the Sesqui Commission would be obliged either to cancel most of its bookings — including NBC's Doc Severinsen — or to declare bankruptcy.

But all of that paled, as I gathered from the papers and my sources, beside Richard Cerretti's wrathful visage upon the city throne. On June 4 the first of many Cerretti/council showdowns had flared, and Cerretti had been bloodied. The mayor had launched an attack against Harvard Ebers, the administrator in the controversial 312 loan program involving the Lyng brothers in 1981, and subsequently appointed city engineer by Mayor Lyng. Cerretti had tried to force Ebers's resignation. The council had voted 11 to 0 to renew Ebers's contract.

Already rumors were circulating that the deposed John Lyng was running a shadow city government from the back room at Fitzgerald's, setting out a series of parliamentary traps for the new mayor.

I couldn't stand it. I had to get back there.

To be sure, my restlessness was double-edged: on recent visits, my homesickness for my wife and sons had begun to press in on me from the flowered wallpaper during those bottomless summer nights in those restored "period" guest houses. My initial delight in the antique desk lamps and the quilted bedcovers had begun to fade toward an awareness of the waiting American Express Card machine. The desk lamps were hard to read by; the quilts were useless to me in the summer. Downstairs in the period parlor the television sat waiting. There was never a radio.

I had conquered my self-consciousness about moving around in Hannibal during the daytime. Nearly all my old friends and new acquaintances — the reporters in the *Courier-Post* city room, say — were used to seeing me by now. Meeting a familiar face no longer meant an awkward interval of explanation and ceremony. But the nighttime was a different matter.

At night in a small town, one's aloneness was blatant; it was a condition that practically required a civic response. There were invitations to dinner at people's houses. I accepted many and declined some. I wanted to avoid a pattern of forced hospitality. The dinner evenings satisfied a need for good talk and companionship without the subtextual combativeness of wit-maddened dinner parties in New York. But these evenings ended early — the empty cashew dish, the unfilled wineglass, the growing gaps between conversation. My hosts liked to be in their offices by eight the next morning. For me the Hannibal night stretched ahead. On evenings without invitations, the night was infinite — filled with the intimation, but not the substance, of other times, other friends, other rituals. It was strange that my intact memory of the town was furnished mainly with night images, but during these times of my return, it was night that most brutally exposed the artifice of reentry.

The remedies were scarce. The Bordello was nominally a restaurant. In fact it was an enclave of serious, huddled drinkers within the joke decor; a vestige of implosive riverfront bars all up and down the Mississippi for a century and a half. And there were older taverns along North and South Main that made the Bordello seem like a study in suburban high kitsch: taverns where the iconography of beer ululated in twisting, phosphorescent gizmos of fluids changing color and illuminated waterfalls that seemed to move with urinacious seduction on the walls — taverns where semicoherent tenderloin menus slanted downward along chalkboards, then trailed off like unfinished sentences; taverns where the frycook/bartender and the socket-eyed, cowboy-hatted clientele seemed equally capable, in their next lurching move, either of offering me a cuestick for a game of pool or of braining me with it. There were intelligent people in Hannibal who cherished these taverns. I could never unclench the muscles to certain vital organs once inside them.

Fitzgerald's was an unhappy alternative. I felt more at home in Fitzgerald's, with its spiffy polished hardwood and its done-up clientele of politicians and newspaper people and young town squires. (If John Lyng was running a shadow government from the back room, he certainly wasn't running it while I was in the vicinity.)

But in the very conviviality at Fitzgerald's lay my dilemma. These amiable people, who kept handing me over rounds of beer in frosted mugs, were the very people whom I would inevitably be writing about, not necessarily in the most salutary of terms. They knew that, and they handed over the beers anyway. The beers were not offered as inducements to kind treatment; they were gestures of an honest and reflexive hospitality.

I couldn't deny it — I liked these people. Hell, I felt more comfortable with them than with most of the people I knew in New York. But there was an agenda between us. I was there to inquire about a process that had seized their lives and the life of the town, a process that had blown in on them from somewhere else and swept them into extremes of choice and behavior that not even they could have dreamed possible before it all happened. And here came I, the detached and untainted observer, to ask them questions and draw inferences about their choice and behavior.

I was untainted not because of any moral superiority, but because of the accidental fact that I no longer happened to live in the town. What choices might I have made if I had still lived there? How would I have interpreted the early promotional promise of the sesquicentennial? What perspective would I have had on its possible consequences? *Would I have done any goddamn better?* These were the questions that hovered unasked over the frosted beers. Because I could not answer them — or perhaps because I feared that I could — I all but stopped going to Fitzgerald's after my first couple of visits back to town.

There was one other disquieting aspect of evenings at Fitzgerald's. The leading people of Hannibal talked about one another there, and not in the Emersonian chords of common democratic bond. God help the regular customer unfortunate enough to be missing on a given night. This was a pastime I had noticed in other venues of the town, but at Fitzgerald's it took on the solemnity and dedication of Florentine court gossip.

"Gossip" was not exactly the word for it — not gossip in the sense of speculation over people's alcoholic or sexual secrets, although those lines of discussion were hardly unknown. Low-grade character assassination might be closer to the mark — a steady *sotto voce* hum of withering opinion, casually and mordantly volunteered.

So-and-so was beyond his capacities as head of that civic service organization. He was isolated. No one took him seriously. So-and-so was a cowboy, reckless and naive. He'd gotten himself too far on the outside of his power base. So-and-so was a sycophant. He was too obvious in the way he cultivated the inner circle. Most of the real movers and shakers avoided him now. So-and-so tried too hard to get her way on the sesqui committees. No one had anything to do with her anymore. So-and-so was the real reason for her husband's failures — so gauche, so *blatant.*

So-and-so, I began waiting to hear someone declare, was overrated as a writer. He was an irresponsible child. Fundamentally barbaric. Why, the son of a bitch was as profound a biological failure as America has produced.

In the beginning, I was fascinated. I took an anthropologist's delight in the talk. Here, I thought, was an ideal way to begin indexing Hannibal's political and social factions. But as I became accustomed to the telltale symptoms — the narrowing eyes, the lowering voice, the pressure of fingers on my arm — I began to understand that Hannibal's factions were divisible down into units of one. There were no real alliances in this town; none, at least, that added up to a coherent agreement on what the town's long-term interests were. There was little inclination, in fact, even to speak of the long term beyond vague affirmations of the need for "growth" and "industry." There were only the opinions, harsh and ad hominem in their nature, round-robin in their cumulative travels around the bar: no one seemed beloved, immune, spared. I wondered whether this bleak and desultory letting of venom was a direct result of the sesquicentennial's blasted illusions, the dashed euphoria of common cause — or whether it was a symptom of something more fundamental to America's corroding image of itself.

Christopher Lasch's view of contemporary society as a "war of all against all" had a model in Hannibal, it seemed, as did the argument of the Berkeley sociologist Robert N. Bellah — recalling Tocqueville's warning — that American individualism has in our time grown cancerous; that it is destroying the integuments of community life.

I didn't know for sure about any of these connections. All I knew for sure, as I left Fitzgerald's bar at the ends of those evenings, the skin on my neck prickly, was that I wondered what they were saying about me. And what I would say about them.

There was one person in Hannibal about whom the opinion at Fitzgerald's was unified, and that was the small, wispy man who now sat opposite me in the mayor's office at City Hall.

"Cerretti will set us back," Larry Weil had assured me over a beer one night at Fitz's. "I'm told that the Department of Housing and Urban Development thinks he's a nut." In the next breath, Weil had verified John Lyng's status as the town's "shadow" mayor: "I've been there," he confided in a hushed tone, jerking his head toward the back room, "where councilmen come in seeking his advice."

The object of all this derision and intrigue merely smiled and shrugged his shoulders when I suggested to him that a narrow cabal was reputedly in charge of the town.

"It was the same with the sesqui," Cerretti remarked, as though the two of us were sitting on a bench in Central Park and shooting the breeze about the crazy folks across the street in City Hall. "John Lyng and Larry Weil — single-handedly, or in consort with Dick Halsor at Buckhorn, were intimately and by themselves controlling the business of the sesquicentennial. That is more fundamental to your understanding of what's happening in this town than anything else going on — that, and the fact that the local press was controlled."

I asked Cerretti whether he had declared for mayor to end this sewed-up approach to running Hannibal. What I learned was that, like so much else that happened in the town, the political rise of Richard Cerretti had its odd connectives.

He had never entertained a thought about politics virtually up until the day he filed for mayor of Hannibal. He had never even set foot in Hannibal for the first twenty-four years of his life, having wandered with his Bible-believing family around the towns of the Midwest, little towns in Illinois, Wisconsin, Kansas, while his fierce father preached the Gospel as revealed by the Moody Bible Institute of Chicago, Illinois.

"My father was a tyrant at home, though a preacher," said Cerretti, dreamily phrasing the sentence as though it were a written line from an inspirational book. "He showed me about hypocrisy."

He attended a tiny college in Kansas, a college named Sterling. "My father had gone there," he said. He met his future wife, Dorothy, there — a woman who bore him three children, a thin bespectacled woman who gazes somewhere to one side of the camera lens, from her kneeling position in front of the fireplace, for the official campaign portrait, and is otherwise missing from Cerretti's public universe. The two young Christians moved on together from

Sterling to the state teachers college in Pittsburg, Kansas, where Cerretti enrolled in some biochemistry courses, then switched to journalism. He ended up training himself to teach kindergarten.

He remembered clearly the decisive moment in his conversion. "I'd been taking some psychology courses at Pittsburg," Cerretti said. "Behavioral psych. I remember that one day, one of my teachers said, 'If you want to do anything beneficial to society, *get out of psych and into kindergarten.*'

"In other words," Cerretti interpreted, "instead of trying to deal with screwed-up adults, mold five-year-old children."

So profoundly taken with this wisdom was Cerretti that when he received a telephone call in 1970 from the superintendent of the Hannibal public schools, notifying him of a teaching opportunity in the sixth grade, the young educator firmly stood his ground.

"I said I would teach kindergarten or I would teach nothing at all," Cerretti proudly recalled.

The superintendent relented and the Cerrettis made their way to Hannibal.

Over the next four years, Richard Cerretti molded Hannibal's five-year-old children; in the summers, he worked toward a master's degree in early childhood education at the University of Illinois. By 1975 his pursuit of his life's destiny was earning him an annual salary of $8,750. He and his wife wanted to start a family. They needed first to find some other source of income.

The answer came swirling in on a flood. It was a Mississippi flood that lifted Richard Cerretti out of obscurity and deposited him in the main channel of Hannibal's civic life.

"I was in the National Guard during the big flood of 1973," Cerretti said. "The Guard had needed a photographer, so I was their photographer. I knew nothing about photography. Well, along came the flood and the armory was under ten feet of water. The colonel said, 'I want pictures.' I went up to a local studio in town — Don Sigler — and he taught me the trade. That's how we became acquainted."

(I remembered Don Sigler. A small, brisk, curly-haired man

with a high forehead and a permanently sweat-beaded brow — all those years of hot studio lights, no doubt — he had induced momentary blindness to generations of Hannibal schoolkids as the official high-school yearbook photographer. Each spring, as another consignment of sophomores, juniors, and seniors clattered toward the end of the production line, Don Sigler stood by with his lights and negative plates and black light-shielding drape, ready to capture us in attitudes that transcended our day-to-day grubbiness and distraction. His images of us somehow emerged like rows of unflagging high opinion on the glossy pages: the girls gazing poetically into the higher reaches of the universe or peering with muted allure over their cashmere shoulders, the flattopped boys staring foursquare into the destiny of the lens, pre-Vietnam faces, blandly assured.)

In 1975 Richard Cerretti bought out Don Sigler for a borrowed investment of $40,000. "It was a leap of faith," he told me with an enigmatic smile. Four years later he was doing well enough photographing soft-haired wedding couples and mortarboarded seniors to abandon his kindergarten career and move the business from its storefront on Broadway near the old Rialto Theater (now Robinson's Paint) building to a converted residence on the slopes of North Fifth, up behind the deserted YMCA. Richard Cerretti Photography now operated out of a handsome old Victorian stone house, the front door of which was festooned with a sticker that displayed the requisite community spirit: "PUSH for the Pirates / PULL for the Pirates."

Richard Cerretti might have gone on taking pictures of robust farmboys in their chocolate prom-night tuxedos for the rest of his days, had it not been for a bizarre and murky episode that thrust him into a public leadership role and provided him with an instantaneous constituency of five thousand citizens: the case of Sheriff Harold White.

In the meager inventory of Marion County success stories, in all of northeast Missouri's blasted landscape of striving, overmatched, inextricably mortal men, Harold White had once stood aloof and inviolate, a colossus, an almost solitary living ideal of midwestern manhood.

He had been elected sheriff of Marion County in 1976, at age forty-three, and reelected in 1980. His tenure as sheriff had generated a kind of giddy euphoria among the people of the county, these people so buffeted and maddened by so many crushing, abstract forces — the collapse of their scrupulously sustained farm economy and the culture it had defined; the cynicism and drift of their sons and daughters; and the growing obsessive conviction that nameless anti-American conspiracies in Washington were somehow at the root of it all. For nearly ten years these dazed and resentful people could take comfort in one deeply satisfying assurance: that if any communistic drug-dealing homosexual son of a bitch stepped out of line in Marion County, he would have Harold White in person to deal with, God help the sorry peckerwood.

I had heard Harold White's name mentioned around town before my conversation with Mayor Cerretti. "There has *never* been a law-enforcement officer I had more respect for than Harold White," Chris Straub, the principal of Hannibal High School, had told me. White, said Straub, had been just about the only grown-up on the local scene who could penetrate the glazed indifference that teenagers routinely awarded their elders. In the mid-1980s the Hannibal public school system faced an 8 percent annual dropout rate, two percentage points higher than the state average. (In Chris Straub's opinion this relatively high rate reflected one of the more unfortunate aspects of Hannibal's ties with its past — the old agrarian belief that a ninth-grade education was enough schooling for any child of the prairie.) Nearly half the students who remained in school were enrolled in a vocational (as opposed to a college-preparatory) curriculum.

"The scariest thing," Chris Straub had told me, "even scarier than the dropout rate, is the kid without any plans." Increasingly, the behavior patterns of these young people replicated the aimless pathologies associated with "street" kids in the urban poverty ghettos: depression, pregnancies, alcohol, drugs.

"The use of drugs by Hannibal High School students is way off," principal Straub had insisted to me — and then had added, ruefully, "unfortunately, the use of alcohol is way up. I don't care how many 'activities' they're involved in — sports, music, scholastics — they're drinking. A *tremendous* amount of peer pressure is exerted on our teenagers to drink. The depression that we see, and the drinking, are interrelated."

In February 1985, just days before my first visit, depression had claimed one of Hannibal High School's most promising students. A star football player and an honor student had shot himself to death.

The one living bulwark against this sort of nihilism had been Sheriff Harold White. The teenagers respected him. They listened to his cautionary talks, they admired his martinet's bearing, they feared his knock-heads approach to enforcing the law.

"You have no idea what kind of influence he had around here," Jim Cary, an old schoolmate of mine and now a leading Hannibal attorney, told me. "He brought so much class, so much decorum, to his job. He was the first sheriff to insist on uniforms for himself and his deputies. He came on like a spit-and-polish Marine. *Very* nattily dressed; every hair in place; slicked back; the Wildroot look. Not today's look at all. Shoes shined, razor creases in his pants, sunglasses.

"Harold was enormously popular in Marion County. It was like he lifted up everyone's standards. His personal charisma was just unbelievable. In a lot of ways, he was the best thing that ever happened around here."

It seemed to me, as I had listened to testimony after testimony regarding Harold White's epic stature, that the area had had a worthy successor to Officer Capp. In fact, about the only negative aspect to Harold White's law enforcement career, the only blemish on his image as a role model, was that on June 3, 1985, he began serving a ten-year federal prison sentence in Big Springs, Texas, on a conviction of conspiracy to distribute marijuana and two counts of perjury.

White's indictment, in 1983, had been the result of a two-year surveillance operation against the sheriff conducted by Missouri highway patrolmen and agents of the federal Drug Enforcement Agency. The surveillance turned up evidence that Sheriff White had accepted money from a marijuana dealer in the neighboring town of Palmyra. In return, White had supplied warnings about the extent to which the dealer was being tracked by federal agents.

The case produced several bizarre twists. Much of the evidence against White was secured via an unauthorized wiretap of the suspected drug dealer's telephone. (By that time the suspect, whose name was Rey Orta, had already been arrested by federal agents and had accepted an arrangement as a government witness in return for cooperating in the investigation against White.) During his trial, Harold White admitted he had made the damning remarks contained on the tape — "All eyes are on you," he warned Orta in one exchange — but denied that he had made them with criminal intent. "I was conducting my own investigation," White insisted. "I created the thought in his mind that I would help him and he needed me. Over several months, I purposely set the stage for that." White said he was taking matters into his own hands because he suspected that Orta was paying off members of the Palmyra and Hannibal police departments.

The law-enforcement authorities who were tracking White seemed almost equally confused in their mission. The wiretap had been ordered by the Palmyra police chief, a man named Junior Chamberlain, who later testified that he knew the tap was illegal, but did not realize that it was a federal offense. This innocence was shared, as it developed, by the Marion County prosecuting attorney, Warren Wells. Wells had allowed the tap to continue for nearly a week in April of 1983 before discovering how severely it was frowned upon by American jurisprudence.

Warren Wells — who received a great deal of publicity for his vigorous prosecution of White — shared law office space in Hannibal with John Lyng.

Despite all the bumbling in the wiretap matter, Harold White was unsuccessful in his attempt to get the case against him dropped on the ground of inadmissible evidence. A United States district judge named James H. Meredith upheld the evidence, commenting that "a criminal prosecution is more than a game in which the government may be checkmated and the game lost merely because its officers have not played according to the rules."

Meredith sentenced White to a ten-year prison term following his conviction. A panel of three appeals judges upheld the conviction, maintaining that the DEA had gathered enough evidence beyond the illegal wiretap to make their case against White.

The conviction hardly seemed to change anyone's high opinion of Harold White. Newspaper accounts described reactions of "shock," "grief," and "disbelief" when the verdict came in. Early in the trial, a group of citizens, including several ministers, had formed a legal defense fund for White — a fund that eventually raised more than $40,000. The group called itself SOS — Save Our Sheriff. Its chairman was a Palmyra pastor. Its treasurer was a Hannibal photographer named Richard Cerretti.

"White always struck me as a good man," was Cerretti's bland explanation for his involvement in the campaign. "I said, 'I wanna *do* something for that guy.' It's a very complex story. Not all the truth has been told yet. Not all the evidence has been presented." When I asked Cerretti what the truth was, he referred me to a tape-recorded interview that the drug dealer, Rey Orta, had made with a St. Louis television correspondent. "That reporter impressed me," Cerretti said. "He's told me he would stake his life that Rey Orta was telling him the truth, and that Harold White was not criminally involved."

(Some months after White's trial, Orta was arrested in St. Louis County and charged with unlawful use of a weapon — a single-shot Uzi submachine gun.)

SOS was not able to save Harold White from a criminal conviction. But the organization did help to sweep White's top deputy, Dan Campbell, to victory in the November general election by a margin of a thousand votes. And it created a constituency for Richard Cerretti.

The mayor acknowledged this with a shrug and a smile. "When it was time for the mayoral race, the SOS people came to me. I told them I didn't know precinct captains, I didn't know politics. I had no organization. I had no money to spend on a campaign. But I went to my pastor, and he told me that God wants Christians ruling the world, instead of heathens. So I lost not a minute's sleep worrying about anything. I always knew that I was going to win." Richard Cerretti paused, his knees pressed together, his pale hands crossed like a pair of gloves in his lap. He leaned forward, squinting for the next question, this starch-shirted claimant of Sam Clemens's old town, this mysterious stranger in his modern-day Eseldorf, drowsing in its own peace in the deep privacy of a hilly and woodsy solitude where news from the world hardly ever came to disturb its dreams.

It struck me that this hadn't been a very successful interview. I had learned a fair amount about Richard Cerretti's wandering history and his religious absolutism (if little about his theology) and his almost eerie — or miraculous — creation as a candidate. But I had learned almost nothing of how he felt about Hannibal, and certainly nothing about his political intentions — every question of that sort had been deflected with a serene shrug, a smile, a blink. In those endeavors, I had not been more successful than the voters of Hannibal. And yet the voters of Hannibal had elected him.

I decided to make one last attempt. Noting the difficulties he had already encountered with the City Council and the town's well-established suspicion of all leadership, I asked the mayor whether he thought Hannibal was ungovernable.

Richard Cerretti shrugged and smiled. "I hope not," he said mildly. "I hope not. I don't understand politics. I have tremendous faith in the people to make the ultimate decisions in what they want. . . ."

"There is talk that some of them want to impeach you," I said.

Richard Cerretti smiled. He shrugged. He leaned forward. "If impeached," he said, "I'll file again and I'll run again. And I'll win."

CHAPTER XVIII

I DASHED down the stairs and burst through City Hall's glass doors like a kid on the last day of school. No offense to His Honor, but I'd rather be outdoors. The June midday air brushed over my skin, and I smelled pollen from the green bluffs. Down at the end of Broadway the Mississippi surface burned white under the sun from a river-blue sky. The drowsing town stirred with hollyhocks and mailmen. This Monday was a clear note from a bassoon, a note held long and low.

I was beginning my longest stay of the summer in Hannibal—a week and a day. There would be time enough for me to explore the town and its festival in each of my guises, as an insider and as an outsider. The Air Supply concert was scheduled for the coming Saturday night at the amphitheater. I had bought my $10 ticket, and I would go and cross Bear Creek on the pontoon bridge and climb the bank and stand on the asphalt slab with a crowd that everyone prayed would number in the thousands. This would be the first rock concert I had ever attended; how amazing that it would prove to be in Hannibal.

The "insider" aspect of my holiday involved another sesquicentennial event, the first annual (it was hoped) Mark Twain Writers' Conference on the campus of Hannibal-LaGrange College. This was the event that, in the original projections of John Lyng, Larry Weil, and their consultants, would attract 30,000 participants. The actual number of faculty, staff, and enrollees was shaping up to be more like about 59, which was some 29,941 below peak estimates. But then, that was roughly consistent with other dropoffs in the sesqui.

As masterminded by Henry Sweets and Jim Hefley, the writers' conference promised to be a smorgasbord of scholarly and popular forums on writing. Henry had pulled together a small but impressive faculty of regional authors and Twain scholars. His prize attraction was Justin Kaplan, the distinguished Twain biographer — the Hal Holbrook, as it were, of literary exegesis — who would deliver the Thursday evening keynote address, "Huckleberry Finn and the Censors." The conference would encompass most of Henry's hopes for whatever serious attention the sesquicentennial might actually pay to Mark Twain's legacy, and Henry Sweets had overlooked nothing on the scale from art to commerce.

Classical genuflection would be served, in addition to Kaplan, by workshops on "The Recomposition of Huckleberry Finn"; on "The Literature of the Illinois Frontier"; on "Mark Twain from Archetypal Perspectives." For connoisseurs of the literarily arcane, there would be get-togethers on "Photography and Poetry: An Interdisciplinary Approach," and on "Kodalith, a Highly Contrast Film for Publication and Color Problems: Maximum Effect with Minimum Cost" — both sessions to be helmed by the redoubtable Dr. Al Beck of Culver-Stockton College — and on "Writing Turn-of-the-Century Melodrama." Finally, a bow to the participants' ineluctable brass-tacks priorities would be achieved through discourses on "Breaking into Print"; on "Submitting Your Manuscript"; on "Writing for Yourself: Getting Started"; on "Maintaining Control of Your Characters"; on "Making Your Story Current (as Mark Twain Did)"; and in the welcoming lecture, to be delivered on Tuesday morning by Marti Hefley, the Hannibal-LaGrange director of drama, world traveler, and coauthor of more than forty books with her husband, Jim. Mrs. Hefley's address was appetizingly advertised as "The Seven Steps to Motivation."

And there would be me.

Through Henry's influence, shamelessly, I had managed to get myself invited onto the faculty as a guest lecturer. On Thursday morning, I would offer some remarks on the topic of "Writing the Story of a Town." The easy, knowing jauntiness of that title was at odds with what I had already begun to appreciate as an almost unattainable quest. Judging by the notes I had taken and the couple of chapters I had already tried to sketch out, the gulf separating the tantalizing, orange-glowing town of my clandestine memory and my flailing attempts to embrace it was oceanic — galactic — infinite. "The Story of a Town," I had privately begun to suspect, was a fool's errand, a tortured dream of endless pursuit over a night-blackened landscape laced with sealed doors, ghosts, tunnels leading nowhere. For every wisp of remembrance that came hurtling back to me there were a thousand essential details that were forever beyond — just beyond — my grasp. Would the good, motivated, mostly Baptist students of the first annual Mark Twain Writers' Conference be prepared for these dark insights into the writer's challenge?

They would never have a chance to judge. They would never be troubled by a lecture so bleak. Writerly doubts aside, I was looking forward to my Thursday appearance with an eagerness that bordered on megalomania. Lord knew, it was not to be a seminal occasion in the history of the town, of the sesquicentennial, of the writers' conference — for sheer volume of impact, my talk would not rival the Thursday-morning turnover at Fern's White Rose Diner. And yet for me, numb and buzzing with my summer-long shuttle from present to past and back again, my appearance at the Hannibal-LaGrange lectern would represent nothing less than a culmination, a triumphal return to the kingdom that had known me only as a boy.

While still in New York, I had agonized for days over what to wear. Should I ascend the podium in the careless garb of the roguish writer, all bush-jacketed and open-collared, an artist who laughed at society's restraints? Or would it be more seemly to respect the decorum of the institution in whose hall I was speaking, and to appear in a self-effacing coat and tie? My deliberations had taken me to the men's furnishings floor of Saks Fifth Avenue, where I had myself fitted for a double-breasted seersucker suit with a thin stripe of robin's-egg blue — a suit versatile enough to wear either with a necktie or over a reckless open-collar shirt, depending on my last-minute instinct for the occasion.

(It was only after I had gotten the suit home that I came to grips with the fact that the necktie question was irrelevant — the seersucker made me look like nothing so much as a small-town Mississippi police chief, a sort of bearded Rod Steiger in *Heat of the Night.*)

There was another reason why I felt like skipping as I left City Hall. On this trip, I didn't have to sleep in the contrived and hollow ambience of some "period" guest house. This time in, I was sleeping at home: I was at Rose Hill. Mrs. Winkler had come back north from Florida, and had invited me to stay as her guest.

I was in Johnny's room, the second-floor room of Dulany's enigmatic and intellectual older brother — I had spotted a copy of *The Idiot* on his bookshelf while in high school and assumed it was a spoof of some kind, possibly a thick special edition of *Mad* magazine. Soft-eyed, aristocratic Johnny had been the son most like his father — he retained much of John Winkler's single-mindedness and his smoldering intensity — but the eldest son had quickly fled Hannibal and his father's ghostly preoccupations with the town: Johnny had set off for larger universes, better times. He found them at the Massachusetts Institute of Technology, where he earned a master's degree in physics; he lived on in Boston as a consultant for several engineering think tanks and, later, for the video software industry. The other three Winkler children had emulated Johnny's exodus: Chris, the youngest son, had set up a graphics-design firm in Milwaukee. Laura, the youngest child and only daughter, had pursued an artist's life in California.

And Duly — ah, the connectives, the weird finishing loops in the Story of a Town. After service as a Marine sharpshooter in Vietnam, feeling the concussion of a North Vietnamese bullet as it whined past his ear, Duly had become a radioman, a voice on the airwaves, a disc jockey and talk-show host in a string of towns and cities across America. He courted a beautiful raven-haired woman, became engaged, and lost her to a rival. A few years passed. The beautiful woman returned to him, a small daughter in tow, her husband disappeared into the radical underground. Dulany and Doris were married in May at Rose Hill. This time the newspaper notices were not so grand. The new family departed immediately for Dulany's next on-air gig, which happened to be in the state capital, Jefferson City. They bought a house on Tanner Bridge Road, which happened to be exactly two doors down the street from the house where Paul and Elvadine Powers lived.

Thus, in his late middle years — this was 1971 — my father found himself the neighbor of the rich boy from the mansion whose kitchen he had once penetrated; the rich boy who had once eaten all of his pancakes. And my father found himself listening to Dulany's voice on the radio as he dialed, searching the airwaves, as always, for larger universes.

I raced down from Chicago, where I was working, and Dulany and I went bear-hugging and circling one another, bawling out insults like Mississippi raftsmen right out on Tanner Bridge Road. Doris's daughter Michele served as flower girl in my sister Joyce's wedding. It was as if Duly had come back from the longest summer vacation in history; it had been twelve years since high school. And despite the diverging cities we have lived in since, and despite the various airwave names that Dulany worked under (Art Duly, Art Snow), we have never let the friendship lapse again.

But now Dulany was a radioman in Texas, and I was alone in Johnny's room. Rose Hill without my friend was something a little other than Rose Hill.

(There had been no question, curiously, of my staying in Duly's old bedroom just down the hall; the room with shelves of paperback books and magazines from the 1950s still intact; with Polaroid photos and records and tennis rackets strewn about, approximately as we had left them in the spring of 1959, in the waning weeks of our boyhood. I didn't ask, and Mrs. Winkler didn't offer; perhaps we both understood.)

The windows in Johnny's large, dark room faced west. They gave onto the lawn that sloped under fir trees and honeysuckle toward a hedgerow that, half a century ago, had bordered a meadow, the down-sloping meadow that leveled off at St. Mary's Avenue. The neighborhood bungalows and paved plunging streets had been in place throughout my lifetime, but the *essence* of meadow remained, somehow shading out the impermanent-seeming structures on its surface. At night I lay awake and listened to the familiar constant grind of gearshifts from the eight-wheel rigs passing through the Junction away and below, revving up from the four-way stop sign or lurching out from Fern's lot — probably the one noise in Hannibal, besides the river's rush, that had remained constant for the last fifty years.

"You know where everything is," Dulany's mother had said as she greeted me with her usual laugh — a soprano's trill that rose as from a lawn party of umbrellas and parasols. At seventy-one, Estelle Mahan Winkler was still very much the *doyenne,* the mannered mistress of two estates whose majesty was undiminished by the abiding silence within and around those estates.

Her staff of maids and groundskeepers was depleted now; she paid strangers to come and mow the lawns and trim the rose garden, and anguished at the results. Rose Hill had not resounded with children's voices for a quarter-century; it was shut down half the year. But even Rose Hill fared better than the crown jewel, Skylands.

Skylands had brooded vacantly on its peak (save for occasional guests) for two years, since the death of its sole occupant — Sara Mahan, Estelle's mother and the Colonel's daughter-in-law. The old woman had lingered for more than ten years after suffering a stroke, and widowed Estelle had seen daily to her every need, transporting her off to Florida in winter and Minnesota in summer, while at the same time administrating the medical care of her own diabetic daughter in California. The society matron who had consecrated my father's Fuller Brush career with a $50 purchase nearly fifty years ago had found, as Hannibal seemed to find in so many aspects of its being, that the very taproot of blessing contained the seeds of curse.

Not that Estelle Winkler lived in the past, or let any unmowed grass grow under her feet. She had her network of friends in Hannibal, the backbone of the country-club set; she played golf and bridge with people who had been fleeting figures in the background of her wedding movie.

The past, however, was inescapable. As we sat talking and laughing over coffee one morning in the kitchen, the telephone rang. Mrs. Winkler excused herself to answer it, and when she returned, the humor had drained from her face.

"Time and temperature?" I asked her. She nodded, standing in the center of the kitchen, kneading her hands thoughtfully. "Time and temperature," she repeated.

I needed no further explanation. I had come across Mrs. Winkler's time-and-temperature problem during a brief visit to town the year before. After our conversation had been interrupted then by four or five mysteriously brief telephone calls, Mrs. Winkler had explained the dilemma.

"The phone company put in a second exchange here a while back," she said, "two-four-eight. Well, as luck would have it, the new exchange, plus the last four digits of *our* number, are the time-and-temperature number. So naturally, people here keep dialing the *old* exchange, two-two-one, out of habit, and then our four digits, and get me. They usually hang up before I can tell them the right number to call. Then they call right back. Same mistake. Swear and hang up on me. Happens day and night. Just drives me crazy. I spoke to the telephone people, I wrote letters to them, but they say they can't do a thing about it, and that's that."

At that time, I had asked Mrs. Winkler a question that might have seemed perfectly rational to an outsider, but one that immediately branded me as someone who had been away from town too long. "Why don't you," I blurted, "change your number?"

"That telephone number," replied the *doyenne* of Rose Hill, making each word sound like a door clanging shut, "has been in our family for ninety years."

Tuesday was overcast. "You must've brought this weather with you," we Hannibalians had always liked to joke to visitors. It was beginning to seem that I, the visitor, invariably brought clouds with me to Hannibal. I didn't want to dwell upon the implications of that notion.

I spent a good part of the day in my rented car, driving from Rose Hill out to the Hannibal-LaGrange campus, then back downtown for my rounds — library, newspaper city room, the historic district for tourist-watching and sesqui-sampling, the Becky Thatcher Restaurant for pork tenderloin, the offices of various businesspeople for the ever-available cup of coffee, information, gossip. Then back to Hannibal-LaGrange for another snippet of the writers' conference.

As I drove around, I kept part of my attention on a piece of business ghoulishly typical of the late twentieth century, the details of which were filtering in on the radio airwaves to the white town.

A TWA airliner, bound from Athens to Rome, had been hijacked and diverted to Beirut, Algiers, then back to Beirut. The hijacking had developed a couple of days before I left New York. The news had occupied my weekend. Reflexively, my journalist colleagues and I had immersed ourselves in the unfolding details: the number of hostages, the name of the murdered Navy officer, the emergence of the enigmatic Nabib Berri, "leader of Lebanon's dominant Shiite militia, Amal. . . ." Efficiently we absorbed the inevitable accumulating dossier of tangled, temporary factoids. We absorbed; we spoke authoritatively and coolly to one another about the subtle geopolitics involved; we exchanged knowing ironies about the president's paralysis in the crisis, in light of his own criticisms of a previous president's paralysis. We absorbed, and we disgorged.

Now, in Hannibal, I continued to follow the story. But now a shift had occurred. Now I was aware of the unfolding details in a different context, a filtered level of intensity. The filtering was explainable only in part by the remoteness of national media: a strong network station in St. Louis came through on the car radio with continuing updates; Mrs. Winkler and I watched the morning talk shows and the evening newscasts on her parlor television set; the *Courier-Post* ran copious wire stories every afternoon — REAGAN: NO CHOICE BUT WAIT, ran one headline over a report that indeed brought up the ironies relative to Jimmy Carter's hostage crisis.

And yet the hijack story was a different entity here. The facts, the factoids, the swelling scraps of data seemed to lose their individual importance, or self-importance; they distilled, coalesced into a unified wave of bad news, a calamity from afar being swept into the town's consciousness as on the river current — a scrap of worldly knowing to be weighed and assigned a judgment, an emotion — but only after being fitted into the mosaic of town agenda, town concern.

The people of Hannibal understood what had happened; they were hardly oblivious to the outrage, the sense of violation — Mrs. Winkler watched television with a handkerchief crushed in her hand, her mouth set and her eyes red — but they were not so likely to memorize names, factions, data.

The TWA hijack crisis was terrible. But it must take its place alongside the arrival of a vintage steam engine, no. 611, in Hannibal on Monday; alongside the showdown City Council meeting set for Tuesday night; alongside the hopes for the Air Supply concert.

It occurred to me that I had had the rare occasion to view the transmutation of what my profession liked to call a "major" news story. I had seen it being assembled in the hyperclinical, intensely data-oriented news laboratories of the East for delivery out into America — and then I had flown to one of the points of its consumption to see the story broken down, reprocessed, reconstituted for absorption into the local fabric, the local preoccupations, the local idioms of anger and grief.

Something very much like that process, it struck me, had happened to the processing and the consumption of the Mark Twain Sesquicentennial.

Certainly the TWA crisis was not paramount in the main auditorium of Hannibal-LaGrange College Tuesday morning, where Mrs. Marti Hefley was about to deliver her lecture on "The Seven Steps to Motivation." Perhaps half of the fifty-nine participants in the Mark Twain Writers' Conference were scattered among the seats as Jim Hefley, acting as master of ceremonies, introduced his wife. Judging from those present, the student body did not differ radically from the demographics of writers' conferences everywhere: white, mostly female, mostly solemn — if "solemn" can be defined as a demographic unit.

"Solemn" did not seem to define *anything* in Marti Hefley's vocabulary. Upon her introduction, she floated forth toward the podium with practiced good posture, maintaining eye contact with the audience all the while.

"AREN'T WE FRIENDS?" she demanded, sending a ripple of shock through the torsos of the widely scattered enrollees. Hands on hips, feigning high dudgeon, Marti Hefley looked right and left.

"I'm of the school," she continued, projecting to the far reaches of the rear seats, "that says, if you want to get good grades, you sit in the front row!" She surveyed the now perfectly rigid assemblage. "It's fun to talk, bounce ideas around once in a while!" Now the students were doing their best to emulate statues, filled with helpless dread at what was surely to follow.

Marti Hefley waved an encompassing arm. "*Come down to the front rows!*" Like people about to be deprived of our constitutional rights, we slid out of our chosen seats and slouched lizardlike into one happy, friendly, good-neighbor compound. Satisfied, Marti Hefley got on with the business of literary instruction.

"When you produce a book," she began, "you want to make it the best product possible." Several heads bent dutifully over writing tablets. "There is an element of truth," continued Mrs. Hefley, "that everyone has at least one good book in them." Switching gears abruptly, she posed a topic question: "*How do you write someone else's story?*" A pause of one beat. "For example — *How to Win,* a motivational book by David Dean! David was selling books door-to-door! Now *that* takes discipline! *That* takes motivation! David told Jim his Seven Principles! I've read that your mind works four times faster than you hear! I was listening to David give his Seven Principles of Selling! And I was thinking — " here Marti Hefley paused just long enough to "tease" us into wondering whether she could *possibly* salvage this anecdote into any kind of literary axiom — "thinking *this applies to writing!*"

Marti Hefley enumerated the Seven Principles, which by implication were interchangeably applicable for selling books or for writing them. They were:

1. Accept Your Situation.
2. Be Willing to Fail. ("I think," Mrs. Hefley said as an aside, "that's a biggie.")
3. Make Daily Preparations.
4. Be a Professional.
5. Live in the Present.
6. Do Your Best.
7. Let God Help You.

There were more rules, more tips, more steps — a veritable upended handbag of rules, tips, and steps — "quotables," as Marti Hefley herself called them, or "underlineables." My scribbled notes began to merge and blur, so rapidly did the underlineables tumble forth. There was something about running five miles every morning; something about cassette tapes. A quotable: "Plan your work and work your plan, so you can wake up employed every morning."

I shuffled up the aisle, out of the auditorium along with the other enrollees, a bit awestruck and more than a bit abashed. I didn't think I was going to measure up very well to Marti Hefley's standard of teaching writing, even after a two-day grace period. At some point during her lecture, I had flipped my notebook over and sneaked a look at the outline I'd been compiling for my remarks. A sentence sprang out at me: "One of the first great achievements of American writing was to free itself from the hidebound cultural memories of Europe." Help me, Jesus. There was not a seersucker suit in America that could save me now.

I drove down to the riverfront. Hannibal was finally beginning to look like a festival town. The volume of tourists had increased; people in sunglasses and shorts and lime-green pants, people carrying white purses or sporting billed caps and holding cigarettes, were photographing one another in front of the Boyhood Home, or in front of the Haunted House across the street. A few took cursory squints at the informational plaques that George Mahan had put up around the buildings in the district:

> In 1845, little Sam Clemens saw a man shot down on Main Street around the corner and watched the man die on the floor of Grant's Drug Store located in this building. The incident was used many years later in "The Adventures of Huckleberry Finn."

Near this plaque, a perspiring man with a mustache sat on a bench, reading a paperback book. I glanced to see whether it was *Tom Sawyer* or *Huckleberry Finn* that had caught his imagination. The title of the book was *Why I Drink Lemonade.*

The Mississippi was busy with excursion boats, scaled-down imitations of the great old wedding-cake paddlewheel steamers and filled with sightseers. The red-and-white boats tootled down past Lover's Leap and back, looping prettily through the narrow channel between Shuck's Island and Jackson's Island near the Illinois shore. I could hear the pilots at their microphones, reciting facts for the tourists.

I stood for a while and watched the boats and gazed at my old friend the Mark Twain Bridge, arcing high and silver over the water, stabbing the far bank. The bridge was the locus of so many of my dreams. Why did I dream so often of crossing that bridge back into Hannibal by crawling along the top of the superstructure? Why was the river always frozen? And why did I always fall?

Today, though, it was summer and the river was flowing. At my back, halfway up Hill Street, just beyond the Home, came the exceedingly undreamlike, amplified sounds of money being made. The Twainland Express was pulling away from the Mark Twain Dinette (featuring Mark Twain Golden Fried Chicken) for another educational tour of the town. The Twainland Express was a yellow Ford pickup truck that pulled a canopied trailer full of people sitting on benches.

The amplified voice of the Twainland Express guide, a young woman's tenor rich with the singsong of officious rote, competed with the amplified pilots' voices floating in off the river:

". . . Also we ast yew not to stick your head or arms out while the vehicle is in motion . . . also, yew people on top . . . there are a few low branches in Hannibal and yew could get hurt . . . okay, ready? We hope to give yew a brief account of ahr rich heritage. . . ."

I wondered what the people were looking at — what they saw through their Polaroid glasses. Did they look west from Third Street and see Tom Sawyer's elemental hill with its dense wood, its mossy spot under a spreading oak — "the dead noonday heat having stilled the songs of the birds; nature in a trance that was broken by no sound but the occasional far-off hammering of a woodpecker"? Or did they see the B. F. Goodrich Tires and Batteries sign as it passed over their heads? Or what?

What was the transmuting process between George Mahan's great bequests and these consumers of rich heritage? What future awaited the historic district? Encircled and encroached upon by mechanical vultures and the rust of a decayed river culture, had it become no more than an interim diversion until some truly professional consortium could unload a serious Heritage Theme Park package over at Mark Twain Lake? And then what would happen to Hannibal? Who would bother to come? "*The only thing that differentiates Hannibal from a hundred other ratty-assed river towns up and down the Mississippi is tourism!*" Dick Halsor had blurted in his moment of candor. What if he were right?

Perhaps it would only fulfill Twain's own subtle prophecy, I thought, as I recrossed the railroad tracks and headed back to my car. No visitor, however Polaroided or Instamaticked his eyes, could help but notice the fact that it was Tom Sawyer (who stayed), and not Huckleberry Finn (who fled), whom Hannibal had selected as its defining symbol: Tom the stout lad of the land, not Huck the questing dreamer of the river current. Tom the entrepreneur, the slick swapper, the get-ahead politician of the whitewashed fence — the embracer, in the end, of the adult burgher values — Tom Sawyer would have understood all this tootling, amplified enterprise. Perhaps he would have figured out a way to keep it going. A boy mayor, he might have been. He would have stuck a gift shop on that elemental hill.

CHAPTER

XIX

I TOOK an early dinner with Estelle Winkler and then left the house again for downtown. This was to be the evening of the confrontation between Mayor Cerretti and the council over the issue of Harv Ebers and his contract as city engineer.

Harv Ebers did not naturally incite wild passions in Hannibal. This sallow man was an issue because Richard Cerretti had made him an issue. Most people barely knew, or cared, that Ebers had been suspended as a HUD 312 administrator (no criminal charges were filed) after facilitating the loan to the Lyng brothers for Fitzgerald's. But the matter seemed to obsess Cerretti. To him, Ebers embraced a number of concepts that struck at the values of any born-again Christian, any talker in tongues, any dancer in the spirit. From Cerretti's point of view, Harv Ebers stood for the proliferation of liquor-serving taverns, for cronyism (with those Lyng brothers), for defiance of authority (HUD) — even, perhaps, by association, for the downfall of Sheriff Harold White. (Wasn't Ebers a friend of John Lyng, who shared office space with Warren Wells, who had prosecuted White?)

So Cerretti stewed. He did more; he acted. Without advertising the fact, he had obtained, via a Freedom of Information request, a copy of HUD's 312 audit — the Who's Who of the loan program's administrators and recipients. Using this document as his text, Cerretti had launched his campaign to expunge Ebers from municipal service. In doing so, he had handed his political opponents — an ever-growing category — a convenient device on which to build a unified opposition. Harv Ebers became a symbol far more powerful than his actual threat, or importance, to the town's interests. When Richard Cerretti let it out that he intended to veto Ebers's contract as city engineer, it became axiomatic that nearly everyone else would defend Ebers — particularly when it became apparent that in withholding his signature after council approval of the contract, Cerretti might be violating the City Charter. It was in this context that talk of a move to impeach Cerretti had begun.

For the three days I had been in town, people had been talking about this meeting with the faintly prurient relish normally reserved for impending barroom fights. Several had asked me whether I had gotten my "ringside seat." I had laughed — an outsider's laugh. But I had kept Tuesday evening clear.

The early-evening sun had broken under the clouds and thrown a lovely, orange-purplish light across the town and its hills. This was the hour when the local radio stations concentrated on sports — thirty-five years ago it would have been the hour of Bobby Benson and the B-Bar-B Riders. It was the hour when mothers fried pork chops in black skillets, when fathers read the Iced Paper — or so it had sounded to my ears when my dad used to unroll the *Courier-Post.* (It took years for me to grasp, as I did one backward-drifting day, that he had been muttering about "t'night's paper.")

I had more than an hour to kill before the council meeting, and baseball was on the airwaves, so I drove down to the South Side, to Collier Street, below the cliff where South Fifth came to its abrupt end; I drove to Clemens Field.

I had put on my seersucker suit for the meeting, and I felt self-conscious wearing it into the old concrete, canopied clamshell of a grandstand, where mothers in pink Bermuda shorts and dads in overalls and no shirt at all watched their children play ball. But I couldn't help it. I needed to see some baseball. I needed to sit in Clemens Field again. Maybe everyone would think I was a scout.

The teams on the field were probably made up of eleven- to thirteen-year-olds. They wore uniform tops and blue jeans. There wasn't much flash or rah-rah showboating on the field, nor did the parents give vent to any of the temper tantrums that have become such a cherished adjunct of American kid baseball. These were working-class families, the very core of town life, and they took their ball games with silent, serious respect. The mothers kept the box score in official-looking spiralbound scorebooks and poured themselves iced tea out of thermos bottles, passing the cups around. The dads watched motionless under their billed caps for long frozen moments, then stretched out their muscled arms to clap two or three claps in the classic baseball way.

I leaned back against the concrete and threw my elbows up on the empty wooden plank behind me. I could smell the faint staleness of old beer, beer that had been spilled into the concrete thirty, forty years ago when Hannibal fans came to root for minor-league teams in the St. Louis Cardinals farm system, and to razz Ed O'Neill as he climbed the swaying stepladder to the aerie of the press box, to cover for the newspaper, act as official scorer, handle the public-address chores in his side-lisping voice, and toss down cartons of cigarettes to hitters of home runs. My seersucker suit may have looked stiff, but I was totally at peace in the baseball twilight — more at peace than at any time since I'd started coming home.

No public-address system crackled on this evening. The game wasn't even important enough to merit the arclights. Out on the mound, a lean, bespectacled kid — "Doc," he might have been called in my time — was throwing with an easy, fluid sidearm motion. I watched him with envy. He was a master of that special, endlessly cultivated nonchalance that in my boyhood had been as much the point of playing baseball as trying to win. In this most time-free of games, nonchalance was nothing less than a declaration of immunity to time. We tried to instill it into our playground games by incantation, we fantasizers of big nights at Clemens Field — we'd supply our own radio play-by-play even as we gazelled and swung and flung. *"Powers drifts over,"* I'd announce, drifting over for one of Dulany's characteristic towering popups, *"and says, 'I'll handle this one, Larry' — aaaaaaand it's three up and three down. . . ."*

"Doc," dealing sidewinder from the mound, retired the side in order for a couple of innings, and then the hostiles began to measure his offerings with their aluminum bats. *"Toiing! . . . Toiing! . . . Clunnk!"* Ah, the timeless sound of Alcoa on horsehide. An adult male surfaced from the dugout in a flawless rendering of the Universal Managerial Deathwalk, chin on his chest as though meditating on some Agnus Dei of the diamond, and yanked the kid — sent him over to first base. The first baseman embarked for center field, and the center fielder came trotting in, as from a distant bull pen, to quench the fire.

I felt a little anguish on behalf of Doc. There are few moments in sports in which failure is more isolated, more public, than the moment of banishment from the pitcher's mound; it did not seem like something that should happen to a thirteen-year-old. But Doc's poker face showed no hint of humiliation. He walked to first base, turned, and put his hands on his knees as matter-of-factly as a laid-off auto worker taking up a part-time job. I watched for a few more minutes and then left these grave, silent people, so absorbed in their druidic enactment of the game. The shadows were general on the diamond; at any moment the players and the watchers might fade into them, to reappear, dimly, the following evening. It was time to head for City Hall.

Before I even got through the glass doors to the ground floor I was conscious of heat, sweat, humidity, lights, whites of eyes. My friends had not been kidding about a "ringside seat." City Hall was a jostling mass of excited people; it looked like the obligatory mob-citizen scene of a Frank Capra movie. Neckties were actually askew; sheafs of rolled-up paper actually protruded from sports coat pockets.

Squeezing my way up the stairs to the council chamber, I kept pressing against people I knew: old friends, a few former high-school teachers, some new acquaintances from my rounds about

Hannibal This time, there were no easy greetings, no pleasantries. People nodded and looked away, or searched my eyes, smiling peculiar half-smiles.

I understood this behavior; I had seen it before. Years ago, when I covered suburban municipal government for a St. Louis newspaper, I had had my fill of grass-roots democracy in action. The regular governing meetings were usually models of parliamentary efficiency and dullness — that is, until some hapless victim of a mayor or an alderman or a cop or a city worker blundered into public controversy of any sort — a falling-from-grace that tended to happen with almost ritualistic frequency. And then the meetings turned primitive. They became arenas, inquisitions that drew from the community a deep, almost erotic compulsion to gather and witness the mortification, and hopefully the complete civic excommunication, of the miscreant in question.

I was spared having to kibbitz the proceedings from the outside corridor by virtue of my vague status as a reporter. I edged my way into the standing-room council chambers, lighted brightly for Quincy television, and made my way to the press table at the foot of the high, curving dais of councilmen's seats. I sat cross-legged on the floor, feeling conspicuous, highly seersuckered and at least as foolish as everyone else in the room seemed to feel — and at least as avid for inquisition.

The subject of the evening's entertainment looked almost radiant. "It's a real pleasure to have all you folks here tonight," announced Richard Cerretti from the center of the dais. "I want to invite you all back tomorrow night for the Army Corps hearing on flood control." I brightened; here was a talent for irony not previously revealed. Perhaps there would be some real thrust and parry before the bloody consummation.

The councilmen arranged on either side of the mayor did not seem amused. They had on their dour, interests-of-the-city expressions; they had just come from executive session. There hung about them all a profound ineffable southernness, something ancient, muted, a little dangerous, but manly, grand: a fierce silent mood at once hair-trigger and infinitely biding. These city fathers had come here not for arena; they'd come resolved to take control of the town's affairs if need be. They'd come with a stoic awareness of Hannibal's isolation from the outside world with its airplane hijackings and its theories of redress and compensation and utopia. If anyone was going to save Hannibal from sliding utterly into chaos, it struck me as I sat on the council floor, it wouldn't be the conspicuous mayors or the mayors who replaced the conspicuous mayors — it would be people like these, the nameless councilmen and women, as silent and determined and continuous and druidic as the shadowy baseball children on Clemens Field. The citizens. The sum, the collective, the aggregate people who lived in the town.

Having finally settled an old question of mine — if this was a kingdom, who was king? — I settled back to watch the sideshow.

There was some preliminary business, a few appointments, a few announcements as the packed spectators fanned themselves. And then came the main event.

"I want to say to the City Council," said Cerretti into his microphone, "that two weeks ago I told you I did not have a copy of the HUD's three-twelve audit. That was true in the sense that I *did not have a copy at City Hall.* I did have a copy at my house."

Laughter and hoots from the crowd. Here was the mayor, the paragon of Christian rectitude, falling back on a fine-point distinction to justify an evasive statement.

A councilman named Lutterbie asked: "Is it true — I've kept hearing that this was a 'criminal' investigation — that the word 'criminal' appeared nowhere on the report?"

Cerretti leaned into his microphone again, his rimless glasses flashing in the television lights. "This is the disposition report of the HUD office," he said, speaking slowly in his whispery voice. "It is not a criminal report." Several councilmen exchanged glances. "But there *is,*" Cerretti added suddenly, "a criminal report!" More laughter.

Cerretti declared that he had vetoed the contract renewal. The question of an override was called. The council voted for the override, 12 to 0.

The mayor pro tem, Paul Arnett, now asked the payoff question: "Do you intend to sign the contracts?"

As the spectators leaned forward to hear the answer, the mayor turned to whisper with the city attorney. This gesture brought a few sarcastic jibes. It seemed to me that Richard Cerretti's political legitimacy, if not his prospects for impeachment, might hang on his answer.

Cerretti adjusted his microphone. "I will reserve judgment on that," he announced, "until tomorrow morning."

The council chamber exploded with laughter. A woman's piercing voice cried, " *'Fraid to make a decision!*" I could see the mayor's Adam's apple working. There was a moment when it felt as if the pent-up energy in the room were going to release itself in some insane rush to the dais, or at least in a hooting so fierce that Cerretti would flee the chamber. Neither happened. This was Hannibal. The people yelled and called out insults and pawed dismissively in the air for a few minutes — and then a sort of shrug seemed to settle over everyone. "What are you gonna do?" the crowd seemed to say. People folded their arms; set their mouths; settled back.

John Lyng, the repudiated mayor, strode to the floor microphone to speak on behalf of some tavern owners anxious about Cerretti's liquor-licensing plans. He received a hero's round of applause. Half an hour later the meeting was over. The irate citizens of Hannibal filed meekly down the stairs and out into the June night. They looked like people resigned to waiting four years to settle this latest mayor's hash. Their opportunity would come sooner, and in more bizarre fashion, than most could have dreamed.

Two mornings later I sat on the edge of a front-row seat in Hannibal-LaGrange College's main auditorium, wearing a nondescript blue blazer and tie — the seersucker suit appeared wrinkled, for some reason — and listened guiltily to a gracious, warm-spirited introduction from Jim Hefley. Advancing to the podium under tepid applause, I noticed that the normally sparse ranks of writers' conference enrollees had been swelled by a claque: Mrs.

Winkler had come, and had brought with her two friends — Mrs. Lester Smith, the mother of Ward, an inner member of Duly's old crowd; and Mrs. Virgil Dent, who had been my speech teacher at Hannibal High School. Mrs. Dent happened to be sitting directly in my line of sight.

The applause died away. Mrs. Dent, who was suddenly the only figure in God's universe, sat smiling expectantly. I stood gripping the podium, wasting precious seconds of my triumphal return to Hannibal, trying feverishly to recall what kind of grade Mrs. Dent had given me a quarter-century ago. Mrs. Dent and I were locked into each other's field of vision. I used to caddy for her husband. He'd had a way of grinding his teeth quite audibly when I would stroll, bags on my shoulders, across the putting green. I wondered whether he had discussed my caddying behavior with his wife over dinner. I wondered whether she would hold it against me after all these years. I thought of invoking Marti Hefley's trick — get everybody way down in front; then I could yammer away without having to look at anyone. I couldn't bring myself to do it. I lacked the panache.

I also lacked a lecture. I had jettisoned all the notes I'd put together back in New York — all the authoritative, confident lit talk that I'd been so sure would endear me to everyone. "Waning sense of historical time," I remembered writing into my outline, and, "instrumental view of knowledge," and one chummy-sounding sentence that went something like "I want to be very careful to avoid terms such as 'self-discovery' or 'heightened self-awareness' as a goal." The hell. What I should have been careful to avoid was persuading Henry Sweets to get me into this.

The students — and Mrs. Dent — and Mrs. Smith — and Mrs. Winkler — all were smiling in anticipation. It was time to begin.

I leaned my forearms on the lectern and told a good one on Henry Sweets. I got a pretty good hand by saying that in future years we'd all take pride in remembering that we were present at the *first* Mark Twain Writers' Conference. I talked a little about how hard it was to write a book about a whole town. About how little, I realized, I really knew about Hannibal — why, I'd lived here when the Bordello was a bordello and hadn't even known it. Silence in the Baptist confines. A possibly poor choice of anecdote.

I moved quickly to the topic of nonfiction writing. There's a waning sense of historical time, I believe I said. The past is a political and psychological treasury, I averred, from which we draw the reserves that we need to cope with the future. *Let me illustrate what I mean,* I added hastily, perhaps shrilly, into the silence surrounding Mrs. Dent's smile. *Let's get down to cases.* It happened that I had with me a few preliminary drafts for the book I was presently working on — and coming here and talking about a book that you've come here to write is sort of like being in an echo chamber, ha-ha, I jested.

I thumbed; I flipped; I found what held some promise as a noncontroversial passage; I read aloud. It was about my father — about how my father had died having reported a taxable income of just under one thousand Fuller Brush dollars. The words, as I read them, sounded brutal. "Some of you are probably wondering why I would disclose something that personal about my father," I ventured, leaning an elbow casually on the lectern as the inner voice of every acquaintance in the auditorium screamed, *WHAT IS HE WRITING PERSONAL ABOUT ME?* I explained that what I was getting at really had to do with the ironies of fate and choice; and that besides, my father had had some excellent years as a Fuller Brush man.

I forged on. I offered some thoughts about how people ought not to just try for beautiful sentences, but should concentrate on clarity and getting through to the truth of the subject matter. I talked about what an important and honorable branch of literature nonfiction writing was, even though it didn't have the glamour of novels, and how no one present ought to overlook it as he or she sat down to choose a mode of literary expression.

I threw it open for questions.

Mrs. Smith spoke without bothering to raise her hand. "Your

father," she informed me in a voice that carried to the farthest reaches of the auditorium, if not the town, "*was the best Fuller Brush man I have ever known.*"

Let us, as Mark Twain once suggested, draw the curtain of charity over the rest of the scene.

On Thursday night, Justin Kaplan delivered his keynote address to the Mark Twain Writers' Conference, on the topic of "Huckleberry Finn and the Censors." My notes from the address are incomplete. The auditorium was perhaps a third filled. The members of the Hannibal Writers Club, whose poetry was regularly published in the *Courier-Post,* turned out as a got-up, flower-printed bloc. They sat very quietly in the middle of the auditorium, along with the rest of the audience, as Justin Kaplan enumerated the various and interconnected epochs of repressive reaction toward Mark Twain's masterpiece. The quiet in the auditorium was impressive . . . sustained . . . singular . . . absolute . . . claustrophobic. After a while Mr. Kaplan himself seemed to succumb to its hypnotic thrall; his voice took on an interestingly hollow aspect, and he gripped the podium as though it might yield a secondary use as a deflective instrument.

Someone should have told him that this was Tom Sawyer's town.

The writers' conference ended with a fried-chicken luncheon in the Hannibal-LaGrange cafeteria on Friday. I sat between Henry Sweets and Jim Hefley. The featured speaker was Bill McLinn in his role as Mark Twain Himself. If Justin Kaplan failed to arouse the passions of the conferees by discussing Twain the victim of jingo suppression, McLinn did not fare much better in his somewhat disputatious rendition of Twain the antiwar activist and spokesperson for human rights.

It was a strange performance in a strange setting. There in the basement of the ancient administration building, we writers-in-chrysalis and learned faculty sat at our long dining tables with their surface coverings of white industrial paper, our Jell-O salads melting into the cold remnants of our green beans, and watched with increasingly fixed smiles as this entertainer in his graying (not white!) wig and his black (not white!) frock coat, the makeup pencil's streaks giving his face a mannequin look, held the floor for about an hour and fifteen minutes. During the vast bulk of that time McLinn spoke "out of character" in his own rich, actorish voice. It developed that McLinn's and Mark Twain's social sensibilities were of the same high moral order. As McLinn in his stage makeup delineated the points of his and Twain's liberal-Democratic agenda, my thoughts drifted toward the famous caveat at the beginning of *Huckleberry Finn:* "Persons attempting to find a motive in this narrative will be prosecuted; persons attempting to find a moral in it will be banished; persons attempting to find a plot in it will be shot." I also recalled the hazy outlines of an observation contained in a Twain letter from the Sandwich Islands, which I later looked up: "His tongue is in constant motion from eleven in the forenoon till four in the afternoon, and why it does not wear out is the affair of Providence, not mine."

At least it was comfortably cool down there in the basement. Bill McLinn for climate, I decided. Marti Hefley for society.

CHAPTER XX

I AWOKE in Johnny Winkler's big dark room on Saturday morning, a train-whistle receding in my brain. An endless freight had dawdled and curled its way around the town in the night, as one did every night — waddling down the Burlington-Northern road beside the Mississippi, then making the big curve to the west along Bear Creek, past the disused bridge where my grandfather and I used to watch from the Packard. The stressed groan and shriek of its thousand wheels on the curving track vied with the whistle in my night-town dreams. The freight had been a good two miles from Rose Hill at its nearest point, but sound carries to Hannibal's hilltops. The waddling boxcars could have been below my window. I'd lain half-transported to another hilltop, Union Street Hill, and my grandparents' house. For a while my grandparents were alive again. It was they whom I had come back to find after twenty-six shameful years, a terrible, inexcusable gulf of neglect for two dear figures so beloved. . . .

The ringing telephone downstairs brought me fully awake. Time and temperature, no doubt. I dressed and went down to the sunlit kitchen, where I found Mrs. Winkler standing in the center of the floor, chin in her hand, elbow tucked into her side, lost in thought. On the breakfast table were some open scrapbooks — she had been researching family history to verify some of her reminiscences with me.

It was a pose I recognized as deeply characteristic of the Winkler people, especially inside Rose Hill. I had seen Dulany transfixed in that dreamlike, unconsciously heroic stance, reminiscent of a child sleeping, when the two of us had reconnoitered briefly in Hannibal a year before. Something of the house, its imperial assumptions, its manifold associations, its uncertain future must have borne heavily upon the Winklers who came back here. I certainly felt it, and again I felt the absence of Duly. Being here in his unchanged house, knowing that Duly was changed and gone — fortyish, in Texas — was too much like my half-dream of the night before to be bearable. I talked with Mrs. Winkler for an hour over orange juice and coffee — the subject was weddings, and the pleasure of her remembrance burned away some of my gloom — and then I headed for the riverfront.

Saturday had dawned warm and cloudless over Hannibal. The sesquicentennial had come out-of-doors for its eighth weekend. The big food-and-beverage tent was up at Bird and North Main streets. Barbecuing slabs of sausage and pork sent pungent puffs of blue smoke curling into the sky. People in sunglasses and Bermudas formed lines for big waxed cartons of Pepsi and Coke.

Street singers and musicians were setting up their acts — gospel, country, string jazz. It seemed to me that about a third of the local population was in costume. A Mark Twain and his Livy strolled and pointed. Dozens of young Toms and Hucks and Beckys (I spotted no Jims) scampered up and down North Main, looking rather alarmingly professional in their artificial freckles. Watching them, I could not help thinking of Larry Lewis, the president of Hannibal-LaGrange College, and his vision of Hannibal as a permanent costume-party parody of its past.

I thought of a more recent conversation I'd had with an architectural designer from Quincy, a maker of what he happily described as "supercontemporary buildings," an artful dresser of a man, a man of taste whose indignation over Hannibal's comedown of a festival, and general neglect of its heritage, moved him to great flourishes of admonition.

"Where were the historical seminars in this sesquicentennial?"

he had demanded as we took Sunday brunch in a restored wing of the century-old Federal Building, its three granite stories now mostly gutted and vacant. (It had housed the Hannibal Post Office when I was a boy.)

"There is *so little,*" this authority had gone on, "in Hannibal of a cultural nature today. Hannibal is like Oz," he had sniffed, "with Mark Twain as the Good Witch of the South. Look at the carnival art that greets visitors as they come across the bridge! When I hear the words 'historic district,' " the architect had declared, "I want to throw up.

"The people of Hannibal," this man had summed up, wiping his lips with a pink napkin, "don't realize *that they owe this to themselves and to the whole world, goddammit — to restore the whole aura of Mark Twain's mind!*"

This cultural vigilante had a solution. His solution was to turn Hannibal's downtown over to a giant corporation for refurbishing as a thematic restoration of the Mark Twain period. The corporation he had in mind was the Disney Corporation.

"I believe," the architect assured me, squeezing a few last drops of fresh lemon into his cooling cup of tea, "that they can be trusted to do a tasteful, responsible job."

Now, as I gazed at the Saturday festivalgoers in their bright clothes, their period costumes, I caught myself wondering, for the first time, whether it might all make some garrison, last-ditch sort of sense. In any case, it seemed inevitable: Hannibal's looming fate — its dismantlement as a town and reconstitution as a cartoon mockery of its townhood, its Twainhood — appeared to be only a matter of time. Blessings and curses.

There was no doubt where the weight of opinion lay. The advocates of transformation, the promoters of history as heritage and community as curiosity, the demographic disciples and the spearheaders of sponsorship opportunity, the capital planners and projectors and image-hustlers, all the Wakers Up to Missouri and redeemers of the ratty-assed river towns came rushing at me now like voices on an airwave search for better times.

Michael Jenkins would have transformed Hannibal surely; welcomed it as a suburb of Mark Twain Lake. I thought of Alfred Stern with his "magic letter" and Jim Gladwin with his visions of a mini-World's Fair. I thought of Marjorie Beenders — "*Hannibal could be another Williamsburg!*" — and the silken Quincy architect with his Xanadu dreams of Disney.

Those were the outsiders. I thought of the insiders, the town's guardians, the people elected or appointed or self-appointed to keep Hannibal economically alive.

Only one of them, at least among those I had met, had seemed indifferent to the lure of liquid-streams-of-gold fantasies: Gale Newman, the dual executive director of the Chamber of Commerce and the Hannibal Industrial Council. Newman had been working tirelessly, at times single-handedly, often in the face of open hostility from others in the town, at the grubby, piecemeal business of recruiting business and manufacturing plants for relocation to Hannibal. (Later in the year Newman's efforts would pay off with announcements that two sizable employers, one of them headquartered in Japan, would establish plants in town. The other firm, a wire-cable operation, agreed after forty-seven negotiating sessions with Newman.)

As for the rest? Proponents of Hannibal-as-museum, to some degree, everyone. I thought of Dr. Lewis, and Dick Halsor, and of course Larry Weil and John Lyng. Among all of them, Lyng had been the linchpin, the necessary agent in the first, failed onslaught. I recognized Lyng as most nearly like myself in his sense of the town, his unmistakable passion for it that shone through his unmistakable ambition. Lyng was defined by the town and his own father's place in the town. He had worked on the *Courier-Post,* assisted John Winkler at the Becky Thatcher Home, had become the boy mayor — had woven himself more deeply into Hannibal's fabric than I could ever hope to do. And yet Lyng had been ready to hand the town over to the synthesizers, the costumers, the corporate colonizers. Only a certain lack of finesse, a certain fatal residue of the old town's sealed-with-a-handshake folkways — a certain *Hannibalness* — had thwarted him. I asked myself again: What had John Lyng come to terms with, as a lifelong citizen of the town, that I resisted, as an exile? Which of us was right? And how differently might I have felt about Hannibal's hopes for a self-determined future, had I remained?

A remark of Lyng's came to me as I stood there on North Main; an offhand comment he'd made the day we toured the amphitheater site. I'd assumed at the time that it was a joke. "Someday," John Lyng had said, gazing at the Mississippi, "that will be a viaduct. We'll be able to drive under it."

I wondered now to what extent he had been kidding.

And would Hannibal really object all that much to being converted into a town-size museum, or theme park? I spotted Hannibal the Frog frolicking with his Aunt Polly partner in polyurethane, and wondered again.

The Sesqui-That-Might-Have-Been imposed itself on the street scene before me. I looked at these people, the locals and the visitors from not too far away, the grandmothers and the barbered Jaycees and the ain't-seen-nuthin'-yet clumps of teens — looked at these people as they ambled and window-shopped the storefronts and photographed one another and gaped at the street fiddlers, and I tried to conjure those imperial corporate pavilions and citified folk operas and pre-Broadway runs; all those gussied-up storytellers and hustling humorists and those fireworks and parades, that skyful of hot-air balloons and that river chockablock with sternwheelers like bump 'em cars. The permanent theme stage. All the U-Hauled hardware of huckstered heritage, the modular amusements of a packager's promised-land perpetrations, finding its way inexorably to the white town. I imagined it five years later; three. I thought of the World's Fair craters in Knoxville, New Orleans; of the peculiar odorless rot, the inorganic compost of all the new-concept ventures in America that suddenly are no longer new, but are damned never to age and decay: the marginal shopping malls, the forsaken theme-condominium villages with their knockoff architecture and their bogus pilings from New England fisherman's wharves.

I imagined my father tipping a period bowler to a housewife on her doorstep, wriggling his fake Charlie Chaplin mustache as the Twainland Express floated by, tourists pointing and applauding. Perhaps the housewife was in a hoopskirt. I imagined my grandfather in a pillowy baker's hat; my uncle Abe in a striped vest with garters on his sleeves, his hair parted in the middle, tending his theme-bar and bawling a song. A 12 rating and a 14.7 customer share. Dr. Lewis I conjured in a celluloid collar and clawhammer coat, pounding the theme-pulpit like Ichabod Crane. Theme-floods, I imagined, and hard-times pavilions; a citizenry that talked among itself in up-tempo dialect and danced to exciting choreography. There would be sixteen songs. It would be the story of man's individual rights to freedom, family, home, and community.

Hannibal had just escaped this sort of purgatorial fate — by accident, and for the time being. Did Hannibal have a chance to escape forever and still retain its vital systems as a town? Or was its future preordained in the winking green screens, the databank cross-hairs of some as yet unrevealed refurbisher? Did *anyone* line up on the other side?

Someone was playing a fiddle on North Main. I could hear the indistinct phrasings of an excursion-boat captain out on the river. Less than a block from where I stood, at 110 North Main, was a small women's shop called the Famous. Every small town in the Midwest had its Famous, or did at one time. This one had been established in 1902 by the Louis Rubenstein family and had been family-owned ever since. Together with Peg's Winning Look, next door, the Famous represented the last remnant of the old downtown shopping district — dime stores, furniture stores, dry goods, and women's ready-to-wear — back in the days when Genial Gene Hoenes was the Man on the Street and my grandfather drove by in his Packard. The Mississippi flood of 1973 had driven nearly every other merchant across town, to the nascent shopping centers on the western rim. The Huck Finn, one of them was called. Peg's had moved briefly to the Huck Finn, but then had returned to North Main. The two stores were putative competitors now, but more resembled elderly allies in their isolation.

I wandered inside the store, feeling a little oversized and bearish. Women in pantsuits were slowly spinning circular racks of women's pantsuits. I found Marilyn Cohn in her tiny office, eating a franchise-food hamburger and talking on the telephone. Marilyn waved her burger in greeting when she saw me, and I sat down to wait, letting my eyes wander around the creams and reds and bold floral prints on their hangers. I remembered what a mutual friend, the wife of a Hannibal dentist, had told me about Marilyn and her store.

"She knows what colors I like to wear," the woman had said. "She knows what colors everybody likes to wear. She knows sizes. That's why she has such loyal customers. She prevents them from going to the chain stores by knowing what they want as well as they do, or even better. That's what's so special about the Famous. Marilyn will keep certain dresses off the display racks, in the back, because she knows they're just right for certain customers. When there's a big party in town she keeps tabs of what everybody is buying, so that no woman will go dressed like somebody else.

"She does something else you'll *never* see in a chain store," the woman had gone on, shaking her head at the very thought of it. "A stranger will come in, buy a dress — an *out-of-towner* — and maybe not have the cash to cover it. Marilyn will offer to send the bill to her home address. Peg's is the same way, of course. But they're not in competition. They don't cut one another."

Marilyn Cohn hung up the telephone receiver, tidily wrapped up her burger remnants, and waved me in with the match for her cigarette. She was a hearty, dark-haired woman in her midthirties, with some of the practiced ironies of the New York University undergraduate — which she was before she decided to return to Hannibal and carry on the family business.

"There's not much downtown left," she agreed when I told her a little about my readings of Hannibal's future. "But I'm not so sure Walt Disney is the answer." She gave a sharp laugh. "The shopping malls have hurt us, sure," she went on, "but you know what? Not even the little shops in the shopping malls are making it." She ticked off a couple of marginal stores within the Huck Finn Shopping Center. "It isn't just the mall," Marilyn Cohn said, "it's the gigantic discount stores that anchor the mall. Wal-Mart is killing business for everybody in the area. Bowling Green, Monroe City — they have no stores to speak of anymore."

I asked her why the Famous had not pulled out of downtown and joined the exodus west. She shrugged, blowing smoke. "*I* don't know. Tradition. The family always located down here. Of course I'm not going to sink fifty thousand dollars into renovation as long as we're in the floodplain."

"Why can't you get some protection?" I asked her.

Marilyn Cohn smoked hard for a minute. "I think," she said, "that one plain and simple thing that could save downtown Hannibal — make it a real downtown again — would be a good flood-protection plan. Not a *wall;* that would be unbearably ugly. But a terraced levee; some landscaping; some gradient that would protect us and still look good."

"Why isn't there such a plan?" I asked again.

"People don't want it. They think they'll be paying tax money on something that only benefits a few. Hizzoner gives lip service, but . . ." she let it trail off, and shrugged again.

I had heard this dilemma expressed before. Here, it occurred to me, was a dismaying shred of evidence that the cynicism of certain city leaders was not totally unfounded. Hannibal's people may hardly have been cretins, but neither could they be relied upon to act unfailingly in their own long-range self-interest. Their suspicion toward the historic district and its potential for authentic commerce, which manifested itself in the defeat of municipal tax-increase bills and riverfront flood-control plans, was as radical, in its way, as the most lacquered visions of the heritage exploiters. It was a standoff. And in such a standoff, it seemed to me, only the corporate-development opportunists could win. A matter of time.

I selected a cream-colored pantsuit for my wife with help from one of Marilyn Cohn's salesgirls — I asked that the bill be sent to my address in New York — and drove away from the festival streets, back to Rose Hill. I wanted to spend some time wandering around the house, packing for my departure the following day, and resting up for my first rock concert. Tonight was Air Supply.

Rivers of people poured through Hannibal's downtown streets. It was a little after 6:00 P.M., nearly two hours before concert time, and already a great multitude was gathering its mass: east on Broadway, south on Main Street, and through a dozen other streets and alleys and along the riverfront railroad tracks it ambled and funneled and edged in its cars, toward the pontoon bridge at Bear Creek, toward the amphitheater.

I could watch the crowd take shape from high on Bird Street Hill, where I had parked my rented car. The people who lived in the old frame bungalows on the slanting street were sitting out on their front-porch swings, fanning themselves and drinking beer and craning their necks to see down into the bowl of town where I was headed. They might have been sitting on those swings since my grandparents' time, for all their dress or their expressions revealed.

Now I became part of the swarm. I hurried down Bird Street, slipping back into a Hannibal hillside gait that I'd forgotten, my toes jamming up into the tips of my shoes with each downward, braking step. At Third Street I looked around to see who my fellow rock buffs were. I suppose I was expecting to find a heavy vein of out-of-town funk: St. Louis rockers, Kansas City bikers, black leather and chains and dyed hair.

I saw nothing of the sort. I saw instead the town; the town and the farms beyond the town. I saw cowboys and cowgirls; curled straw Stetsons and bellies over belt buckles. I saw muscle T-shirts and maternity blouses over Bermuda shorts. I saw white-haired women in groups of two and three, carrying their folded aluminum-and-canvas chairs like purses under their arms. I saw trim dads in their striped J. C. Penney polo shirts and moms in their starched Lady Hathaways. Many of the moms were pushing strollers. Many of the dads dandled kids on their necks.

I saw teenagers and children, of course; currents and eddies and swarms of them. I spotted some stabs at the New York club look: some Bad Girl pullovers and some wraparound shades. I saw some facial insignia and an earring or two clamped to unaccustomed lobes. But these were last-minute affectations, like the artificial freckles on North Main Street. At some subtle but impervious line, the costuming in this crowd gave way to . . . *clothes*. Beyond some sensed level of decoration, these kids, like their parents, were coming to the concert not as someone else's idea of an American rock 'n' roll crowd, but as themselves. The internationally famous rock band named Air Supply may have come to knock Hannibal's sox off, it struck me as we ambled, but the knocking would be on Hannibal's own terms. The sox, by God, were over-the-calf Supp-hose.

We funneled, we converged, we bumped shoulders, we said excuse-me. The sky over the Mississippi was a cloudless deepening blue, and the low sun behind us fired the Mississippi Bridge into a blazing skeleton. The bridge burned down, mostly unremarked, upon the backs of all the figures in this oddly rural, oddly sacramental procession swarming dreamlike toward the amphitheater; swarming to gather at the river.

In Nipper Park, just yards from where Bear Creek emptied into the river, families were spreading out bedsheets on the ground. No point in crossing on over until it was time for the show to start. On one of the sheets a baby, naked except for the fluffed sac of her diaper, lifted her arms and did a dreamy backwards dance.

The town fathers had turned on the circular stone fountain in Nipper Park, the old Board of Public Works fountain put up in 1931 with its sequence of seven colors of light playing on the central spout. I had not seen this fountain working since early boyhood, and I sat down on the grass to watch it. From the amphitheater stage on the far side of Bear Creek we could hear the amplified bass thump of recorded rock music, interspersed with the live baritone witticisms of some local deejays there to warm up the crowd.

There was something ancient and familiar about the mixture of sensations I felt here on the grass beside the river. The colliding dynamics of the situation tugged at my memory. Here we all were, Hannibalians waiting for the start of a show, a big show; a famous specimen of entertainment in from the outside world. All of us subdued, a little awestruck, by the imperial fun about to be visited upon us, by this impending brush with the nation: and yet the event almost unconsciously softened, rendered *safe* by the murmurescent local voices, the very sacrament of our collective waiting.

I lay back on the grass and let the sounds and feelings take me back thirty-five years. I remembered the air-conditioned strangeness I felt sitting in the Tom Sawyer Theater, waiting for the screen to crackle and boom with whatever concatenation of imagery awaited me — nervous, perhaps, at the well-advertised prospect of terrible robots from flying saucers beaming death rays from their eyes — *The Day the Earth Stood Still.* My jitters increasing to reverential terror as the movie opened with a whine of sirens, police cars pouring out of headquarters; my nine-year-old soul obsequious with a kind of mannerly fright — only to have the terror reduced, contained, sweetened somehow by the common-sense drawl of a woman's voice in the row behind — "*Earth Stood Still,* huh? Looks like it's on the move to me!"

The sun lowered and the colors on the river deepened and we began to rise from the grass and shake out our blankets and make our way to the pontoon bridge. The bridge bobbed under us on its green barrels. Bear Creek trickled into the river a few feet to our left. It seemed such a modest event, this confluence, like a hallway opening onto a living room. We handed over our tickets to some elderly officials in red caps, and got a stamp on the wrist. There were some local police milling around, and a few youngish men wearing orange plastic vests imprinted with the legend "Crowd Control," but there was nothing to control. We were not your common rock 'n' roll mob, we Hannibalians. Some Jaycees had a concession stand working atop the far bank. The usual orderly lines had formed for cola and barbecue. Behind the concession stand were the portable outhouses, and beyond them arose the Parthenon skeleton of the amphitheater stage, hard on the bank of the Mississippi, facing a widening cone of hushed people. There must have been eight thousand of us.

We milled and gossiped and took pictures and straightened out our aluminum folding chairs until showtime; and then a disk jockey onstage snatched a microphone to his mouth and bellowed out something thunderous and important, and from the trailer dressing rooms on the far side of the amphitheater a band of men in pink and spangled clothes came sprinting for the stage, and the colored lights on the amphitheater scaffolding began to wink and sweep furiously, and a great shrieking roar escaped the crowd, and the Air Supply concert was on.

We screamed and danced and shrieked, we Hannibal rock fans. The young girls waved their arms and called out the soloist's name and beckoned him with shrieks as he waved first to this section of the crowd and then that. We screamed and danced and shrieked, and the musicians waved to us, beckoning *us,* trying to draw us into them. The music crashed into the valley corridors of Hannibal, and the performers flirted with the crowd, struck shimmering attitudes, pointed into sections of screaming girls and vamped for applause; the Air Supply performers dared the crowd to let go. And there was an interval somewhere within that concert, beneath the music, when I thought that something hung in the balance; that some quality of will, of identity, was in contention, some weight that might finally swing either way — toward the figures on the stage or toward the crowd. Toward Hannibal.

The sky deepened into cobalt above us, and the old universe spread out — a quarter-century, or a century and a half, was less than a flicker under it — and the winking stagelights gained in definition, and Air Supply sang, "Nothing at All." And all the young girls in the crowd crooned and swayed. I turned to look at the riverbank near the foot of the stage and saw that it had filled with pinpoints of orange light: the running lights of speedboats. About a dozen speedboats had tied up just off the amphitheater, and their shadowy occupants had disembarked to hover waist-deep in the river, watching the show. It was the first time I had ever seen anyone actually stand in the Mississippi, and it put to rest an old childhood assumption, never actually tested until now, that the river was bottomless.

I turned to look back in the opposite direction, toward the rear of the amphitheater crowd. I glimpsed the unmistakable figure of Mad Dog Manus in full battle dress, black Bermudas and a black T-shirt pulled tight over his torso, stalking a parapet above the throng, stalking and pacing, a shark, a terminator guarding his brood.

The river vanished and the night became absolute; only the winking stagelights separated the riverfront from total darkness. And as Air Supply rocked on and the flashbulbs glittered around the crowd, I felt that I knew which way the weight had swung. The people of Hannibal had claimed this night. They — we — had come to cheer and celebrate and ogle the rock stars, but we had come only so far. We had dressed in our own clothes, and we had brought our aluminum chairs, and we had held the line at dissolving into an adjunct to the spectacle, a collective prop, an interchangeable mass of Americans herded into one more ceremony of adoration of one more panoply of mass-marketed gods. We had gathered at the river and performed a different sort of sacrament.

Streaming back across the pontoon bridge to Nipper Park and the cars parked on the levee, we could see the grain terminal and the dim bridge behind it. A spotlight illuminated an American flag at the top of the elevator. I had never cared for the grain terminal, nor did I usually warm to showy displays of the flag, especially those that violated the etiquette of display. But tonight the terminal and the lighted flag looked about right. A few thousand of us hung around the historic district for a few hours — there was a jazz combo on the patio outside the Bordello and an amplified country band on North Main — and then we went on home.

Hannibal had reclaimed its sesquicentennial. On this night the town had repudiated its assigned status as a colony; it had defined the terms of its role in the festival. Perhaps whatever future colonizing force awaited the town would find the same subtle resistance, the same inchoate, unyielding strata of town integrity. The old moral coordinates held.

The next morning I bade Estelle Winkler good-bye and left Rose Hill for New York. For the first time that summer, I did not feel as if I were leaving the bedside of a dying relative.

CHAPTER

XXI

SAMUEL CLEMENS rarely returned to the white town after he left in 1853. He came back to lecture in 1867 as Mark Twain, a young satirist just on the verge of his great fame, and found Hannibal desolate. The railroads, for which his father had lobbied on town committees, had arrived to banish the steamboat trade, but had not yet been harnessed to the lumber trade to ignite Hannibal's great boomtown years.

Clemens did not return again until 1882, a towering author and social lion and confidant of generals now, a legend whose nom de plume was emblazoned on the hulls of riverboats. This time he wept at the sight of the town, stayed six weeks, and returned east to complete two long-postponed works in which the elegiac past and the river predominated — *Life on the Mississippi* and *Huckleberry Finn*.

He was back again three years later, and again a mood of sadness and unbearable recall overtook him. He spoke of the "infinite great deeps of pathos," and anguished at the encounter of a childhood playmate, rendered deaf and dumb from a fall into the river while skating with young Sam forty years before.

Sam Clemens had left his home on Hill Street at the age of eighteen, dreaming — as he wrote in a young girl's autograph album — of destiny. He returned for the last time in May of 1902 at age sixty-seven, having conquered destiny and dreaming of nothing so much as dreams.

He had come back home to America only a couple of years earlier after ten debt-ridden years of wandering the world — the last five spent in grieving exile in England and Europe. His beloved daughter Suzy's death in 1895, of meningitis, the news of which reached Clemens in London, had nearly driven him into catatonia. He had lived for two years in a trancelike state, obsessed with dreams and the dark symbols of dreams.

But at the century's turn, Mark Twain's financial fortunes began to stabilize — *Following the Equator* had sold well enough to retire his debts — and something of the old life force had returned. He had sailed with his wife, Livy, to New York in October 1900, and was welcomed by a nation eager to honor him as a literary and cultural hero.

His final visit to Hannibal came on the crest of a great valedictory season of tours, honors, banquets, and wealth. The occasion was an invitation by the president of the University of Missouri at Columbia to accept an honorary doctorate of laws.

An unusual and graceful account of Twain's pilgrimage exists in the files of the *St. Louis Post-Dispatch*. The newspaper had assigned a young reporter and book reviewer named Robertus Love to board the author's train as it approached St. Louis, and to remain with Clemens for his visit to his old hometown. Robertus Love, whatever else he might have accomplished, proved to be Twain's ideal Boswell. His observations of Twain on the streets and in the lecture halls of Hannibal are tender, and almost contemporary in their rendering of mood and detail. They are also the only thorough record of Twain's last visit home.

From his vantage point alongside the distinguished passenger, Love wrote,

> Mr. Clemens showed heightened interest when the train reached the Mississippi river. He craned his neck to look up and down the stream, once so familiar to him as a steamboat pilot.
>
> "See those ripples and curlicues," said the author to a young woman who entered his drawing room to get his autograph — and she got it, too, with a smile and a pat on the shoulder.

(N.B. — I promised not to mention this. Mark Twain says he has writers cramp and is scarcely able to make his "mark." Autograph hunters, he says, should respect age, unless they are unusually pretty girls.)

Clemens stayed in St. Louis that day only long enough to have his photograph taken at the *Post-Dispatch* and to take a nap. He boarded a train for Hannibal at 2:00 P.M. Love found himself required to explain a Twainian utterance that contained potentially indelicate implications:

"While in St. Louis he took a nap at the Planters Hotel. On the way downtown from Union Station, he remarked: 'St. Louis reminds me of several cities — Philadelphia and other places.' Then he went to sleep."

Clearly horrified at how this morsel might be interpreted, Robertus Love hastened onward:

"But it must not be taken for granted that Mark Twain went to sleep because St. Louis reminded him of Philadelphia. He courted a siesta because he was sleepy. He was sleepy because he needed sleep. It was the most natural thing in the world."

The Hannibal that greeted Mark Twain in 1902 was Hannibal at the height of its might and glory. This was the Hannibal of eighteen thousand residents, of fifty-six passenger trains and thirty-four freight trains a day; the Hannibal of one hundred twelve factories, a street-car system, the largest Portland cement plant in the world. The Mark Twain Hotel was under construction, thanks partly to the financial sponsorship of George A. Mahan. This was Hannibal the booming, dreaming, unsuspecting husk — the town whose demise was already prefigured in the played-out timberlands of Wisconsin and Minnesota.

On Friday, May 30, Robertus Love filed the first of his dispatches from Hannibal:

> Mark Twain at 10:30 o'clock visited and identified the old house on Hill street where most of his boyhood was passed.
>
> "Yes, this is the house," he said, while a large crowd of adults and children gathered around him.

Mr. Clemens did not emerge from his room until 9 o'clock, clad in a fresh suit of clothes to match his hair and a real Panama hat of the circular type.

He promises to make a speech if he can think of a subject. . . .

Many oldtimers crowded about the great man to shake his hand in the hotel office. Among them were W. H. C. Nash, Chas. W. Curtis and Edwin Pierce, all of whom he identified as playmates.

"How are you doing, Eddie?" he inquired of Mr. Pierce.

"Like yourself, Sam," replied the schoolmate.

With a light and springy step, Mark Twain walked up the street with his old cronies to the Farmers and Merchants Bank, where an informal reception was held.

"If we had known he was aboard that train," remarked a citizen, "the Union Depot platform would not have been big enough to hold the chairmen of committees."

Love's descriptions indicate that Hannibal caught itself up in the spirit of its famous guest, and transformed itself into a village the likes of which Twain might have caricatured in a story — and also into an unwitting presagement of its heritage future.

"Today," wrote Love, "Hannibal is full of Huck Finns, Tom Sawyers and Beckys. There are more 'originals' of Huck, Tom and Becky in this town since Mark Twain arrived than one would expect to meet in a staid old town with 23 respectable Sunday Schools and a Salvation Army."

But Mark Twain's mood of good-spirited reunion abruptly gave way to shocking pathos. Speaking before a meeting of the Labinnah Club ("Hannibal" spelled backwards), Clemens, without warning, dropped his head and wept.

Robertus Love wrote,

It was the almost wailing voice of an old man who realized that the years are behind him and that he is bidding farewell forever and ever to the haunts and comrades of his childhood days.

Mark Twain apparently had forgotten all save his early life and the consciousness of increasing age. He had forgotten his world-wide fame, the plaudits of princes. . . .

Nothing remained to him save the past of half a century ago and the insistent clamor of that inward voice crying across the years, "Farewell, farewell!"

> Since he came here two days ago the consciousness that he came not to say, "Howdy, boys," but, "Good-bye, old men," has been growing within him. . . .

Love described how the transition from humor to tears had descended upon Mark Twain.

> A moment before, the scores of beautiful girls and matrons and the clubmen and their friends had been laughing heartily at the flashes of Mark Twain's characteristic wit. . . . Everybody was saying to himself: "He is the funniest man on earth."
>
> Then Mark Twain's whitened head was bowed for a moment and his shoulders shook. He seemed to be groping for words. He mumbled something that was not understood, and at last he looked up into the now tense, sympathetic faces of his auditors.
>
> Every face showed much more than mere admiration for a literary celebrity. They showed love for the town's foremost citizen, who has proved upon this occasion and many others, that he loved his old home.

The next day Mark Twain preached an informal sermon at the Baptist Church, dropped the information that he smoked fifteen cigars a day, took a drive with a schoolmate's pretty daughter, and boarded a train for Columbia to accept his doctor of laws degree. He would never again return. But in spite of the sorrow and yearning that always seized him in Hannibal, Mark Twain saw to it that he exited the white town on a ripple of laughter.

One of Clemens's last acts in Hannibal, Robertus Love reported, was to ask the Reverend Everett Gill of the Baptist Church to walk to his hotel with him.

"It will give me a better standing in Hannibal," announced Mark Twain, "to be seen on the street with a preacher."

CHAPTER

XXII

A WEEK after the Air Supply concert, the Sesquicentennial Commission reported a deficit of $13,465 on expenditures of $349,844. The shortfall appeared to be relatively modest partly because it did not include a separate debt of $122,000 on loans made by the Commerce Bank in Hannibal to the Mark Twain Sesquicentennial Commission, Inc. — the independent fund-raising corporation that reporter Mary Griffith had dubbed "The Inc."

The chairman of the finance committee expressed confidence that July revenues would be high, owing to the attractions of Tom Sawyer Days and concerts by Survivor and Doc Severinsen. John Lyng announced that jazz trumpeter Al Hirt had been added to the list of performers. "He attended the Cincinnati Conservatory of Music," Gene Hoenes noted on the front page of the *Courier-Post,* "where he played nothing but the classics."

Thirty thousand people came to watch the Lions Club parade that kicked off Tom Sawyer Days on the Fourth of July. Wally's Smooth Shoes performed that afternoon at the amphitheater; the Kiwanis Club sponsored tricycle races and Barbara Stewart's Dance Studio held forth on the bandstand in Central Park. Mayor Cerretti and Gale Newman played checkers on a giant board in the park. The game lasted two hours before ending in a draw.

Erma Bombeck, the famous humorist, was on hand with a television crew from "Good Morning, America." ("It will be interesting to see what Erma writes in her column and says on television about her visit to Hannibal," ventured the ever-present Gene Hoenes in his front-page story. "More than likely, it will be complimentary with a Bombeck bounce.")

But these were merely the nickel-and-dime diversions, the lounge acts. The events that had made Tom Sawyer Days a nationally recognized event, the masterstroke of the Hannibal Junior Chamber of Commerce, were unfolding as well.

There was the fun run and the pet show and the beautiful-baby contest. There was the celebrity mud volleyball event at Front and Hill streets (an original prospective site for the permanent theme stage). There was the Tom and Becky look-alike competition. There was the venerated frog-jumping contest on Broadway — described in the Jaycee brochure as "the third jewel in Frog Jumping's Triple Crown."

And there was the centerpiece, the fence-painting contest. Held on three levels in recent years — local, state, and national — and "sanctioned" by the United States Congress, the fence-painting contest had long since grown too complex and sophisticated to be held at the restored fence beside the Boyhood Home. It had been moved to a quasi-Olympic setting before a bleacher crowd at Broadway and Third, near the levee. Contestants, dressed in the obligatory Tom Sawyer frayed jeans, plaid shirts, and suspenders, were required to race one another for about fifty yards, each heading toward a paint bucket resting beside a section of disembodied fence. They sloshed whitewash on the fence boards, covering them as quickly as possible, and sprinted back to the finish line.

The fireworks display had to be postponed one day because of thunderstorms. But Doc Severinsen did indeed blow his trumpet at the amphitheater on Saturday night, and stayed around to eat some cold watermelon presented by Pam Lyng. It made the front page of the *Courier-Post.*

The *Courier-Post,* as things developed, was my closest link to Hannibal for the ensuing four months. There would be no more impulsive airplane trips back to Missouri, no more rented-car dashes up the Mississippi to the white town, for the rest of the summer and most of the fall. I had been letting Hannibal and its concerns, its mysteries, overwhelm the rest of my life. I had turned my study at home into a small Hannibal museum: books, newspapers, files of notes and maps and correspondence. When either of my small sons wandered in to see what I was doing there, I could usually disengage myself enough to welcome him, hold him on my lap, give him a few spins in my swivel chair. But as the summer lengthened, I had taken to barricading the door with the end of a sofa so that they would not come in at all. This was no good. Emerson had written that Infancy is the perpetual Messiah, which comes into the arms of fallen men and pleads with them to return to paradise. But here I was, in the very throes of returning to paradise, and locking out my own infants from their efforts to reach me.

After a quarter-century of trying to find a way back to the white town, I needed to escape it. I needed to feel once again the reality of my family, and my chosen place, and my profession.

So I stayed home. I reread *Life on the Mississippi* and *Huckleberry Finn*. At night I lay awake and thought about the town, the river, and the bridge. I wondered what I would do if I had enough money to take my wife and children back there to live — given the unlikely chance that my extremely reasonable wife would consent to such an upheaval. I was not so far gone that I didn't grasp the paradox embedded in this thought: I earned enough money to live in one of the most expensive metropolises in the world, but I would probably go broke trying to live in a town where most people earned less than $18,000 a year. Neither my wife, a scientist, nor I possessed any skills remotely useful in the economic marketplace of Hannibal — at least while Gene Hoenes had a lock on featured bylines at the newspaper.

And so I followed my hometown's fortunes from half a continent away.

On July 15, Mayor Cerretti announced that construction for the sesquicentennial theme stage could begin by August 15. On the same day former mayor Lyng affirmed the possibility that the celebration might finish in the black.

The following night, the mayor acted out a fresh show of quixotic defiance toward the council, inviting another unanimous repudiation. Cerretti's council agenda had called for discussion of an Army Corps of Engineers proposal to repair beach erosion near the amphitheater. At the meeting, Cerretti announced that he would forbid such discussion. "I changed my mind," he blandly explained to the council, adding that he had not been given "adequate information" about the project. (A copy of the corps's application had indeed been handed to the mayor — but by his nemesis, City Engineer Harv Ebers.) Cerretti's stonewall was shattered by one of his own devices. A councilman moved from his seat on the dais to a floor microphone that the mayor had set up for citizens' comments, identified himself as a citizen, and continued arguing the point. Later the council voted 10 to 0 to formally consider the matter in two weeks.

On Wednesday, July 24, the rock group Survivor drew a record crowd of ten thousand at the amphitheater. Sixteen girls fainted from head exhaustion during the performance and a band member was overcome after the show.

The Army Corps announced that it would not do the beach-restoration work near the amphitheater.

On July 25 Mayor Cerretti struck again. He issued a directive that all government and private agencies doing business with the city must go directly to his office, and not to the department that would normally handle the matter. The mayor said he made the move "so I will know what is going on." Most of the transactions listed as examples by Cerretti involved the Department of Public Works. Two city councilmen immediately claimed that the directive was a personal vendetta aimed at Ebers — who in addition to city engineer was public works director. Cerretti said it wasn't so.

A new attraction was added to the sesqui calendar. Gene Hoenes broke the story: Halley's Comet would appear in the heavens in time for the windup of the festival.

At an August 6 council meeting, Cerretti's fixation with Ebers again dominated the proceedings. It came out that the mayor had refused to include the public works director in a bridge study project, sending queries to outside consulting firms instead. (Cerretti explained, irrelevantly, that "I just received this proposal recently.") The mayor was further challenged over a move that would limit Ebers's ability to make long-distance telephone calls from his office: an order to remove his direct-access long-distance phone lines. (Cerretti cited his concern over "an increasing number of unlogged calls" — a concern that the assistant city clerk later dismissed as negligible.)

Cerretti's maneuverings regarding Ebers seemed to be forming a fixed, if incomprehensible, pattern: an all but unmistakable move to thwart or isolate the city engineer, followed by attempts to explain why no snub should possibly be inferred.

The Oak Ridge Boys, the Osmond Brothers, and Ralph Stanley and the Clinch Mountain Boys came and went. The sale of radio station KHMO was approved — from a company based in Springfield, Missouri, to a company based in St. Louis and Palmyra. On August 19, an obviously ruffled Gene Hoenes went front-page in the *Courier-Post* with an article expressing local anguish over a waspish piece about the town that had appeared in the *Wall Street Journal*. The *Journal* writer, Hoenes noted, "concentrated on what he called a city divided over the Mark Twain Sesquicentennial Celebration. He spoke of civic restiveness, financial problems and a mayor's defeat at the polls."

If Hannibalians had their "druthers," Hoenes supposed (without actually having polled any), they would prefer an article about Hannibal written more than twenty years before by "the New York–based columnist Russell Baker." Apparently that column was handy. "All over the world," Hoenes quoted Baker at the beginning of a long citation, "wherever men can read, everyone knows Hannibal. Everyone has lived here for a precious moment and there are few men who do not revisit it still in search of forgotten tranquility and lost dreams. . . ."

On August 20 it was regretfully announced that the theme stage would be further delayed. There was no chance that it would be ready for the Autumn Folklife Festival in November. The State Highway Department, acting as the soul of prudence, had suggested that the city not advertise for bids until the local authorities decided exactly what kind of structure they wanted to build.

On the same day, the local paper carried cryptic news of a three-hour, closed-door session involving Mayor Cerretti and several councilmen. The topic was the mayor's relationship with Harv Ebers. Not many details were available to reporters — one councilman did go so far as to allow that there existed a deep communications problem between the two men. A *Courier-Post* reporter pressed the mayor himself for details about the meeting. Cerretti answered almost every question with "no comment." Asked why he commented to other news media but not to the Hannibal paper, Cerretti replied, "You know why." Cerretti was then asked why he agreed to speak to the reporter yet would not answer any questions. "Courtesy," the mayor explained.

Two days later, a city councilman reported that Cerretti had prepared a letter of impeachment against Ebers. The mayor would not comment.

At a four-hour council meeting August 22, a session infused with a certain encounter-group aura, it came out that some of Mayor Cerretti's willfulness toward Ebers was rooted in the mayor's hurt feelings over the lack of respect shown him by the council. In a rare disclosure of his innermost emotions, the mayor admitted that he felt personally affronted when the council overrode his veto of Ebers's contract with the city. "The council was taking my authority away from me and I deeply resented that," Cerretti confessed. A councilman replied that authority in Hannibal government lay with the council, not the mayor. Another councilman suggested that Cerretti go home and read his Bible.

The Beach Boys came to the amphitheater for a Labor Day concert — "basically the last big weekend of the celebration," John Lyng told the *Courier-Post.* Mad Dog Manus told the paper he had been working with the Beach Boys for the past twelve years, since the Joliet Jam in Joliet, Illinois, in 1973.

On September 10, the City Council voted to decrease its next allotment to the Sesquicentennial Commission by $2,900 in order to pay a bill presented by the designer of the proposed theme stage.

The next day, the three main corporate contributors to the theme stage withdrew their support for the project. The companies were Southwestern Bell, Watlow Industries, and the *Courier-Post.* Festival director John Lyng said that he was disappointed, but admitted that a stage would no longer be of real use to the sesquicentennial.

The riverboat *Mississippi Queen* visited Hannibal and unloaded dueling Twains. Both Bill McLinn (who always wore a black coat) and Roger Durrett (who always wore a white coat) were on board and eager to be interviewed. Durrett told the *Courier-Post* that he was like a kid on Christmas morning, being in Hannibal and performing as Mark Twain. He added, perhaps pointedly, that it was very important to him that he was licensed by the Mark Twain Foundation.

McLinn, as usual, took a larger perspective. He let it be drawn out of him that he was traveling officially for the American Cigar Association and that he was about to embark on a five-day visit to the Soviet Union. He declared his intention to disembark from the plane in Moscow dressed as Mark Twain. "I hope I don't have any trouble with my visa," he confided to Gene Hoenes, "because the picture on the passport is without my makeup."

Mark Twain's mother came to town. A woman named Ecky Broad, of Chagrin Falls, Ohio, gave a performance at Hannibal-

LaGrange College in costume as Jane Lampton Clemens. Her tag line was: "I'm his mother. I ought to know." Mrs. Broad told Gene Hoenes that her husband sometimes portrays Orion Clemens, Sam's brother.

On September 17 the sesqui chairman, Dick Halsor, admitted that unpaid pledges to the festival were beginning to concern the commission. He estimated the total of unpaid pledges to be about $40,000. "We borrowed money against these pledges," Halsor said. "Without those pledges, we will not have a solvent program."

The City Council voted officially to delay further action on construction of a theme stage.

Gene Hoenes reported in the *Courier-Post* that a man named Dick Oitker had resigned as executive director of the Marion County Ambulance District. Pressed by Hoenes for the reason, Oitker unveiled what may have been a dry wit. "I just thought it was time for new blood," he said.

Up With People's cancellation for the sesquicentennial's Opening Day had been the first of two very large shoes to drop. On September 20 came the second: Dick Halsor announced that Hal Holbrook would not be able to appear as *Mark Twain Tonight* for the November 30 finale. Holbrook had accepted a movie contract, Halsor said, and would be "on location." Halsor said that commission members were thinking in terms of what could be done to present a fitting finale to the sesquicentennial.

The Hannibal-based gospel group Proclaim and the Rock City Boys of Chattanooga, Tennessee, presented the final concert on a cold night at the riverfront amphitheater. Autumn arrived in the town on Sunday, September 22, with heavy thunderstorms. A circus came to town.

Up With People finally arrived in town for performances at the high-school gymnasium October 19 and 20. Gene Hoenes reported in advance that the group's current show was "Beat of the Future," an entertaining but thoughtful look at life in the twenty-first century where there are floating cities, interstellar travel, song-writing computers, and the global community of mankind.

On October 9 the sesqui finance chairman, Dean Eshelman, announced that if all outstanding pledges — totaling $163,000 — were paid, the festival would finish with a profit. He said that the $122,000 debt to Commerce Bank had been reduced to $96,000.

On Saturday, October 19, three councilmen signed a document at City Hall listing charges of impeachment against Mayor Cerretti. A special council meeting was called for the following Tuesday night.

It appeared that the councilmen had pounced on an opportunity to exploit the mayor's scabrous feud with City Engineer Ebers. The central impeachment charge fairly vibrated with high dudgeon:

> That on or about Oct. 15, 1985, Richard N. Cerretti, in violation of the ordinances of the city of Hannibal, directed Charles Salyer, superintendent of the Street Department, to use street department crews and equipment to open a sodded waterway located on private property between the residences of Mrs. Francis Laswell and Mrs. James Patterson. The action was taken by Richard N. Cerretti after the city engineer's office had advised Mrs. Laswell that the matter was a private matter and not the responsibility of the city of Hannibal.
>
> Not only was the action taken by Richard Cerretti in direct violation of the city charter and ordinances, but was clear evidence of continuing oppression of the city engineer's office. This constant oppression has continued unabated since Richard Cerretti's election. . . .

The device at least offered a certain vengeful symmetry. In his own election campaign, Cerretti had professed stern outrage over the fact that Mayor Lyng had approved construction of a brick sidewalk (in the historic district) despite a City Charter provision that all sidewalks be made of Portland Cement concrete. VOTE FOR

THE MAN WHO WILL OBEY YOUR CITY'S CHARTER! Cerretti's newspaper ads had thundered.

John Lyng told the *Courier-Post* that he had no interest in running for mayor again.

A letter in the newspaper stated: "You know the world conveniently, so they thought, crucified Jesus. But, praise the Lord, He overcame death and now we all have a chance to live forever.

"Now our city council is trying to crucify Mayor Cerretti."

On Tuesday, October 22, there began a tragicomic opera without precedent in Hannibal civic life.

At the special meeting the council voted 7 to 5 to suspend the mayor pending an impeachment hearing late in November. Cerretti's attorney argued that the three councilmen who had brought impeachment charges should not have voted. Cerretti thereupon declared that the motion had failed. He returned to his office the following morning.

In the meantime, Councilman Paul Arnett, the mayor pro tem, claimed the duties of acting mayor. On Wednesday night Arnett ordered the building maintenance supervisor to remove the telephone switchboard from Cerretti's office. As the order was being carried out Cerretti himself burst into the office, brushed past the supervisor and a couple of policemen, and snatched a hidden tape recorder from a cabinet. Arnett later said that the recorder appeared to have been attached to the telephone system. Cerretti then vanished into the night.

On the following day Cerretti sent his wife, Dorothy, to the *Courier-Post* with a press release in which he offered to resign his office if all members of the City Council would also resign. "Paul Arnett has forcibly assumed the duties of the mayor," the press release argued, and added, "while things may look bleak at the moment, Richard Cerretti and the overwhelming populace of Hannibal will prevail and justice will be done. Arnett and his endorsers will come to justice for their illegal acts."

On that same day, the front page of the *Courier-Post* displayed a bizarre photograph: the building maintenance supervisor scaling a ladder to the second-floor window of the mayor's City Hall office to secure city documents in a file there. Cerretti had locked his office and refused to hand over the key.

"Hannibal today is a town torn asunder," editorialized the newspaper. "The people are suffering. The city is suffering. . . . The story is big news not just in Hannibal but across the state. We're in the spotlight, and it's a harsh glare; our problems are now common knowledge to the rest of Missouri, and even beyond state borders. . . ."

CHAPTER
XXIII

I FLEW back to Missouri on October 31. The day was a Thursday: a somewhat wristwatchy, attaché-case day of the week for levitation and time-travel. On the other hand, it was Halloween.

Fog and rain had turned Lambert–St. Louis Airport, by midafternoon, into a phosphorescent swamp. Landing airplanes fishtailed and sent up greenish plumes of spray. The rain made ungainly little stains on my rented car's windshield, like tiny eggs bursting, and the classical station out of St. Louis was quickly crushed under sickening thunder rolls of static. The rock 'n' roll stations came in just fine.

I wallowed west for an hour on I-70 in a funereal file of early commuter backup. It was like breaking free from civilization's own great gloomy cortege when I hit the exit ramp north to U.S. 61 and plunged into the sleepy-hollowed stillness of the old two-lane countryside. The Halloween fog enveloped me, but I was born and bred in this briar patch. I tailed trailer trucklights on up 61 into the dark town.

I had wanted to make Hannibal before pumpkinlight. I wanted to sit in my car and watch the trick-or-treaters on St. Mary's Avenue, to see children costumed in the color orange ringing doorbells under orange porchlight.

No doubt there was a sentimental element buried somewhere within this wish. I couldn't help that. For me, Hannibal had always reached its apotheosis in October, and the color of its apotheosis was orange. Orange flooded the field of my boyhood vision: the tinny, gummy transient orange of drugstore jack-o'-lanterns and Halloween crepe, the heavy preternatural orange of construction-paper harvest moons cut in Mary Wiehe's art classes to be pasted on dark blue nightscapes and hung on doors, innocent as hexes; the waxy orange of candy corn, yellow-tipped like bad teeth, that grinned in its aggregate from clear glass dishes in the living rooms of aunts — and the larger, elemental orange that hung about the town itself, ushered down from the north perhaps on the river current, and investing the town's fallen leaves and the husks of its gardens and its cold twilit air with a temporary and interior light of the kind that lingered for a hopeful moment in the tubes of an old radio after the dial had been switched off.

Perhaps a cynic could find sentiment there. My own unsentimental sense told me that the sentiment was doubtless in vain: there were not likely to be all that many trick-or-treaters abroad on this Halloween, not even in Hannibal. This was the age of the razor-bladed apple and the cyanide cookie. And it was the age of true bogeymen: as a bearded stranger lurking in a parked car, I could probably expect to throw a legitimate scare into the few remaining kids and parents brave enough to risk being poisoned, and perhaps get myself hauled off to the new police station in the process.

I could have waited for the weekend and still have seen the Autumn Historic Folklife Festival and talked to the people I wanted to see. But it was the last day of October in Hannibal, and the orange was fading, and so I went.

My Halloween dreams were moot by the time I reached town. The Junction was a wet blot of neon floating in the six o'clock darkness. St. Mary's Avenue would be as black and depopulated as it sometimes appeared, horribly, in my dreams. I ate a fried-chicken dinner at a table at Fern's — I was the only customer except for a couple of coffee-drinkers at the counter; the waitress was dressed up as a witch — and then I found a coin telephone, out by the gas pumps. I called the home of a couple who had often served as my guides in Hannibal; the woman had steered me to the Famous and Marilyn Cohn.

"There are some parties in town," the woman acknowledged to me now, "but you should go to the armory if you want to see children — families. The Police Department puts on a Halloween party for kids. It's nothing fancy, but it's at least safe. You'll see the real people there."

She offered to meet me there. Her own children were elsewhere, but she seemed determined that I not miss the party at the armory. Her instincts about Hannibal had been unfailingly shrewd and subtle — "They don't know what they're destroying," she had said of Jim Gladwin's big-deal planners early in the summer. "People come to Hannibal from everywhere just to touch the way we live" — and so I agreed.

Frank Sinatra had sung from Harry James's bandstand during the armory's dedication ceremonies in 1939. I had watched Bear Creek's floodwaters amputate its foundations from my grandfather's Packard and traced, with my hand, the long enclosing granite wall along Collier Street that joined its compound to Clemens Field. I had worn a Boy Scout uniform on my last visit inside, around 1955, when Bobby Schweitzer and I teamed up in the fire-by-friction competition during a Scout Jamboree. We caught the imagination of the crowd that night. So deeply immersed were we in the frantic grinding of looped string around a stick to ignite our wood chips that when we paused to catch our breath it took a few seconds before we became aware of the stillness in our vicinity. Small fires were burning away on the floor around us. Only gradually did the scope of the stillness widen in our consciousness (I remember our heads rising slowly, together) until we grasped the extent of the catastrophe. Everyone in the armory, *everyone* — competing Scouts, Scoutmasters, parents in the bleachers, God — was staring at us with a kind of fixed fascination that went beyond mere hilarity. We had been sawing for perhaps fifteen minutes. The two of us had suspended the forward progress of the entire jamboree. We had bequeathed Troop 100 a record for fire-by-friction ineptitude that, to the best of my knowledge, still stands.

Now the armory was a granite cave in the autumn night rain. Silhouette shapes slipped past me in the darkness, flitting for the entrance, and flickered into people in the pale orange light. I spotted my friend just inside the doorway. Behind her, on half an acre of echoing floor space, Hannibal was having its Halloween.

The decoration committee had been frugal: a few twisted lengths of crepe paper — orange alternating with black — hung from facing basketball backboards. Several plywood booths were clustered below the crepe, in the center of the floor. Around this hub shuffled and milled the Halloween merrymakers in a kind of dreamy, unhurried gavotte — an oblong, amiable donut of citizenry in denim and spangled taffeta. Costumed kids held their parents' hands; the whole mass progressed clockwise a few steps at a time, paused, bumped ahead again. I thought of crowded airports on holidays, but these people showed no anxiety. They were home. The gathering seemed to embody its own purpose. Now and then someone would step out of the promenade to line up at a booth and bob for apples, toss rings, pitch coins into jack-o'-lanterns. The booths were run by Boy Scouts, Girl Scouts, the Retired Senior Citizens Volunteer Program, and a sorority my mother had belonged to when it met at the Mark Twain Hotel, Beta Sigma Phi.

"These," my companion remarked, nodding toward the swarm, "are the people that didn't get to play." She was referring to the sesquicentennial and its early snubbing of local committees, local volunteers.

We plunged in. The costumed children were rampant around us (it was intermission of the costume contest; there were microphones on floor stands on a raised stage), but I spied no Toms or Beckys. Witch gowns with matching conical hats were popular, with lots of glitter stuck to whitened faces. I saw rubber gorilla masks, Frankensteins; I saw ballerinas and zombies. There seemed to be a high concentration of babies with cat whiskers penciled on their cheeks. An old man wandered about placidly in a rabbit suit.

The costumes were singularly timeless — I scarcely saw anything that referred to current pop icons. Many of the garments and masks had surely been taken down from shelves, and would be returned there tonight for another year's use.

I spotted Henry Sweets in horn-rims and shirt sleeves, but he was manning the free refreshment center and too busy to do more than wave. The light was orange, and I began to think of the Fall Festival.

My friend from the town was thinking her own fixed and bitter thoughts — thoughts that had hardened into dogma for her by now, but thoughts that I had trouble disputing. "This is what they wanted to take away, in favor of their smoothness," she said, sweeping an arm. "All this fun. All this down-home jerky fun."

Leaving the Halloween celebrants at the armory, heading toward my lodging as October trickled away, I thought of the lead paragraph of a story I had read on the front page of the *Courier-Post* over dinner at Fern's: "The city will be able to make its third payroll this month, despite a shortage in city funds. . . ."

On Friday it was still raining. I paid a visit to Richard Cerretti at his photography studio in the converted graystone on North Fifth. I had not called him to say I was coming, but when I pulled open the front door to his reception room ("PULL for the Pirates!"), he seemed not at all surprised to see me.

"Things are *so* ripe now for constructive change," he commented as he came forward to shake my hand. The onslaughts of the past ten days might have descended on some other man; the mayor of the town, say. The placid burgher-businessman who greeted me was the picture of serenity. The light-blue shirt collar was starched and smooth as an eggshell, as usual, its surface broken only by the gleaming bars of the fish insignia. The rimless glasses flashed as he sat and pressed his knees together; the voice was reedy with diffidence.

He was blandly uninterested in discussing the stepladder, the tapes, his breezy suggestion that Police and Fire Board members "take the day off" on the day of his suspension — a suggestion that had set the city boards scrambling to clarify their chain of command in the event of emergency. Nor was he concerned with the petition that had begun circulating the previous day, calling for the recall of the mayor, the city attorney, and all council members, and a special election for their successors.

"Let the people decide," he suggested in a way that sounded a little practiced. "I have the people's support."

There were the dissenters, to be sure; the enemies. Richard Cerretti dwelt for a moment on the death threats. He told of his eleven-year-old daughter answering the telephone at night and hearing a man's voice say, "We're gonna shoot your daddy and burn your house."

But anti-Cerretti violence was not the real threat, the suspended mayor proposed. If any violence broke out, it was likely to arise from Cerretti's own followers, the vast majority of Hannibalians, already at the limits of their tolerance for the abuses visited on their mayor.

"I wouldn't be surprised," Cerretti remarked, mildly, "to hear about some broken windows . . . attempts on councilmen's lives . . ."

We were sitting in a softly carpeted room of antique sofas, gold-flecked wallpaper, leather-bound photographic scrapbooks, ceramic statuettes of Tom and Becky. This was Hannibal, and outside an autumn rain was falling. I was not sure for a moment whether I had heard Cerretti correctly.

"And what would you say," I asked him after a strange silence, "as a Christian, to someone in the grip of this sort of — passion?"

Cerretti's smile was so warm that he seemed briefly to disappear behind it. "At this point," he said, "I'd encourage it."

It seemed a propitious moment for changing the subject. "Do you see yourself as mayor of this town six, seven, eight years from now?" I asked him. Cerretti nodded; his glasses flashed.

"I do," he said. "I do. I know I have the ability to manage the city. I have the people's support."

"What might you do differently?" I asked him. Cerretti smiled his radiant smile again. "Given the opportunity," he said, "I would get some new people in key positions."

I thanked the mayor for his time, reached for the doorknob — "PUSH for the Pirates" — and escaped into the rain.

The next day I found Mary Wiehe. I opened the telephone book to the W's, and there indeed was the old art teacher's name: a deadpan little row of typography, no more or less remarkable than WHOLESALE KITCHEN SUPPLY or WIESE PLANNING & ENGINEERING INC. I looked at the small name in the column and thought of the Jubilee Chorus.

Her voice on the telephone was the same as I remembered it from a quarter-century before — hearty, intelligent, faintly ironic. She remembered who I was, and said that if I didn't mind her having to excuse herself early — there was some discomfort in her stomach — I could come out and see her.

She was living with her companion, a small woman in marcelled hair named Beulah Doer, in a ranch-style house near the college campus on the western rim of town. Miss Wiehe and Miss Doer had dressed for my afternoon visit. Mary Wiehe greeted me in a pink woolen jacket and matching skirt. She had pinned an oval brooch at her throat and put on earrings. She had rouged her cheeks and applied a thin line of lipstick. Her once-shaggy hair was white and lacquered as a British magistrate's wig now, and she had gained some weight — who hadn't? — but a quality that I now recognized as bohemian sass still animated her. Miss Doer, who announced her age as eighty-six, wore a navy dress and a string of pearls.

"I'm teaching Beulah to paint," Mary Wiehe said as we stood in the living room. "I've been getting after her for her outlining, but she does nicely with color." Hand on hip, feet planted apart in her old teaching stance, she gestured toward a small framed watercolor on the wall — a rather explicitly rendered pastoral, with lavender flowers anchoring the foreground and a Grecian swirl of cumulus clouds — obviously Beulah Doer's signature touch — cascading from above.

"The clouds are exquisite," I told Miss Doer, who lowered her head at this effusion and cast a shy glance at her tutor. I recognized some of the other landscapes as bearing Mary Wiehe's own touch — a thick, impatient, almost cursory stroke, as if she were making a point of defying the lyric possibilities presented by nature.

As we made our way back to the sun porch (the rain clouds were breaking up now; light was pouring through) I asked Mary how long she had known Beulah. "Since . . . ?" Mary raised her eyebrows at Beulah. "Since nineteen forty-one." The year of my birth. "That was when Beulah came to town to teach at Hannibal-LaGrange, wasn't it, Beulah?" We sat down on sofas. The screened porch offered a view to the glowing college campus beyond a neighbor's satellite dish. "Beulah came to live with me in nineteen sixty-two, the year her father died — didn't you?" On a nearby shelf were the blue-bound Harvard Classics, a print of the Praying Hands, a copy of Van Gogh's *Sunflowers*.

"I taught art for fifty-one years," Mary Wiehe said. She tugged absently at her hem. "I taught at the college for forty-four. I'd teach at the college in the mornings, then I'd teach the elementary schools and the high school. Evenings I'd teach at the YMCA. Fourteen-hour days. I never made a salary," she observed with a kind of triumph, "above four figures."

"They named a wing after her at the college," put in Beulah Doer.

"The Mary E. Wiehe Art Building," confirmed Mary Wiehe.

The long trail began to unwind again in her memory. She recalled asking permission from the school superintendent to complete her master's degree in fine arts at the University of Iowa in 1941. "He said, 'Well, hell, Mary, go ahead; it'll look nice on your tombstone.' " The thought of it triggered a horselaugh. She remembered how she had studied under a redheaded artist in a white suit, who was Grant Wood, the great regionalist. She recalled how she refused to lay out her pallette Grant Wood style; and how she damn well got her MFA anyway. The orange sunlight deepened on the green campus beyond the window screen.

Emboldened by the wash of memories, I leaned forward and asked Mary Wiehe: "Do you remember the Jubilee Chorus?"

The question confused her. She looked from me to Beulah Doer. Beulah, who had been woolgathering, came alert at Mary's glance. "What's that, baby?" she said softly, lifting out her hand.

"I read about it," I told Mary. "You were in charge of staging it. It was a concert at the high school in nineteen thirty-five. It was part of the centennial, I think. The Jubilee Chorus."

Mary Wiehe shook her head slowly. "I don't remember any Jubilee Chorus," she said. "But I remember the centennial. And I remember when Franklin Delano Roosevelt came to town to dedicate the bridge. Do you know who it was," she said, tilting toward me, her face suddenly bright with conspiracy, "that stretched the ribbon across the bridge for President Roosevelt to cut?"

Now I came alert. I stared at the old woman. Hannibal imploded. I thought of a missing face in a newspaper photograph of a crowd of seventy-five thousand. I thought of the town, the river, and the bridge. The moral coordinates. The connectives.

"Who," I asked Mary Wiehe, knowing the answer.

"He was sitting in that open limousine," Mary Wiehe was saying, her eyes fixed on something that Beulah Doer and I could not see. "Harry Truman was right beside him — he was still a senator then. I was trying to get the ribbon over his stomach. And it wouldn't quite stretch. He was already on crutches then, and he had a pot belly." A grin of girlish naughtiness spread on Mary Wiehe's rouged face. "I said . . ." — she shifted her bright gaze from the past to Beulah Doer beside me — "I said, '*Mister President, would you mind pulling in your stomach?*' "

I saw John Lyng at the restaurant that had been built into the old Federal Building. He was with his mother and his brother and a flock of other Lyngs. They had drawn two tables end-to-end, family style. John Lyng sat in the middle of a row, busy with passing a bowl of something down. He was dressed in a woolen plaid shirt with the sleeves rolled up, and looked hardly at all like a former boy mayor. In fact the entire tableau had a slightly displaced, archetypal quality — an outdoor Sunday dinner on a Missouri farm from some mythic long-ago, re-created here within this hopefully with-it restaurant that itself was planted within a gutted, used-up building whose function no longer obtained. In its crazy, forged logic the scene was pure Hannibal — it defined everything that had happened to the town.

My last glimpse of the Mark Twain Sesquicentennial was on Sunday, the final day of the Autumn Folklife Festival. A great prairie wind from the west had blown the remaining thunderclouds away and left the town gleaming in the hard cold November light. Puffs of white breath curled from people's mouths on North Main Street, then flattened into the breeze. The booths and exhibits had a buckskin-and-calico motif, and Hannibal, as usual, was in costume: there were women in frontier gingham selling fried apple fritters, street fiddlers in fringed vests and broad-brim hats. Young men dressed in Union blue and Confederate butternut from Saturday's Civil War skirmish strolled arm-in-arm with their wives and sweethearts. Quick children in Indian headdresses darted like panthers in the crowd — a wigwam of some sort had been erected in a parking lot. A bagpiper in kilts and tam-o'-shanter stood outside the Bordello and skrawked out "Amazing Grace."

I am looking at some handmade leather belts at a booth at the foot of Hill Street near the river, and I understand that it is over. I have one thing left that I want to do. I walk rapidly up Hill Street, past the Boyhood Home and the museum and the Becky Thatcher Gift Shop and the Haunted House; I walk to Third Street where my rented car is parked. I get in and drive two short blocks and make the right turn up onto the approach ramp to the Mark Twain Bridge.

When men are innocent, wrote Emerson, life shall be longer, and shall pass into the immortal as gently as we awake from dreams. Mine is the only car on the bridge. For a few moments the auspicious upward cant of the approach blocks my view of the river itself; and then my car passes through the bridge's mouth, the spot where Roosevelt cut Mary Wiehe's ribbon, the spot near where my father may have stood straining in the crowd. I had forgotten how narrow and cocoonlike the old bridge was, how small and naked it made one feel to move out upon its long arched roadbed toward the East.

And then the Mississippi spreads out below on either side of the cocoon, deflected from the limestone bluffs and flowing south — flowing from past to future or from future to past; it depends upon the dream. Glancing quickly over my right shoulder I can see the proscenium sweep of Hannibal's riverfront and the people, in costume, along North Main, gathered as if for a curtain call. The riverfront has become its own theme stage. But the town, the river, and the bridge are themselves, intact, inviolate.

I drive on into Illinois and slow to a standstill for a few minutes, hushed and motionless, the universe briefly perfect. Half a continent in front of me are my wife and two sons, my job, my friends — my true life. The next day I will depart Hannibal without shame or regret — still innocent, no doubt, but having gently awakened from the dream.

I dial the car in a half-circle on the old tar-caulked two-lane, laying down just a little judicious patch of rubber to boost myself back up off the shoulder. And I head back for the bridge.

On November 8, Mayor Cerretti complied with a subpoena and surrendered to the city his covert tape recorder, a transcript of a telephone conversation, the files in his possession, a box of blank tapes, and an adaptor. Four days later the City Council accepted the resignations of Cerretti and the three councilmen who filed impeachment charges against him. All four men announced that they would run for reelection in a special election set for February 4. Councilman Paul Arnett would serve until then as mayor pro tem.

Gene Hoenes reported that the Sesquicentennial Commission would need at least $30,000 to close out the celebration in the black. John Lyng announced that a Mark Twain "birthday gala" would be held November 30 at Rockcliffe Mansion, the night Hal Holbrook was to have appeared for the grand finale, with tickets available at $100 per couple. The *Courier-Post* quoted Richard Halsor as saying, "We are asking for community support."

On November 18 Richard Cerretti formally filed as a candidate for mayor of Hannibal. By filing deadline, five men — John Lyng not among them — had declared for mayor.

The newspaper said that it rained on the night of the closing ceremonies. Only about eighty people turned out for the "birthday gala" at Rockcliffe. John Lyng and Richard Halsor cut a birthday cake that won a contest sponsored by the Mark Twain Senior Citizens Center. The occasion moved Richard Halsor to oratory. "What Mark Twain did for Hannibal and for the world — that's what we're celebrating tonight. He was a real literary giant," Halsor averred.

"With the coming of Halley's Comet, maybe another Mark Twain will be born here today," Halsor went on. "There were so many coincidences in his life, you can't help but think that maybe the coincidences haven't ended."

John Lyng, ever more practical and ever hopeful, announced that a "memory book" of the sesquicentennial, containing color photographs of the events, would soon be available at $20 the advance order.

Richard Cerretti was not among the top two finishers in the February 4 special election for Hannibal's mayor. On February 18, in a runoff, a thirty-five-year-old salesman and former schoolteacher named Richard Schwartz defeated a businessman named Charles Bindemann and became mayor of the white town. There were no broken windows, no attempts on councilmen's lives.

The special election and the runoff cost more than $5,000, double the amount set aside in the town budget.

In late February Gale Newman relinquished all his directorates in Hannibal to accept a position as executive director of the Chamber of Commerce in Naples, Florida. The Sesqui Commission released a final set of figures: its net balance from the festival, on expenditures of about $900,000, was $55,776 in liabilities, partly offset by $41,119 in "assets." Listed among the sesqui's "assets" were $36,371 in pledges that had not been received and $11,098 in inventory that had not been sold.

"If we had it to do again," John Lyng told the *Courier-Post,* sounding as though he could hardly wait to get started, "I think we would lighten up on the cultural aspects of the celebration. The exhibits, writers' conference, and free concerts cost us about $30,000. . . ."

"Ours is an age of elegy and of loss," says the poet Paul Mariani. Mark Twain sensed it more than a hundred years ago, while the nation was still galloping toward unlimited gain, the wind of the Century of Progress in its face. "Down in my heart of hearts," he wrote to his wife, Olivia, as a young man of thirty-five, "I yearn for the days that are gone and the phantoms of olden time."

Mark Twain's phantoms, and his white town, were of a different order from my phantoms and my town. I cannot more than hazily imagine the textures or the comforts or the deep adhesions of his lost Eden with its prairies covered with wild strawberry plants and its drowsy towns awash in shingle-shavings, waiting for the steamboat that would bless and curse them with its access to larger universes, better times. (Such a steamboat ultimately swept Mark Twain from his frontier Eden to the Gilded Age, and he went willingly, hell-bent for the better times.)

I cannot imagine back into Mark Twain's Eden, but I think he saw sharply ahead into Eden's fall. His Hadleyburg, that most honest and upright of towns, was corrupted by a stranger bearing a sack of gold; its amended motto at the end was "Lead Us Into Temptation."

It was gold that doomed Arcadia, in Mark Twain's own experience and view: the California Gold Rush of the 1850s, which incubated, after the Civil War, its parasite culture of robber barons, its ruthless railroad promoters and craven capitalists who followed the money west and left deep scars on the land: Jay Gould and John D. Rockefeller and J. P. Morgan and the rest. Twain lived to witness a quarter-century of moral rot triggered by a westward stampede of openly corrupt and corrupting industry, followed by the seedlings of a utilitarian, transient social order indifferent to the old allegiances of community and church and continuity — indifferent, if not hostile, to the very notion of "past." Twain died before the gold rushers were supplanted by the apostles of liquid streams of gold, but he would have recognized and understood them; and he would not — contrary to a comfortable assumption among the predators — "have laughed and counted the house."

He would instead have said — as he did say — that the onrushing civilization was "a civilization which has destroyed the simplicity and repose of life; replaced its contentment, its poetry, its soft romantic-dreams and visions with money-fever, sordid ideals, vulgar ambitions, and the sleep which does not refresh; it has invented a thousand useless luxuries, and turned them into necessities, and satisfied none of them; it has dethroned God and set up a shekel in His place."

I look into Hannibal from the bridge, and see myself looking back, in the costume of a boy. I cannot stop approaching, nor can I shed my costume and get off the levee and onto the bridge, heading east. I cannot escape Hannibal, and I cannot return. It is on the bridge where I belong, perhaps, with my invisible father, watching the president cut a ribbon to let the future in.

ABOUT THE AUTHOR

Ron Powers is a journalist, novelist, and nonfiction writer. His criticism of American broadcasting has appeared in several newspapers, magazines, and books, as well as on television. In 1973 he won the Pulitzer Prize in criticism for his TV columns in the *Chicago Sun-Times*; in 1985 he received an Emmy for his commentaries on "CBS Sunday Morning."

White Town Drowsing is his first nonfiction book about American town life. The second, *Far From Home*, is also published by Anchor Books. Powers hails from Mark Twain's hometown, Hannibal, Missouri, and presently lives in Middlebury, Vermont, with his wife and two sons.